£14·9X

DESIGN S S

Frederick
WISEMAN

---

a guide to
references and resources

A
Reference
Publication
in
Film

Ronald Gottesman
Editor

Frederick
WISEMAN

a guide to
references and resources

LIZ ELLSWORTH

G.K.HALL&CO.

70 LINCOLN STREET, BOSTON, MASS.

Distributed in the United Kingdom and Europe
by George Prior Associated Publishers Ltd.,
37-41 Bedford Row
London WC1R 4JH, England

Library of Congress Cataloging in Publication Data

Ellsworth, Liz.
  Frederick Wiseman : a guide to references and resources.

  (A reference publication in film)
  Bibliography: p.
  "Archival sources for further research": p.
  Includes indexes.
  1. Wiseman, Frederick--Bibliography. I. Series.
Z8979.2.E44   [PN1998.A3W63]   016.79143'023'0924
ISBN 0-8161-8066-0   79-117

Contents

Preface

instructive.
(to teach).

Unless otherwise noted, the information presented in Part I of this volume is compiled from a presentation Wiseman made in Chicago at the 1976 Midwest Film Conference, and from two interviews I had with Wiseman, one in 1976 and one in 1978. Material for Part II is adapted from an analysis of Wiseman's films which I prepared for a master's thesis project at the University of Wisconsin-Milwaukee. As part of that project, I prepared detailed shot lists for Wiseman's films. Four of of those shot lists appear in this volume in Part III. *Titicut Follies* is included because it is Wiseman's first film, a film critics consider a classic of American documentary filmmaking, and Wiseman's most didactic film. *High School* is included because it is the most widely seen of his films and is representative of the films that characterize the institution as an agent of socialization. *Hospital* represents the films that show institutions' attempts to relieve the crises and pressures of a disintegrating society. *Primate*, a recent film, is the most controversial and abstract to date. It depends, like *Meat*, primarily on images and film structure for development of themes and meanings.

The shot lists were compiled from repeated viewings of the films on videotape and 16mm prints. The lists and synopses break the films into parts and superparts according to the scheme outlined in Part II. The lists include description of each shot's visual content and all camerawork. Key dialogue is quoted completely and identified with quotation marks. Often, we never know the names of Wiseman's major characters. In these cases, they are identified by assigned labels. Speakers are not identified under "sound" when the visual description makes it clear who is speaking.

Part IV reflects a thorough search in English, French, and German of literature on Wiseman and his films. This includes a search of indexes of Canadian and British periodicals. All *New York Times* articles are included. Criteria for selection of other newspaper articles required that an article contribute new viewpoints or information not already expressed elsewhere.

I would like to thank Fred Wiseman for his assistance with the biographical portion of this volume, and for use of review copies of the films. Professor George Bailey, University of Wisconsin-Milwaukee, provided most of the tools and resources needed in compiling the shot lists, as well as insights and criticism valuable in formulating a critical survey of oeuvre. Ron Gottesman has been indispensable for his close and careful editing and correction of the manuscript. I would like to thank my friend, Susan Straley, for spending long and tedious hours at the typewriter.

I Biographical Background

Frederick Wiseman's success in a genre notorious for nearly insurmountable funding and distribution problems is as unusual as his preparation for making eleven highly acclaimed, controversial, and award-winning documentaries. His first film, *Titicut Follies* (1967), is considered a classic of American documentary film.

Although Wiseman says he has been interested in film from his teens, he did not attempt to make films until his early thirties. Born January 1, 1930, he attended a private high school in Boston and received an LL.B. degree after attending Williams College and Yale Law School. He studied at Harvard for a year as a graduate fellow and worked as an assistant to the attorney general of Massachusetts. He was drafted into the army, and after his discharge, went to Paris with his wife (also a lawyer) on the GI Bill, where he studied and practiced law from 1956 to 1958. While in Paris, Wiseman experimented with 8mm film, making documentaries of Paris street scenes and marketplaces. He attended screenings at the Cinematheque and says that the films that interested him most were classical Hollywood films, as well as those by Fritz Lang and Jean Renoir.

Wiseman returned to Boston University's Institute of Law and Medicine as an instructor. In an interview with Ira Halberstadt, he explained why he decided to produce a film in 1963.

> I didn't like reading appellate-court decisions, because I found they were at too high a level of abstraction and removed from what I thought were the more interesting kinds of issues. So I stopped. And since I have always been interested in film, I decided to give it more of a whirl. (*See* Item 161 below.)

Wiseman bought the film rights to Warren Miller's novel about delinquent youth in Harlem, and produced *The Cool World* (1964), a feature directed by Shirley Clarke. The film used techniques usually associated with documentaries: non-professional actors, script improvisation, and on location shooting. For Wiseman, *The Cool World* was a chance to watch and learn from the professional filmmakers in the project. Financially, it was unsuccessful, costing him the last of his savings and unpleasant encounters with creditors.

1

This first film production experience convinced Wiseman that there was no mystique about filmmaking, and that his real interest was in directing and editing. While teaching at Boston University, Wiseman took his students on tours to Bridgewater, a prison-hospital, to show them where their clients might end up after sentencing. The idea of making a film about the institution grew out of his visits. He had seen documentary films by Richard Leacock and ABC's Time-Life series of documentaries by Drew Associates, and chose conventions of cinema verite while shooting at Bridgewater because he thought they were best suited to the themes he wanted to express. Wiseman says that his unconventional structuring of the film grew out of his own experience with the material and the shooting.

Wiseman funded *Titicut Follies* through lab credit, deferring payment to labs for film and processing until the film earned money back from rentals. In return, the lab had rights to the print business. Wiseman borrowed equipment to use in shooting the film. After it was completed, NET wanted to buy the film and run it as the first program of the Public Broadcasting Laboratory, but a lawsuit had started in connection with the film.

Wiseman was accused of breaking an oral contract giving the state of Massachusetts the right of censorship of the film, and of invading the privacy of the inmates. The trial judge ordered the film to be burned, but that decision was stayed pending appeal. Finally, the Massachusetts supreme court ruled that the film had value for professional audiences like doctors and lawyers, but that it could not be shown to general audiences. That injuction remains in effect. Wiseman must notify the court of each screening of *Titicut Follies*, and who saw it. According to Wiseman, this is the first time a court has found any "publication" acceptable to one audience and not to another.

Despite the lawsuit, Wiseman received a foundation grant in the spring of 1967 to do *High School* (1968). *Law and Order* (1969), *Hospital* (1970), and *Basic Training* (1971) were funded in varying proportions by PBS, WNET Channel 13 in New York, and income from rentals. Wiseman says he began distributing his own films after deciding there was little risk involved, because distributors made money from his films and paid none to him. After *Basic Training*, Wiseman contracted with WNET to do one documentary each year for five years. The contract has been renewed once — *Canal Zone* (1977) and *Sinai Field Mission* (1978) are the first of this second series of five films for WNET that will play on the PBS network. Wiseman says he is able to make a living by combining funds he receives for production, distribution, and speaking engagements. His films are rented primarily by schools, libraries, and film societies.

Wiseman has followed the same basic production scheme for each of the films. After getting approval of the subject from WNET, Wiseman finds someone in the institution to be filmed who is sympathetic and who becomes the internal advisor. He makes it clear that he has editorial control over content and tries to get verbal, taped consent from everyone filmed. He does no research on the subject before shooting — he considers the shooting of the film to be the research. He accumulates an average of 80,000 feet of film over four to six weeks. People in the institution are notified about the filming in staff meetings and through notices on bulletin boards. Wiseman claims that camera awareness has never been a problem, and he is able to sense when people are playing to the camera. But this happens rarely, he believes, because people have a limited repertoire of behaviors, and when in awkward or tense situations, they tend to fall into comfortable, familiar patterns of behavior, seldom looking at the camera. His subjects rarely deny permission to use the shot.

"We don't do anything except hang around," Wiseman said. "Out of 10 hours you shoot two. You talk with the people to get a better idea of what's going on and the usual pattern of events. I try not to alienate them by talking politics or being provocative." Wiseman sees the silent rushes within three days of shooting.

Back in his Boston studio, he views the synched rushes and quickly discards 50 to 60 percent of the footage. Out of the remainder, he constructs an outline of "goodies" that are likely to be in the final film.

> I randomly edit the goodies down without thinking of structure. Ideas of structure may develop then, sometimes through a rational, deductive process, other times through an irrational or inductive process. This kind of trial and error, hit and miss goes on for four to eight months depending on the success I have dealing with the material. The film becomes progressively more absorbing and as the film emerges, I have greater command over the material and make changes faster. Sometimes the sequences you don't think are important turn out to be crucial for feeling and pacing of the film. For example, the corridor scenes in *Hospital* are important for the rhythm of the film and for giving pauses after major sequences — if you abut major sequences you lose meaning.

Wiseman explains that his unconventional documentary style stems from his interest in fiction and novels and from his effort to adapt a novelistic structure to documentary material.

> I try to place the viewer in the middle of events and ask him to think through his own relationship to what he is seeing and hearing. My point of view is given indirectly through the structure. The placement of the letter at the end of *High School* makes it a different film than if the letter hadn't been used or if the letter started the film. When you hear the letter at the end of the film I hope you read the film into the letter. It connects the major themes I think I've been dealing with and hopefully enlarges the context of the film.

In interviews, Wiseman is impatient and unhelpful to people who ask questions about the "meanings" and "points of view" of his films, insisting that the films must speak for themselves, and that it is the critic's job to make interpretations and connections. He has repeatedly said that he makes the films for no intended audience, but for himself, to satisfy his own standards of form and "fairness."

When I first started I believed that there was a connection between documentary and people rushing out to man the barricades
and produce instant social change. I now think this is a naive view
which has an implicit condescending attitude toward the audience. It assumes that they have no other experience, read no
books or see no other films, and that they are waiting for films
and filmmakers to provide swift illuminations. Fortunately, the
reality is different. People make up their minds on the basis of
more experience and thought than the single work can offer
them. If you believe in the idea of the marketplace of ideas, part
of that is the idea that in order to do something about anything,
you have to understand it. And the more information you have —
even information that says it's very complicated — the better
chance you have if you're interested in doing anything about it.
While I understand the feeling that the films are depressing, I also
think the reality is depressing and the only hope to do something
about it is to give some ideas of the dimensions of the issues.

Wiseman has repeatedly expressed an interest in applying documentary techniques to a feature film in which he controls the actors and dialogue, but evokes the
same feelings of reality and density usually associated with documentaries. But
more recently, his interests have shifted toward films like *Days of Heaven* (Terrence
Malick, 1978), which he calls a "very stylized, completely nonrealisitic, and beautiful movie." He is currently writing a film script based on a novel by Anne Tyler,
Celestial Navigation. Wiseman says that the script is about an artist who lives alone,
and it draws abstractions from concerns of ordinary life. "I realize that my films
have been becoming increasingly abstract," Wiseman said, "but I want to deal with
abstractions in a different way. I'm interested in stylization, and in doing with the
writing of the film what I have been doing with the editing. I want to control what
the people in the film say, instead of having to work it out afterward in the
editing."

Wiseman says he has no political commitment to the documentary form. "My
only commitment to documentry is that I like to do it."

II Critical Survey of the Oeuvre

Wiseman's work embraces two traditions of documentary film. In the Grierson tradition, he explores and exposes conditions of society and its institutions that demand change. Yet his films are as much about individuals as they are about impersonal institutions, fusing John Grierson's social journalism with Robert Flaherty's artful humanism, satisfying the artist as well as the activist. Wiseman's fusion of these two traditions and his unconventional style restate once again the hard central questions about film and reality. Each new release provokes a flurry — sometimes a storm — of controversy from critics, the public and the films' "actors" themselves. Critics charge that Wiseman's films are neither balanced nor "objective" in the journalistic sense. But balance implies two sides to a story. Wiseman sees not sides but the murky center.

STRUCTURE

Critics of Wiseman's first film, *Titicut Follies*, had an understandably hard time deciphering this new form. The film introduced a unique, unconventional approach to structure that Wiseman applied to each of the later films. Often, sets of shots share common space, characters, time, and action, much like conventional scenes. But the word "scene" is not appropriate to Wiseman. While he might follow the activities of a "character" through several shots, there is no character development. Representations of space, time, and action are not motivated narratively. There are no traditional structural divisions like clear sequences marked by fades to black, no narration, no establishing shots. Wiseman picks up action directly before its climax and cuts away directly after, leaving us wondering what precipitated the action and what was the outcome.

On first viewing, the films look like randomly ordered collections of these unconventional scenes. But Wiseman's films do have meaningful, complex structures of repetition and thematic or chronological progression of parts and superparts. Into each part, Wiseman groups sets of shots that share some commonality on a standard that varies from film to film, but one which is just as rigid and meaningful as the standard used for conventional scenes. In *High School* and *Basic Training*, Wiseman groups shots into "lessons." Shots of girls participating in a fashion show, a home economics class, a typing class, and a sex education class — disconnected in space, time, and characters — become a lesson in growing up to be a woman. In *Hospital*, each part reveals one of the institution's services (admission, diagnosis, surgery). In *Law and Order, Juvenile Court,* and *Welfare*, each set of shots is a case. In *Primate*, each part is an experiment. *Essene*'s parts compare and contrast the personalities of the monks. In *Meat*, each part is a step in the process of turning animals into supermarket products. In *Titicut Follies*, each part is a set of shots that shows an activity or process within the institution.

But unlike many documentary filmmakers, Wiseman does not construct his films out of clearly distinct, topically arranged parts. Instead, he weaves the loose strands of his gapridden incomplete scenes into a superstructure of symmetrical, overlapping repetition of elements. Settings, nonevents (janitors, hallways), sound, people, and events themselves reappear rhythmically in the films. Each film has its major "characters" (not in the narrative sense) — those people who reappear in longer parts important to the film's primary themes. Minor characters appear less frequently, performing minor "roles." Wiseman's complex overlapping repetition of these elements unifies otherwise disjointed parts and suggests themes of timelessness, circularity, changelessness.

On a second level, the films have superstructures of thematic or chronological progression. In the absence of narration and establishing shots at the beginning of each scene, Wiseman begins the films with short visual introductions to institutions through their admission process or by a series of shots that orient the viewer. Each film ends with shots that either complete a circular thematic structure or send us on a tangent out of the institutional cycle (often into another institution). In *Law and Order* and *Essene*, chronological progression takes the form of parts that are grouped into superparts of film days and nights. Shots of daytime activities are grouped together as are shots of nighttime activities. The superparts are linked with transition shots of dusk and dawn. Although there is no chronological continuity between parts of these or any of the films, the reappearance of major characters a little farther along in their journeys through the institutions suggests another type of weak chronological progression. Thematically, the parts of *Juvenile Court, Titicut Follies, Primate, Basic Training, Welfare, Meat,* and *High School* follow a progression from admission to departure. Parts in *Law and Order, Essene,* and *Hospital* form a larger structure that suggests circularity and the endless natures of the institutions' and the individuals' problems.

On a third level, Wiseman sets up a wave-like superstructure of rising tension and release by juxtaposing scenes that place high emotional or intellectual demands on the spectator with scenes of lighter situations. In *Titicut Follies*, the upbeat birthday party follows immediately after the most unpleasant part, the force feeding. After the camera lingers on the coffin in the death sequence, we cut to the "happy ending" of the Titicut Follies stage show.

STYLE

The style that Wiseman introduced with *Titicut Follies* — called "crude" by one critic — is duplicated in each of the later films. John Marshall photographed *Titicut Follies* and Richard Leiterman photographed *High School.* Starting with *Law and Order,* the remaining films are photographed by William Brayne. Wiseman does his own sync sound recording, allowing him to be in constant close contact with his cameraman and the events themselves. Camera movement is limited almost exclusively to keeping the subject in the frame. The camera is always hand held and most shots are head on. High or low angles seem to be accidents of where the camera happens to be rather than calculated effects. Nearly all shots are closeup or medium. The use of the zoom is free but seldom jarring.

This style of camerawork underscores Wiseman's concern with the human subject — in closeup, throwing the surroundings out of focus and otherwise revealing the environment only in whatever space remains in the frame. The result is often disorienting and claustrophobic.

Working only with available light, Wiseman shoots exclusively in black and white and the images are often of high contrast. Sound functions diegetically except, importantly, when Wiseman overlaps sound between two parts for transition or comment, and rarely, when he continues sound unchanged from one shot to a whole sequence of succeeding shots (the rhythmic machine noise during the surgery in *Hospital,* the crickets during the night maneuver in *Basic Training*). Wiseman uses naturally occurring music as a structural element and as commentary on situations in which it occurs. In *Titicut Follies,* the trombonist inmate plays "Blue Heaven" in the courtyard as accompaniment to shots of inmates relaxing, exercising, masturbating. In *High School,* a hall monitor's barked demands: "Got a pass?" are cut with a girls' gym class doing exercises to the song: "Simon Says." Transitions between parts are simple cuts except when Wiseman overlaps sound to suggest simultaneity, thematic relationship, irony, or comedy. "Nonevents" that act as transitions and releases after intense scenes have become Wiseman trademarks: hallways, custodians, computers, waiting rooms, the sound of intercoms. All of these, of course, are indigenous to institutions. After *Titicut Follies* and *High School.* Wiseman stopped juxtaposing individual shots for what he later regarded as heavy-handed irony or comedy. In the later films, his point of view surfaces through a more subtle and ambiguous comparison and contrast of events across entire films.

THEMES

All of Wiseman's films deal with themes inherent in any institution: socialization, alienation, class relations, control, unhuman bureaucracy, irrationality, legitimation. Each film emphasizes some of these more than others. Minor themes are common to several films. Misfits confront the institutions in *Titicut Follies, High School, Basic Training, Essene,* and *Welfare,* refusing to go along and questioning the institutions' basic premises and values. Their nonconformities force agents of the institutions to justify and articulate institutional values and goals. With a second subtheme, Wiseman shows the interconnective, symbiotic but sometimes antagonistic relationship between institutions. *Basic Training* is a natural sequel to *High School*. High school shares militaristic characteristics with basic training, while basic training relies on high school-like instruction of recruits. Basic training is a year away for many of *High School's* seniors. Northeast's teachers talk about the fate of their graduates now in the army. Similarly, *Juvenile Court* is a natural sequel to *Law and Order*. Many of the problems of the court's young people stem from the family breakdowns we see in *Law and Order* and the social disintegration we see in *Welfare*. *Law and Order* type police officers deliver patients and accident victims to Metropolitan Hospital where Dr. Schwartz of *Hospital* is on the phone, accusing another hospital of jeopardizing a woman's life by the way it transferred her to Metropolitan. *Titicut Follies* gets its inmates from the criminal courts. *Essene's* monastery shelters men who seek retreat from all society's institutions. *Primate's* researchers get their grants from the government and military. The role of the clergy and religion in Wiseman's institutions is another minor theme, as well as another example of the interdependence of institutions. Ministers, priests, or chaplains are present in *Titicut Follies, Hospital, Basic Training, Juvenile Court, Essene, Welfare,* and *Canal Zone*. In each case, the clergy have become ideologues of whatever institution they serve. They become agents of the institutions just like the police officers, doctors, or custodians, and try to help their clients fit in as easily as possible. In *Essene* the clergy try to create their own ideal (though arti-ficial) community and find themselves in yet another institution.

In many ways, Wiseman's films conform to the "rules" of traditional documen-tary filmmaking. He uses native actor and scene, his lightweight equipment lets him have the minimum impact on his subjects, and he insists that meaning be dictated as much as possible by the material. With a point of view, he creatively selects material and edits for the drama and intensity necessary to involve the viewers. But the disorienting absence of establishing shots, the claustrophobic close-ups, the lack of narration (in some films we never hear the name or location of the institution) engenders a feeling of confusion especially unsettling to those who expect his work to be explication and analysis of social problems.

In interviews, Wiseman has said that he hopes the films will incite action to improve the conditions he exposes — but he offers no solutions, or even the hope of solution. He answers none of the questions his films raise. Certainly the films have some journalistic value, recording the natures of the institutions at least partially: their physical plants, their clients, use and abuse of authority, values. But Wiseman says little about these. Critics who call the films "attacks" against the institutions would be hard put to find editing or camerawork to support a claim that Wiseman is in any way angered by what he sees. Each film has a compassionate yet detached attitude toward its human subjects and their plights. Wiseman's camera watches the tragedy and black comedy of the institutions with fascination, moving uninvolved, from example to example of irrationality, helplessness, hopelessness. Its detached interest discourages the spectator from easy emotional responses. The films' inter-lacing structures force us to compare, not to judge. They present themes, not argument or analysis.

Grierson believed that documentary film could and should digest raw information to make it meaningful and useful to citizens who are otherwise paralyzed by information overload. Wiseman's films refuse to simplify to the extent of most documentaries, and instead suggest that a correct understanding of social problems requires that we acknowledge the very complexity, ambiguity, and interrelatedness that Grierson tried to deny. Challenging spectators to decipher the films' unconventional structures and come up with their own meanings and solutions, Wiseman demands a higher level of participation and commitment from spectators than do most documentarists. By shifting the locus of this participation and commitment away from a film's conclusions and analysis and placing it in the process of spectatorship itself, Wiseman puts the viewer through an exercise of active spectatorship that she/he can apply to real life encounters with institutions.

III   The Films: Synopses, Shot Lists, Credits and Notes

The following abbreviations are used in the shot lists:

ECU	Extreme close-up, subject from chin up.
CU	Close-up, subject from chest up.
MS	Medium shot, subject from knees up.
LS	Long shot, reveals the whole subject.
ELS	Extreme long shot, subject takes up less than half of the frame's height.
ZI	Zoom in.
ZO	Zoom out.
LA	Low angle.
HA	High angle.
PR	Pan right.
PL	Pan left.
FV	Front view.
SV	Side view.
BV	Back view.
FG	Foreground.
BG	Background.
(00:00)	Duration of shot in minutes and seconds.

1   TITICUT FOLLIES (1967)

Titicut Follies is set in the Bridgewater State Hospital for the criminally insane in Massachusetts. Wiseman took the title from an annual variety show performed by by inmates and employees. Shots from the show function as opening, middle, and closing scenes for the film. The camera follows seemingly routine days in the lives of inmates, employees, and professionals. Each part is a set of shots that present an example of the inmates' hopelessness in the institution.

The commissioner of correction gave Wiseman permission to film, but after *Titicut Follies'* release, the state of Massachusetts disputed the terms of permission and argued in court that the film abused the patients' right of privacy. The court banned *Titicut Follies* in Massachusetts. Television stations have refused to broadcast the film, and most showings are at university film societies and social welfare courses.

The film won the First Prize for Best Documentary, Mannheim Film Festival, 1967; the Critics Prize, Festival dei Popoli, 1967; and Film Best Illustrating Human Condition, Festival dei Popoli, 1967. Wiseman financed *Titicut Follies* with investments and loans. (87 minutes)

SYNOPSIS

Part 1: Admission

In what amounts to a musical overture, *Titicut Follies* opens with a pan across faces of costumed men singing "Strike Up the Band." Only later do we conclude that this is the institution's variety show. The master of ceremonies turns out to be a guard ("Star Guard") who reappears throughout the film. This upbeat opening, with its glittering costumes and lively music, contrasts sharply with the drab uniforms, hallways, cells, and faces of the admission process that follows.

In the next scene, Wiseman intercuts shots of two parts of the admission process — men exchanging street clothes for uniforms and a child molester's first interview with a psychiatrist. In the admitting room we meet an inmate (the "Prophet") who will reappear, loudly preaching to no one in particular about politics, race, and religion. Finally, we follow the child molester as guards escort him through jail-like corridors and rooms to his cell. He walks to its barred window, and as the camera shoots through the peephole of the cell door, we see him gaze outside. Shots 2–35, (17:00).

Part 2: Free Time

Overlapping sound between shots 35 and 36 bridge the first two parts. We hear a trombone playing a rough blues. The images also act as a bridge: the inmate in shot 35 looks out of his cell window . . . into the courtyard of 36. Part 2 begins with the first of three sets of courtyard shots. Walled in by buildings, inmates exercise, debate, sit alone, talk to themselves, play the trombone, sing. We leave the open courtyard for a dark, unidentified room lit only by a television hung from the wall. A woman on the television sings a love song. Beneath the television, in the same frame, an inmate inexplicably sings "Chinatown." He is playing to the camera, cheerful, and wiggling his ears for his audience. In the next shot he seems to be a different man; older, vacant, unhappy as he walks out of the room and upstairs. Throughout the part, inmates are relaxed and relatively free. Guards show up only briefly, in the background. Shots 36–43, (3:11).

Part 3: Routine Day

Part 3 reveals more of the institution. Inmates and guards go about routine tasks: emptying bedpans, cleaning rooms, washing and shaving. We get to know the personnel and their relationship to the inmates. The "Star Guard" jokes sarcastically about his job and makes fun of an inmate; guards crack racial jokes at a black inmate; others taunt Jim, a naked, elderly inmate, until he shouts and stamps around his room; the "Star Guard" and a second guard chat about how they once used tear gas to subdue an inmate. Finally we return to the Titicut Follies show, where the "Star Guard" and a second man (who is never identified as an inmate or employee) sing "I Want to Go to Chicago." Shots 44-59, (15:50).

Part 4: Who's Crazy

Part 4 is set in the courtyard. The "Sane" inmate, arguing with the psychiatrist from part 1, insists that he is perfectly healthy and should be released. A second inmate argues knowledgeably about the Vietnam war. It's only his last argument about how America is the "female, sex crazy part of the earth," that makes us doubt his sanity. A third inmate steals the trombonist's stage (part 2) to sing the "Ballad of the Green Berets." The trombonist looks on impatiently. Inmates give each other skeptical, wary looks as if to say, "He's crazy." Shots 60-73, (10:21).

Part 5: Force-feeding

The psychiatrist from parts 1 and 4 returns to force-feed an elderly inmate. The psychiatrist's indifferent attitude produces memorable images: he smells the liquid he is about to pour down the feeding tube; he squints through his cigarette smoke as ashes threaten to drop into the feeding tube's funnel. The force-feeding is inter-cut with shots of a mortician carefully preparing the same inmate for burial. After the feeding, guards shut the cell door behind the inmate, and we cut to a morgue, where an employee shuts a cooler door on a coffin. Shots 74-97, (7:52).

Part 6: Birthday Party

Personnel, volunteers, and inmates celebrate a birthday in a bright, decorated hall. Women aides cut cake and direct children's games while a trio of guitar-playing inmates leads a sing-along of "Have You Ever Been Lonely?" The "Star Guard" sings an encore of "I Want to Go to Chicago" from part 3, and gives a one-line preview of the song he will sing in the final Titicut Follies shots. His theatrical, even egotistical, behavior contrasts with the relaxed, lucid inmates. Shots 98-117, (6:46).

Part 7: Trying to Get Out

We meet a second psychiatrist as he sets up an appointment over the phone. He hangs up and turns to a meeting with other doctors and the "Sane" inmate from part 4. The "Sane" inmate still insists that he's well enough to be released, and as in part 4, his seemingly logical arguments contrast with the seemingly arbitrary resis-tance of the doctors. The psychiatrist concludes that his patient is regressing and needs tranquilizers. Shots 118-134, (8:40).

Part 8: Hopeless Cases

Contrasting with earlier parts, here we see behavior of apparently hopelessley insane inmates in a washroom, a commons, and a cell. Shots 135-146, (3:40)

Part 9: Getting Out

Images of dying, death, and burial; and religious references made by the "Prophet," a priest, and a singing inmate link the shots of part 9. After the priest gives the last rites to a conscious, silent inmate, we cut to the courtyard where the

"Prophet" and a singing inmate expound on religion. When we cut back, workers lift a body from a cooler to the coffin, and nail the coffin shut. We follow it to the cemetery where inmates carry it to the grave and the priest prays. The final image before the closing Titicut Follies shots is a low angle, long shot of the coffin on the horizon, alone between the ground and the sky. Sound overlap takes us to the Titicut Follies show, where the "Star Guard" directs the finale. The song is "So Long for Now." The image of the "Star Guard" is low angle, bottom lit, and becomes grotesque as he stares into the audience, grinning, mouthing the words of the song. The final image of the film is a very young inmate, smiling and clapping. Shots 147-164, (10:13).

SHOT LIST

Shot No.	Visual	Sound
1	TITICUT FOLLIES (0:02)	"Strike Up the Band" sung by inmates, played by band.

Part 1: Admission

2	CU ZO to LS of men (inmates) singing on a stage. Slow ZI to 3 shot, MS; ZI to CU of one inmate. Slow PR along faces, ZO to MS as they shake pompons. After song they walk off stage right. Shot is front bottom lit, black BG. (1:55)	Men (inmates) sing "Strike Up the Band."
3	MS master of ceremonies ("Star Guard" who reappears throughout the film) waving on applause. ZI to ECU of him at microphone, bottom lit. He turns and exits through curtain. (1:03)	"Star Guard" introduces next act and tells joke about Father Mulligan (a chaplain at the institution who is referred to later in the film).
4	MS of inmate taking off shirt in what appears to be an admitting room. "Star Guard" crosses in FG, smiling and silent. ZI to CU of inmates' faces as they walk aimlessly in the large bare room. (0:23)	room noise
5	MS of guard searching Russell's clothes, inmates stand in BG, guard gives Russell his clothes, several inmates are naked. ZI to CU guard, ZO to MS guard and first inmate from shot 4. (0:50)	Guards: "Next." "Russell, come around here." "Harold, come here, get your clothes."

6	ECU inmate, ZO to CU of him (child molester) seated across what is later revealed as psychiatrist's desk. (0:22)	Off camera: a man with an accent questions inmate about his sexual relations with children.
7	CU molester, ZO to MS over psychiatrist's shoulder. (0:20)	Psychiatrist asks if inmate was intoxicated when he committed sexual assaults.
8	ECU molester, he bites lip. (1:10)	Psychiatrist asks about crimes, inmate admits sexual relations with his daughter. Inmate: "The way I am right now, if I have to stay like this, I'd just as soon go to jail and stay there."
9	Admitting room, MS ZI to CU inmate, PL to CU guard, inmates standing in BG, ZO to MS of guard and inmates. (0:16)	Guard: "Take off your clothes."
10	MS pile of personal articles on the floor. (0:05)	room noise
11	MS BV naked inmate, guard left, ZI to CU inmate. (0:12)	room noise
12	CU inmate from shot 11, he walks left. (0:02)	room noise
13	MS guard emptying pockets of inmate's clothes, inmates in BG. (0:15)	Off camera: a guard calls Richard over.
14	CU 2 shot guard and Richard, ZO to MS, guard searches clothes. Richard undresses and holds out arms, turning to be searched. ZI to CU 2 shot. (0:37)	Guard: "Take 'um off, come on. Put your hands out, turn around, OK. take your stuff and get over here. Get dressed."
15	Psychiatrist office, ECU inmate from shot 8. (0:04)	Psychiatrist asks how many times inmate masturbates a day . . .
16	ECU psychiatrist. (0:02)	"Or a week?"
17	ECU inmate, eyes, nose. (0:03)	"Sometimes three times a day."
18	ECU psychiatrist, exhales smoke from cigarette. (0:36)	"That's too much." He asks if inmate is interested in "big, tall, husky, luscious, looking female." He doesn't give time to answer. "What are you interested in, big breasts . . .

19 ECU molester, scratches head. (0:04)

"... or small breasts?"

20 ECU psychiatrist, ZO to CU as he inhales on cigarette, squinting through smoke. (0:55)

Inmate: "I never though of it." Psychiatrist asks about homosexual experiences and inmate relates two experiences.

21 Admitting room: CU inmate (stutterer), unshaven, nods and jerks his head sharply. (0:25)

"I told the doctor before I came here I didn't want my balls taken outta me."

22 Psychiatrist office, HA MS, ZI to CU molester. (0:15)

"I know there's something wrong, otherwise I wouldn't do things like that. But that's the way I am."

23 CU psychiatrist. (1:03)

He narrates inmate's criminal record. "And you still say you don't need help." Inmate: "I need help but I don't know where I can get it." Psychiatrist: "Well, you get it here, I guess."

24 Admitting room, ECU inmate who stares into camera, slow PR, ZI to inmates standing in BG, CU of individual faces. (0:30)

Off camera: can hear "Prophet" and stutterer from shot 21.

25 CU and MS of inmates as they walk slowly to right, slow PR to see corridor in BG. "Prophet" (an inmate who reappears throughout the film) enters left, CU, gesturing emphatically with arms, ECU ZO to CU as he faces camera. Corridor and inmates BG. (1:30)

Off camera: we hear "Prophet." On camera he intones "truths" about a parole board, Charles Volpe, John Kennedy, Nazi Party, Israel, interspersing words with nonsense syllables.

26 CU stutterer shots 21 and 24, he grimaces as he listens to "Prophet" puts hands over ears, ZO to MS stutterer with "Prophet" in FG. Stutterer looks angry and afraid of "Prophet." (0:20)

"Prophet": "We all know the truth ..."

27 MS "Prophet" facing camera, inmates seated in chairs BG, ZI to CU. ZO to MS and PR as he walks right, chopping at the air with his arm. (0:40)

"I point them out for I am called Christ Jesus."
"John Kennedy I say you sick boy ... send them back and put sign: 'Niggers we don't want to see you here.' "

28   MS of guards ushering child molester from shot 22 out of a cell and into a corridor. (0:10)

room noise

29   CU BV "Prophet," track forward as he walks left, arms raised as in blessing. Inmates file past him into corridor BG. (0:37)

Intones religious phrases, political names.
"Amen . . . Thy will is done."

30   Reverse angle, view from corridor, MS guard in doorway, inmates file past into corridor. (0:05)

"Prophet": "Therefore, I have completed my mission in life."

31   CU BV "Prophet," inmates in BG, he walks through doorway, hands raised in benediction. (0:07)

"Amen!"

32   MS 3 shot guards and inmate (shot 28) walking down corridor. Camera follows behind them, cells on right, ZI to 2 shot officer and inmate. (0:28)

footstesps
Guard asks a question and inmate nods.

33   Reverse angle, they walk toward camera, past, and camera follows from behind as they pass through door, LA MS as they go up stairs and through door at top. (0:22)

footsteps

34   CU inmate, takes off clothes. ZO to MS inmate and guards, ZI to ECU inmate. (0:25) We follow him through shot 35.

Guards: "Got an empty one?"
"Number eight is empty."

35   Long tracking shot, ECU guards, ZO to CU guards and naked inmate (shot 34) walk down corridor, cells on right. Guards reaches down and looks at inmate's hands, puts cigar in mouth, runs hand over inmate's crew cut, checking hair. Camera tilts up to LA CU of television hanging from ceiling at end of corridor, tilts down, CU guards gesture for inmate to enter cell. He walks in and they close door, ZI to ECU over shoulder of one guard to "8" on door. Hand reaches in to open small window on door, guard peaks in and moves away, camera ZI through window to MS inmate silhouetted by light

footsteps

television sound

Off camera: we hear a trombone

from window across room, he leans on sill, looks out, ZI to CU out of focus. (1:05)

playing "Blue Heaven," mixed with sounds of guards and television.

Part 2: Free Time

36 LS of courtyard, inmates walking, standing, exercising BG. Slow PL. (0:20)

Off camera: trombone plays "Blue Heaven," sound overlap from shot 35.

37 LS BV inmate standing alone in center of courtyard. Trombone player right BG, inmates sit on benches along wall BG. (0:07)

"Blue Heaven"

38 LS trombone player standing next to fire hydrant, inmates on benches BG. (0:10)

"Blue Heaven"

39 CU inmate standing in center of courtyard (shot 37) masturbating, ZO to LS. (0:25)

"Blue Heaven"

40 LS 2 shot inmates sitting on lawn, ZI slow PR to inmates on benches, LS. "Prophet" enters right, PL with him, he gestures widely, but we can't hear him talk. (0:25)

"Blue Heaven"

41 LS BV trombone player, fire hydrant on right, building in BG. (0:08)

"Blue Heaven"

42 CU older inmate, face lit brightly from right, black on left, BG black except for television upper left. Slow ZI to ECU inmate, television upper right. He finishes his song, wiggles his ears and grins into the camera. (1:40)

Inmate sings "Chinatown." This is counterpointed with the smooth love song of the television female singer: "I love Johnny."

laughter off camera

43 Same inmate walks toward camera, leaving television room, MS to ECU, he passes camera and it follows him to stairs, tilt up as he climbs stairs. Seen through grating of the stairs, he's silhouetted against light BG. He looks blank and unhappy as compared to shot 42. (0:32)

footsteps

Part 3: Routine Day

44 Long corridor, "Star Guard" walks toward camera LS to CU, passes camera on right, cells line the left of the corridor. (0:20)

"What time they open up these doors?"

45 CU BV "Star Guard" looking down corridor to two guards at end. He looks around, bored. Guards open doors down hall. Inmate emerges carrying bucket, passes camera on left. "Star Guard" hums to himself, turns to walk around corner down second corridor. Zip left to second guard opening doors down second corridor. (0:43)

Guards down corridor: "In another minute or two."
"Star Guard": "They're not vicious, I hope," he grins and laughs to himself, "a man could get hurt."

"Very interesting work, ahem!" (Sarcastically) "Tuesday, gotta open all the doors."

46 "Star Guard" right, CU BV over shoulder, standing in short hallway, talks through door to someone. (0:28)

"You're going home in 10 days huh? Or some other jail? Oh. You think your stay here has helped you? He thinks there's been a big improvement," he says, laughing, to a guard off camera.

47 LS of corridor, guards open doors, an inmate walks out of cell and toward camera with a bedpan, passes by on right. (0:24)

whistling off camera

48 MS inmate (shot 47) throws contents of bedpan into toilet in room off corridor, walks past camera and down corridor, PL. (0:07)

whistling off camera

49 MS naked inmate standing against brick wall of corridor, PR to guard on right, PL to door of room, janitor sweeping floor, inmate right. (0:30)

Off camera: guards ask about the "messy room."
"Gonna keep it a little cleaner tomorrow?" Inmate nods yes.

50 ECU same inmate, turns and walks into cell, two guards close door, CU. (0:07)

Guards: "OK, see you later."
"Bye, bye now.

51 ECU smiling guard, PR as he walks to next cell, BV as he opens door. Black, naked inmate walks quickly out of door and squats against wall next to door, MS, HA. (0:59)

Guard: "Come on, Tommy, what's the matter?" "You want to go to work?"
Tommy: "Yes, sir."
Guard: "Want to sell watermelons, how about giving us that watermelon song?"

Tommy: "Where can I work?"
Guard: "What do you feel like
doing? "What *can* you do?"

52   CU old, thin, naked inmate, no   "All right, go in."
        teeth. Guard gestures for him
        to enter room, he backs into
        room slowly and two guards
        close door. (0:12)

53   CU guard leading naked inmate to   room noise
        cell, he walks in and to window
        across cell, guard closes door.
        (0:15)

54   MS guards leading Jim through halls,   Throughout this shot, the guards
        he is naked, camera follows from   taunt Jim repeatedly, constantly
        behind. They walk up steps and   asking questions that he has
        through doorway, a guard slaps him   already answered.
        on the face. They walk down cor-
        ridor with cells on right, they turn
        into a shaving room. MS Jim sits
        in chair, barber puts soap on his
        face, guards stand at his side, ZI to
        ECU Jim's face, barber nicks his
        lip and blood runs down Jim's
        chin. Guard takes towel and wipes
        it off. Room is bare brick and ex-
        posed plumbing. (2:35)

55   ECU Jim's face, side view, hori-   Jim: "Thank you very much
        zontal in barber chair. ZO to   indeed. Thank you ever so much."
        CU, ZO to MS barber drying   Guard: "How about a drink of
        Jim's face. Jim gets up and takes   water Jim?"
        a drink from water fountain,   Jim: "All right, on the house, isn't
        walks out door with guards,   it?"
        camera follows into the corri-   laughter
        dor. (0:35)   As they enter corridor, guards taunt
        him again with questions about his
        messy room. He shouts and be-
        comes angry.

56   MS Jim and two guards standing   taunting of guards
        in stairway. ZI to CU Jim, he
        shouts and clenches teeth. They
        move left along corridor toward
        camera. Jim trots through his
        cell door and stands in far cor-
        ner. LS of him stomping   stamping feet
        rhythmically on floor, his hand
        over his mouth. ZI to ECU, he
        walks past window and back to

corner. ZO to LS, ZI to ECU.
He stops and frowns at camera,
walks to window, ZO to LS, PR
as he pounds on window, walks
to corner and stands with hand
on cheek, ZI to CU. The cell is
bare with brick walls and un-
covered floor. (2:35)

57 CU Jim in corner, he salutes
twice, ZO to MS, ZI to CU, ZI
to ECU. (1:00)

Guard: "You play piano Jim?"
Jim (quietly): "Yes."
Guard: "Where do you play?"
Jim: "My home in Pittsburgh."
He gives address.
Guard: "You a school teacher
Jim?"
Jim answers that he taught junior
high school subjects, arithmetic and
mathematics.
Guard: "What college did you go
to?"
Jim: "Pittsburgh State Teacher's
College, Pittsburgh normal school,
Pittsburgh business college, Pitts-
burgh high school."
Guard: "Graduate with honors
Jim?" He doesn't answer.

58 ECU guard, seated, ZO to
2 shot of him and "Star
Guard." ZI to first guard,
CU. They sit in a lounge,
rocking in rocking chairs.
(1:50)

They talk about the effects of tear
gas, the gassing of one of the inmates in the "bull pen," and how
they had to run the fans "steady
for a week" to get rid of the gas.
"I don't like it, it seems to affect
you awfully fast, you know, I
just get one whiff of it . . ."
(first guard)

Part 4: Who's Crazy?

59 Back to the Titicut Follies performance. CU 2 shot of "Star
Guard" and partner swaying in
time to song they are singing.
Black BG. They wear glitter-
ed hats, the "Star Guard"
leans his head on the shoulder
of his partner as they sing. ZO
to MS as they dance, ZI to ECU
guard, PR to ECU partner,.ZO to
MS as they end song and shake
hands. The guard points to his
partner to encourage applause,

They sing "I Want to Go to
Chicagotown."

then jumps to the center of the stage, spreads his arms and shouts: "And me!" ZI to CU "Star Guard" grinning. (1:35)

"Star Guard": "And me!"

60   Courtyard, CU 2 shot of psychiatrist from molester interview, and the "Sane" inmate (who we see again later in the film). ZO to CU 2 shot. (0:45)

"Sane" inmate: "Obviously I talk well, I think well, I am well . . . the principle is I am here obviously well and healthy and I am getting ruined." (He talks with accent.)

61   MS 2 shot of psychiatrist and "Sane" inmate, ZI to ECU inmate's mouth, ZO to MS, ZI to ECU PL then PR to each face, ZO to MS as they walk toward camera. Doctor finally breaks off conversation. Inmates and wall BG. (3:55)

Inmate complains that the tests he was given are useless, that he has been classified schizophrenic because he loves his father and mother.
Psychiatrist: "Then I'm a schizophrenic because I love my mother and father, but I never been in mental institution, nobody thought I should be."

62   LS of exercising inmate, stripped to waist, walks toward camera in courtyard, flexing arms. (0:04)

silence

63   CU BV exerciser, he turns to walk toward camera. (0:10)

We hear the "Communist" inmate off camera. (shot 64)

64   ECU, ZO to CU of "Communist" inmate as he lectures in the courtyard on Vietnam. (0:25)

"Anyone the American government doesn't like they use the term of 'Communist.' "

65   LS ZI to MS of inmates listening, PL along faces, guard BG. (0:15)

"Communist": "I'm not a Communist . . . even though I have Communist affiliation."

66   ECU "Communist" inmate. (1:15)

"A nuclear war is in the offing . . . they get tired of stockpiling and they're like a bunch of little kids, they have toys to play with and they gotta play with those toys. You watch in 1970 you're gonna see the greatest nuclear war of all time."

67   MS bystander inmate, points and argues with "Communist," ZI to ECU, ZO to MS 2 shot, bystander BG, "Communist" FG, ZI to ECU bystander, inmates

Bystander argues that Communists have regimented the Vietnamese people. "Communist": "America's the female part of the earth world and she's sexy crazy, her sexiness

and guards BG, ZO to MS 2 shot, ZI to CU "Communist," ZI to ECU. (2:35)

brings on wars, like the sperm that is injected by man into the woman."

68   CU HA inmates listening to "Communist," they look incredulous, impatient. They are seated against the wall. (0:15)

"Communist": "You mean to tell me that after you've had sex intercourse you feel fine or healthy — you don't."

We hear someone sing "Ballad of the Green Berets" off camera.

69   CU BV of exerciser, camera walks with him, inmates on benches BG. (0:10)

"Green Berets" sung off camera. (shot 70)

70   MS 2 shot singer and trombonist, trombonist looks incredulous, impatient, looks at singer as if he's crazy. (0:25)

"Green Berets"

71   LS inmates get up and start toward door on left. (0:02)

"Green Berets"

72   LS inmate walks to door. (0:02)

"Green Berets" fades out

73   LS, one inmate guides another to the door. (0:03)

silence

ᶦ *Part 5: Force-feeding*

74   Psychiatrist from "Sane" inmate and molester interview scenes, CU, walks left and looks through small window in cell door, ZI to ECU of window, he enters right, exits right, CU window. (0:30)

"Mr. _____ , come here a minute. If you don't eat food we are going to feed you with tube . . . through your nose."

75   Office, ZI MS to CU of psychiatrist on phone, he sits down. (0:40)

He arranges to have two patients prepared for tube feeding.

76   Tracking MS BV, three guards leading old, thin, naked inmate out of dark hall into feeding room, PR to psychiatrist standing next to inmate. (0:50)

Psychiatrist tells inmate if he doesn't drink the liquid, it will be put "through a tube through your nose into your stomach."

77   CU inmate, ZO to MS guards as they tie restraints to his wrists and stand on either side. (0:19)

Guard: "Either drink it or he'll dump it down the tube through your nose."

78	Psychiatrist, CU, guards BG. ZI to ECU as he lifts liquid to smell it. (0:03)	room noise
79	HA MS chest and face inmate lying on table, PL to psychiatrist as he places a cloth across patient's groin. ZI to CU psychiatrist smoking cigarette, ZO to LS, he wipes the tube around an empty jar to grease it. (0:43)	Guard, referring to jar: "Ain't much of anything left." Psychiatrist asks for "any other grease, or oil or anything."
80	ECU inmate's head, ZO to CU psychiatrist's hand, tube is above inmate's head. ZO to MS psychiatrist tries to get grease out of empty jar. ZI to CU his hands and tube, tilt down to ECU inmate's head, psychiatrist pushes tube into nose. (1:10)	Psychiatrist: "Any grease, butter?" Guard: "Swallow, swallow, that's a boy."
⁺81	ECU same inmate, dead, his eyes open, mouth open, fly on forehead, soap on his face. (0:02)	silence
82	ECU head of inmate, hands of doctor, ZO to MS doctor as he pulls chair over and puts one foot up on it. He holds up funnel and pours liquid into it. ZI to ECU funnel, ZO to CU psychiatrist with cigarette over funnel pouring liquid through smoke, LA. (0:45)	Assistant: "The marker's way down there, way down doctor." Doctor: "Get some water, OK?" Guards: "Did Sam work Friday?" "No he didn't work all last week."
83	ECU mortician. (0:03)	silence
84	ECU razor shaving corpse. (0:04)	silence
85	MS psychiatrist pouring fluid into funnel, cigarette ashes longer over funnel, squints through smoke, slow tilt down along tube to CU inmate's face, ZI to ECU. (0:32)	Doctor: "You got more food?"
86	ECU corpse, eyes open, razor shaving face. (0:04)	silence
87	ECU inmate in feeding room, PL and ZO along body, tilt up	Voice: "Leave some for the other the other guy."

at feet to guard holding ankle
restraints, PR to second guard,
CU. (0:25)

88	ECU dead inmate, mortician places cotton in eye sockets. (0:06)	silence
89	ECU corpse, mortician adjusts lids over cotton. (0:04)	silence
90	MS mortician and corpse, he adjusts lids over cotton. (0:04)	silence
91= end 87	tilt down and PR along inmate's body to CU head with tube in nose, ZI to mouth and nose, he swallows. (0:30)	Doctor: "Please get this job over with."
92	ECU psychiatrist, long ashes of cigarette poised above funnel. ZO and tilt down to MS of him and inmate, doctor pulls tube out. (0:25)	Doctor says something about "a little whisky." Laughter. Doctor: "Very good operation, very nice." Guard: "OK, Herr Doctor." "Hey, that wasn't bad at all, he's a veteran."
93	Mortician shakes out cloth after shaving corpse. LA, MS. (0:02)	silence
94= end 92	Psychiatrist places tube to right. (0:04)	Doctor: "I think he's been tube fed before." "All right, that's it."
95	Flash to corpse laid out in suit. (0:01)	silence
96	MS 2 shot doctor and attendant, PL and track LS after two guards leave room with inmate, down short corridor, turn corner to right, lead him to room, they close the door behind him. (0:23)	footsteps
97	Cut on action, HA MS of coffin being slid into cooler. Attendant closes door and walks away. Camera lingers on door. (0:13)	room noise door shuts

Part 6: Birthday Party

98	CU festive sign: Congratulations and a Happy Birthday! (0:03)	silence

99   CU cake, ZO to LS table of in-   applause
     mates, one blows out candles,
     ZI to birthday inmate, women   They sing along with guitars off
     aides look on in BG. (0:25)   camera: "Have You Ever Been
                                            Lonely?"

100 MS woman placing cake on   song
     plate. (0:02)

101 MS inmate smiling, eating cake.   song
     (0:02)

102 MS BV three singers, party BG,   song
     ZI over shoulder to CU woman
     singing along as she cuts cake.
     (0:20)

103 CU singers, wearing matching   Song: "If you knew what I've been
     vests, ZI to one singer, ZO to 3   through, then you know why I ask
     shot, all are inmates, one re-   you — have you ever been lonely,
     appears in final Titicut Follies.   have you ever been blue?"
     (0:45)

104 MS two women, one cuts cake,   song
     other pours coffee, ZI to ECU
     as they sing along. (0:15)

105 CU woman's hands placing   Off camera: "Then you're able to
     cake on plate. (0:03)   stand trial now?"
                                            "Oh sure." "Well good."

106 Track left from BV of inmate   He tells about success of new medi-
     seated at table to FV CU. He's   cation that relaxes him and keeps
     talking to a woman volunteer,   him from getting angry.
     ZI to ECU inmate. (0:25)

107 ECU "Star Guard," ZI on mouth,   He recites words of a song while
     ZO to CU, he recites the words of   pounding rhythm on table.
     a song while tapping the rhythm
     on the table. Singer inmates listen
     in BG. He stands up to leave, grin-
     ning. (0:23)   They clap.

108 ECU eyes of inmate, ZO to CU,   strumming of guitar off camera
     he inhales on cigarette, grins,
     turns and points finger at some-
     one, walks left. (0:16)

109 MS group of nurses, singers, volun-   Nurse reads part of letter from alco-
     teers, "Star Guard," camera PL to   holic and shows medal from him. "I
     focus on individual faces, ZI to   hope we cured him, it makes you
     CU of nurse as she shows medal   feel you're doing a little something
     and letter from a patient. (1:00)   and you feel, well, you at least tried."

110 ECU "Star Guard," his mouth works, he frowns and looks away. (0:03)	room noise
111 CU woman volunteer, ZO to LS, she's standing behind a target that rests on a chair. (0:20)	"Come on boys, show us your aiming."
112 CU BV of inmate walking toward target, camera walks with him. (0:25)	room noise
113 ECU inmate, PL as he rejoins group CU, he walks off left, camera stops on fat inmate, CU. Woman in BG, she points to bull's-eye, ZI to MS of woman and game, ZO to LS. (0:30)	Woman: "Here's the bull's-eye, line it up, come right at it."
114 MS of inmate reaching for dart, ZI to CU. (0:03)	Woman encouraging men to play.
115 LS woman and player, ZI to MS, ZI to CU of woman. (0:15)	Woman: "Come on now, who else?"
116 CU BV woman, PR to inmates BG, PL to woman, inmates BG. (0:11)	"Has everybody tried it?"
117 ECU "Star Guard" at party, he "rehearses" songs that appear in Follies scenes. He struts around room, camera follows, ZO to CU, seated inmates watch BG, he begins to leave room, picks up hat, then walks back into room singing second song, dances out of room left. (1:00)	"Star Guard" sings "I Want to Go to Chicagotown." He sings: "It's do or die for NCI."

Part 7: Trying to Get Out

118 ECU doctor on phone, ZO to CU, ZO to LS of him and desk, woman seated at table right, writing. (1:12)	He arranges an appointment with someone.
119 ECU doctor, hangs up phone. (0:15)	Turns to desk: "OK . . . now."
120 ECU "Sane" inmate. (0:30)	Doctor tells him he will be released when there is enough improvement. Inmate replies it is the institution that is making him worse.

121 CU doctor, he inhales on cigarette. (0:05)

Off camera, inmate: "I want to go back to prison where I belong."

122= ZO to MS "Sane" inmate sitting.
120 in chair, woman at same table BG, inhales on cigarette. (1:05)

Inmate: "I was supposed to come down here only for observation. My mind's perfect. I'm logical. I've been here for a year and a half. Every time I come in here you tell me I look crazy."

123 CU woman (shot 122), looks away, disinterested, inhales on cigarette and blows out smoke, ZO to MS inmate, FG, woman BG, ZI to ECU inmate. (1:40)

Inmate argues that he needs peace and quiet. That there are no sports at the institution. He is losing weight. "Everything that's happening to me is bad."

124 CU BV inmate, second doctor in BG. (0:04)

Inmate: "If you leave me here, obviously that proves . . .

125 CU ZI to ECU doctor, PL as he reaches to light cigarette, ZI to ECU eyes, nose. (0:36)

. . . that meant you want me to get harmed, it's just plain logic."
Doctor: "Well, that's interesting logic."
Inmate: "Isn't that perfect logic?"
Doctor: "No, it isn't Vladimir."

126 CU inmate, ZO to MS as he gets up and leaves with guards, PL, he walks away from camera out the door across the room, camera is behind desk, doctor FG. (0:25)

Doctor: "Thank you Vladimir."

127 ECU doctor, ZO to CU. (0:30)

"He's been much better than this. Now he's falling apart." He prescribes tranquilizers.

128 ECU woman (shot 123). (0:13)

"He argues in perfect paranoid pattern. If you accept his basic premise then the rest is logical, but the basic premise is not true."

129 ECU doctor. (0:25)

Doctor says Vladimir was very closed before, but has opened up recently.

130 ECU older man seated at table. (0:30)

Man says Vladimir sought executive clemency once, and got as far as the parole board at one time.

131 ECU woman. (0:03)

"I really think he's terrified of leaving."

132 CU doctor, ZI ECU. (0:30)

Doctor suggests he be put on tranquilizers to bring paranoid elements under control.

133 ECU second doctor (shot 124). (0:12)

He comments on paranoid behavior.

134 ECU doctor dictating into recorder. (0:25)

He records diagnosis: Schizophrenic Reaction with Prominent Paranoid Features.

Part 8: Hopeless Cases

135 HA CU Al, kneeling in tub and scrubbing his head with soap, ZO to MS of tub and Al. (0:16)

Guard: "That's good, huh?" "Take some of that chocolate pudding off."

136 ECU Al's face and hands as he washes, ZO to MS, he kneels and sticks head in water, drinks and blows bubbles, guard BG. (0:30)

Guards: "Why don't you lay right down in the water to get your back washed." "Yeah, soak your piles." "Don't drown, Al." Laughter.

137 ECU guard talking to Al. (0:04)

"Sit down and face me."

138 MS Al's upper body lying on back in water, he drinks water. (0:10)

Guard: "Don't swallow the water."

139 ECU AL's face in water, lies back and drinks water from the corner of his mouth, ZO to CU of Al drinking from faucet. (0:37)

Guards: "That's a boy Al." "How's it feel?" "Don't drink the water Al." "Here Al, drink out of the faucet."

140 Guard, BV, PL as guards walk Al to left, ECU guard drying him off. (0:05)

Guard: "Feel good?" "Nice and clean?"

141 ECU reflection of Al in mirror, ZO to CU BV Al. (0:12)

Guard: "OK Al, all set Al." "Yeah, had a good time."

142 MS Al, he stoops towards sink, walks toward camera, guards at his side. (0:06)

room noise

143 CU two guards and old inmate, they bring him to cell, he wears shorts, LS of him in cell, he bends double and screams. (0:20)

Inmate screams shrilly.

144 In the commons, inmates dressed in loose clothes wander in room. MS deformed inmate, PL as he walks to LS, ZI to CU as he sits across room. (0:37)

room noise

145   LS 3 shot, deformed inmate and   room noise
      two others, the two swing at each
      other. (0:04)

146   Same three inmates, ZI to CU de-
      formed inmate, ZI to ECU as
      he puts hand to face, grimaces   Sound overlap with shot 147, we
      at camera. (0:40)   hear priest's voice.

Part 9: Getting Out

147   LA MS priest standing right,   Priest reads scriptures.
      shaking oil onto inmate lying
      in bed left. (0:06)

148   MS BV priest, inmate BG, ZI to   Priest prays that inmate is forgiven
      CU inmate, ZI to ECU inmate   for sins committed by use of sight,
      as priest makes cross over nose,   hearing, sense of smell, power to
      mouth of inmate. ZO to MS   walk.
      priest and inmate, tilt down to
      high angle of inmate's feet, CU
      hands of priest as he lifts sheet
      and makes cross on feet, tilt up   "The Lord be with you and with
      to MS of priest and inmate.   your spirit."
      (1:15)

149   CU, ZI to ECU eyes of inmate   "Let us pray."
      over Bible in FG, as priest prays.
      (0:14)

150   Courtyard, CU "Prophet" track   "Prophet": "What is indulgences?
      right and over his shoulder we   Father Mulligan with his confes-
      see the feet and legs of an in-   sional, exposes us and calls us down
      mate standing on his head, ZI   to Warden Johnson. I know every-
      to ECU "Prophet," focus on   thing because I'm psychic. Even
      feet BG, "Prophet" exits right,   Pope Paul is not without sin. The
      tilt down to CU BV head of in-   vicar of the church is Jesus Christ.
      mate standing on his head.   I announce that the rightful Pope is
      (1:20)   now Archbishop Fulton Sheen. I
                                               Borge say so."
                                               We hear singing in the background:
                                               "For the glory of the glory of
                                               Father Mulligan . . . for the glory of
                                               his love and his holiness."

151   ECU FV singing, head-standing   He sings: "For the glory of the
      inmate upside down, inmate is   bishop, of the cardinal, the pastor
      singing with his eyes closed.   and the rabbi."
      Opens eyes at the end of song.
      (0:30)

152   CU singer's feet in air, track right   "Prophet": "Hear him, he's a liar
      to "Prophet" seen through the   and so is Peabody. I say so, I Borge

two legs, "Prophet" walks away, framed by the legs. (0:16)

say so." Song fades in and overlaps into shot 153.

153 Morgue, CU as man pulls body, head first out of cooler, it's wrapped in plastic, hands reach in to lift it, tilt up and to right as it's laid in coffin, tilt down, PL as drawer is pushed into cooler, hands close door, LA MS of guard as he walks from cooler door. (0:42)

room noise

154 MS HA wrapped body in coffin. (0:05)

room noise

155 CU guard in room, walks right. (0:04)

He swears about something.

156 LS of guard tightening lid screws on coffin. (0:02)

room noise

157 ECU hand holding screwdriver at its base, tilt up to ECU hand turning screwdriver, tilt up along arm to head of worker. (0:12)

room noise

158 MS workers bending to lift coffin, they back out door to right, camera follows as they go outside and down steps to hearse. CU BV of guard as he rolls coffin into hearse. (0:55)

room noise

159 At graveyard, LA LS of group of six inmates at hearse, guard pulls coffin out, they lift it, PR as they carry it away from camera. (0:20)

voices

160 ECU flowers, ZO to LS of inmates placing coffin over grave, priest at head of coffin, FG, ZI to MS, tilt down with coffin, tilt up PL to ECU BV priest, inmates and guards BG, PR to inmates on right side of coffin. (0:50)

Priest prays.

161 LA LS group at grave, gravestones FG right. (0:02)

Priest: "Eternal rest grant unto him."

162 LS LA of group at grave, inmates on each side of coffin, priest at head of coffin. Priest throws dirt on coffin, they turn toward camera and file off past both sides of camera. Coffin stands alone oh horizon. (0:40)

Priest: "May he rest in peace. Remember Man, that thou art dust and until dust thou shall return."

Overlap sound from shot 163, Titicut Follies song.

163 Titicut Follies show, LS eight inmates on stage, ZI to ECU inmate on left, slow PR along faces, slow ZO to LS, band director in lower center. PL as "Star Guard" enters left with women aides, LS ZI to CU two women, PR to "Star Guard" singing into microphone, he holds out hand to encourage applause, inmates sing BG. ZI ECU "Star Guard," bottom lit, he mouths the song. ZO to CU "Star Guard," PL to cast, ZO to LS inmates waving goodbye. "Star Guard" enters right and shouts "aren't they terrific?" ZI to MS Guard and two inmates, one is a young boy with a straw hat, ZI to CU boy, he bows several times. ZO to MS Guard and boy, ZI to ECU Guard, bottom lit. PL to boy and across to women, ZO to MS as they throw something to crowd, ZO to LS women as they turn and flip up skirts like a chorus line, ZI to CU of two women. (2:35)

Applause, piano playing "So Long For Now," inmates sing along.

164 ECU boy, clapping his hands, smiling. (0:05)

silence

165 Credits fade in and out. Directed and Produced by Frederick Wiseman. Co-direction and Photography by John Marshall. Editor Frederick Wiseman. Associate Editor Alyne Model. Associate Producer David Eames. Copyright 1967 Bridgewater Film Co., Inc. (0:20)

silence

CREDITS AND NOTES

Producer:	Frederick Wiseman
Director:	Frederick Wiseman
Photography:	John Marshall
Editor:	Frederick Wiseman
Associate Editor:	Alyne Model
Associate Producer:	David Eames

Copyright 1967, Bridgewater Film Co., Inc.
Filmed on Location at Bridgewater State Hospital, Bridgewater, Massachusetts.

Distribution:	Zipporah Films
Running Time:	87 minutes
Released:	September, 1967.

2 HIGH SCHOOL (1968)

The high school is Northeast High School in Philadelphia, an upper middle class school with a white student majority. Wiseman planned to film at a school in Boston, but the board of education was "upset" in the wake of the *Titicut Follies* trial, and a friend suggested that he try the schools in Philadelphia. Northeast High School was generally considered one of the two best schools in Philadelphia. Wiseman filmed at the school for four weeks and chose his footage from 40 hours of film. After seeing the final product, the Philadelphia schools' superintendent and much of the board of education said the film was an accurate picture of the school. But after screening the film again and reading reviews, the principal of Northeast High School threatened censorship. To avoid legal problems, Wiseman has not screened *High School* in Philadelphia. Like *Titicut Follies, High School* shows the routine activities of the institution: classes, assemblies, gym, counseling sessions, disciplinary action. Each part of the film is a set of shots that illustrates one of the institution's "lessons." The National Education Television network has broadcast the film. It was financed by the New World Foundation. (75 minutes)

SYNOPSIS

Part 1: Introduction

Like *Titicut Follies, High School* starts with a song, this time Otis Redding's "Sitting on the Dock of the Bay." We hear it as we ride in a car down neighborhood streets, past a shopping district, and up to a large factory-like building (that we later hear someone refer to as Northeast High School). The part is made up of short sets of shots from throughout the school: students walking in hallways, a teacher reading the thought for the day ("Life is cause and effect, one creates his tomorrows at every moment by his thoughts and deeds of today"), Spanish and French classes, drum rehearsal, and disciplinary action by the reappearing Coach. We are introduced to the setting, the institution's values, and its power structure. Shots 1–23, (5:56).

Part 2: Control

Part 2 is a series of confrontations between people in power and the disenfranchised. A parent argues with — then submits to — a teacher's evaluation of his daughter's work. The Coach from part 1 arranges punishment for a student who tries to defend himself and assert his "manhood" by sticking up for his principles. The Coach replies that to be a man is to be able to take orders. A male teacher patrols the halls, demands to see passes, denies a student the right to call his insurance agent during lunchtime. Wiseman cuts to a girl's gym class doing jumping jacks in time with the record: "Simon Says." Shots 24–46, (8:51).

Part 3: One teacher's way

In part 3 an elderly English teacher delivers a monotonous reading of "Casey at the Bat" to a class of seemingly unmoved students. We cut to the auditorium where girls in gym class swing at baseballs. Shots 47–58, (2:51).

Part 4: Socialization for Girls

In part 4 the school acts as an agent for socialization. Students learn some fundamental skills and attitudes that will help them to fit successfully into 1968 middle America. Boys in a home economics class measure ingredients for a recipe, girls learn to sew and model dresses designed to flatter their figures — they learn how to walk, how to be graceful. Students learn to type, a class of Jewish boys hears a lecture on the Jewish family structure. A speaker at the girls' sex education assembly describes how to use the birth control pill. Teachers call a girl on the carpet for failing to dress formally for the prom and tell her she has insulted her class. Girls compete in physical endurance for gym class. The part ends with a shot of a janitor in the hallway. Shots 59-98, (14:16).

Part 5: Another Teacher's Way

This time a young English teacher tries to interest students in analyzing poetry by offering something more "relevant" than "Casey at the Bat." She plays a tape of Simon and Garfunkel's "Dangling Conversation," to expressionless students who gaze around the room. The part ends with a shot of a cleaning woman in the hallway. Shots 99-115, (4:21).

Part 6: Control

Part 6 picks up where part 2 left off. We see more confrontations between the powerful and the disenfranchised. The Coach berates the "bully" for throwing the first punch, and ultimately for his lack of respect for adults. In a counselor's office, Eileen's mother and a teacher scold Eileen for locking a fellow student in a closet, and ultimately, for being disrespectful to adults. Shots 116-118, (6:01).

Part 7: Socialization

Continuing with Eileen and cutting to Rona (part 2), students, parents, and counselors discuss college plans. Eileen's family's financial position is not strong and the counselor tells Eileen — whom we have heard is a "leader" type — to plan practically in case "none of her dreams come true." This is cut with a discussion of Rona's college plans. Her career goals are limited (as is her intelligence, according to her father), but she has received a $10,000 scholarship that assures she can go to any school anywhere. This part ends with a shot of a janitor in the hallway. Shots 119-131, (4:05).

Part 8: Control

The topic for discussion in part 8 is the relationship between those in power and the disenfranchised. Teachers around the lunch table discuss foreign aid to underdeveloped countries and conclude that no one appreciates anything unless he works for it. The Coach lectures about union-management relations in his social studies class, and his reasons for the rise of unions in America — lack of communication and security — sound similar to the conditions that exist between the students and teachers in Northeast High School. In the following set of shots, students in an extracurricular discussion group describe their school as regimented and unable to address the problems of society. The older English teacher returns to deliver a work ethic motto, and we cut to a shot of a police officer, with club, in a hallway filled with students. Shots 132–166, (9:00).

Part 9: Socialization for Boys

The final part is a male version of the girls' socialization in part 4. Boys graduate from childish, immature imitation of cheerleaders to a sex education assembly where a gynecologist warns them, between jokes, to be prepared for the possibility of fatherhood; to a film that warns them of the consequences of veneral disease; to a conversation between a coach and an alumnus just back from Vietnam about the injuries of a classmate that prevent him from ever playing soccer; to a mock space flight complete with capsule, astronauts, military uniforms, and waiting women. A drum and bugle corps rehearses. At a faculty meeting, the principal reads a letter from a graduate who is on his way to Vietnam. He thanks the school for what it has done for him, and says, "I'm only a body doing a job." In the last shot of the film, the principal smiles and says: "When you get a letter like this, to me it means we are very successful at Northeast High School. I think you can agree with me." Shots 167–195, (1:26).

SHOT LIST

Shot No.	Visual	Sound
1	HIGH SCHOOL 1968 OSTI Inc. (0:02)	"Sitting on the Dock of the Bay," sung by Otis Redding.

Part 1: Introduction

2	LS out of side window of moving car, street scene; brick houses closely spaced, garbage cans, clothes hung out to dry. (0:18)	song
3	CU out of windshield of moving car, sign on back of truck for "Penn Maid Dairy Products," ZO to LS truck, stores and sidewalk right. (0:07)	song
4	LS out of moving car, shops and clutter of signs. (0:07)	song
5	LS out of side window moving car, large building BG, wire fence FG. (0:05)	song
6	LS out of windshield of moving car, pull into parking lot and toward large building (shot 5), tall smoke stacks, factory-like in appearance. (0:15)	song

7	LS LA of hallway, young people file past, girl combs her hair. (0:25)	Song fades out to hallway noise.
8	MS male teacher, blackboard BG, girl's head left FG; she's seated. (0:03)	Teacher: "First thing we want to do is give you the daily bulletin."
9	ECU girl's face. (0:04)	Teacher (shot 8): "You may find a little notice somewhere you think may concern you."
10	ECU mouth and nose of same teacher. Tilt up to ECU his eyeglasses. (0:23)	He says a notice could change their whole lives, the college they go to, the activities they attend. "All right, the thought for today: 'Life is cause and effect, one creates his tomorrows at every moment by his thoughts and deeds of today,' and it's a question of cause and effect . . .
11	LA ECU student resting his chin on his hands. (0:03)	Same teacher: . . . you know, as I say, I might read something that might change, ah, your life."
12	ECU LA Spanish teacher, tile down to ECU waist and hand on hip, PR to other arm, elbow on hip. (0:24)	She questions students in Spanish, they answer in Spanish.
13	MS of class over Spanish teacher's shoulder, she walks between desks, book in hand. (0:07)	same as above
14	ECU LA same teacher. (0:15)	same as above
15	CU LA same teacher, she signals with her arm that students should repeat after her. Turns toward camera and raises arm to give signal. (0:20)	She gives phrases and students echo.
16	MS three students playing drums, PR to CU band director, two students BG. Director signals the tempo, PL to MS three students on drums. Tilt down to CU gong as student strikes it. (0:27)	beat of drum, rhythm of clappers
17	CU Coach (who reappears throughout film), crew cut,	Coach (*impatiently*): "What you mean you can't take gym? You get

glasses, white shirt and tie, seated behind desk. Zip right to students, CU, standing in front of desk. PR to CU Coach ZI to ECU his glasses, ZO to CU as he points pen at student, he stands up, ZO to MS as he comes around desk toward student. (0:47)

dressed in the morning, you get undressed, then you can get into a gym outfit." Student says he has a doctor's note to exclude him from gym, that his mother was in to explain the situation.
Coach: "We'll determine whether you take exercise, or not . . . we'll determine that."
Student: "I'm not even supposed to come to school."
Coach: "Oh, oh look. I'm gonna tell you something."

18 ECU student. (0:04)

Coach: "Don't you talk and you just listen."

19 CU Coach pointing at student with pen, PR to MS student, arms folded across chest, hand with pen enters left. ZO MS student over Coach's shoulder, Coach points to door, PR as student walks out door, LS. (0:30)

Coach: "You come prepared with a gym outfit when you go to gym, is that clear? We're gonna put you in a uncompromising position, but you'll come dressed in a gym outfit."
Student: "I said I would."
Coach: "You're suspended."
Student: "I said I *would*."
Coach: "Go and wait outside."
Student: "Oh man, I *said* I would."

20 MS hallway, students file past. Motto hangs on wall: "Minds are like parachutes, they only function when they're open." (0:08)

hall noise

21 Classroom: CU seated girl, students BG, PL to other faces, ZI CU teacher's hand gesturing. (0:15)

Off camera: teacher speaks French, students respond.

22 ECU girl looking up, listening. (0:06)

same as above

23 ECU French teacher, he's animated, smiling, gestures. (0:30)

same as above

Part 2: Control

24 MS parent seated in chair, leans back, holds up papers, points to them. PR to wife and teacher seated, PL to father, gestures with papers, PR to wife and teacher. (0:26)

Father: "No, no, no, no. A flunking student wouldn't receive such accolades as fabulous!" He argues that the student wasn't warned that she was on the verge of a poor grade. Teacher replies that the grading teacher felt the grade involved more than the papers in question.

25 ECU father, he sits forward, wife BG. Father turns to talk to second teacher who gave the grades. ZO to MS over second teacher's shoulder, father and wife BG. (0:55)

Father: "Is it compassion for a teacher to write 'fabulous' and the girl sees it and figures she's doing it well and then finally she gets her report card, and the girl is stoned, it's another reading."

26 MS first teacher and wife, he points and she nods. (0:10)

Teacher says total mark cannot be based on marks of a few papers. Father: "And Rona, limited in many ways . . .

27 ECU father, he bites lip, looks down, leans forward, swallows, PR tilt down to wife's hand tight on chair, CU. (0:53)

Father: . . . knew forms and types of governments, world events . . ." First teacher: She failed "because she failed all three tests. The world will recognize you only by your performance." Father: "That's true." First teacher: "If you want your daughter to be basically well adjusted . . . you cannot impose preconceived values and dreams on a child. Part of your job is . . .

28 ECU mother's face. (0:03)

First teacher: . . . to deal with Rona as a sympathetic and understanding father . . .

29 ECU father, PR past wife to ECU first teacher's hand gesturing to father. (0:15)

First teacher: . . . if you impose too much your desires on her she may be acting in a way that may be damaging to her too."

30 MS Michael standing, PR to Coach (shot 17) seated behind desk holding card, PL to Michael, ZI to CU, PR to Coach HA CU, PL to HA CU his hands holding card, PR to Coach, PL to Michael, ZI to ECU, PR to ECU Coach. (0:50)

Coach tells Michael he is there for cutting a class. Michael denies any part in wrongdoing, saying that a teacher started yelling at him. "I said I'd go out and talk to her later when she calms down." Coach: "When you're addressed by somebody in authority your job is to respect and listen. She's not asking for blood. You should have showed some character, saying 'OK, I'd go to detention but may I speak to you later.' " Michael: "I don't feel I have to take anybody screaming at me for

nothing."
Coach: ". . . it's time to show a
little character of your own, right?
I would take the detention and
then you come back and say 'now I
took your detention, now can I
speak to you?' "

31 ECU Coach's hands, focus on University of Pennsylvania ring, tilt up to folded hands. (0:13)

Michael: "I won't take it."
Coach: "Why?"

32 ECU Michael's mouth, nose, ZO to face. (0:28)

He says someone else threw books, and he was dragged in for nothing.

33 ZO to CU Coach over Michael's shoulder. (0:08)

Coach: "We're out to establish something aren't we. We're out to establish that you can be a man and you can take orders."

34 CU LA Micahel, PR to CU Coach ZI to ECU his mouth and nose. (0:34)

Michael: "It's all against my principles, you have to stand for something."
Coach: "Yes, but I think principles aren't involved here. I think it's a question of proving yourself to be a man."

35 MS Michael listening quietly. (0:07)

Coach: "I don't see anything wrong with assigning you a detention."

36 ECU Coach ZO to CU, PL to MS Michael. (0:20)

Coach: "You should show you can take a detention."
Michael: "I think I should prove I'm a man and that's what I intend to do by doing what I feel is right."

37 CU Coach, PL to MS Michael. (0:20)

Coach: "Well are you taking a detention or aren't you? I feel you should."
Michael: "I'll take it but under protest."
Coach (*grinning*): "All right, you take it under protest, that's good. Today after school?"

38 LS balding man walking down hall past lockers, camera follows, a student puts something in a locker on left, camera and man pass him. (0:10)

Man: "What are you doing here? Well, go to a lunchroom, goodbye."

39	MS BV same man walking down hall, looks at watch, comes to phones, MS boys on phone. One indicates to wait a minute. Man turns to walk down hall. (0:30)	Man: "Where you going?" "Gotta pass?" "Gotta pass?" "How about you?" "Hang up. Let's go. It's for emergency. Let's get on the ball."
40	LS BV girl walking away down hall. (0:03)	footsteps
41	CU BV same man, walk with him as he returns to phones, MS student on phone over man's shoulder, he hangs up and walks with man down hall, camera follows MS, girl comes toward camera and passes. (0:40)	Man: "I told you to get off of there, let's go." Student: tells person on phone that he has to go, "there's a man yelling at me." He hangs up and tells man, "I had to call my insurance company." Man: "Well, get a pass." Student: "I had lunch." Man: "Lunch means lunch, it doesn't mean phone calls."
42	HA MS legs and feet of same man walking down hall, camera follows. (0:07)	Footsteps, fade in song: "Simon Says."
43	CU same man, camera follows as he goes to a door, PR as he turns to look into window of door. (0:07)	"Simon Says"
44	CU record player, PL to MS waist down of girls doing jumping jacks to time of music. ECU feet and legs as they bend to touch toes. (0:32)	"Simon Says"
45	MS SV girls, waist up, PL as they do exercises. (0:25)	song
46	CU BV girl with long hair exercising arms, tilt down and holds on her behind. ZO to LS girls doing jumping jacks, they sit and move along floor, clapping to song. (0:35)	Song, fade in recitation of "Casey at the Bat."

Part 3: One Teacher's Way

47	ECU older teacher, glasses, bad teeth, ZO to MS, holding open book, blackboard in BG. (0:13)	"Casey at the Bat"
48	ECU girl, listening. (0:04)	same as above

49 ECU second girl's eyes framed by   same as above
    arm of boy FG, tilt up and focus
    on boy FG, hand on chin, class
    ring on finger. (0:10)

50 LS LA same teacher, student   same as above
    seated right, ZI ECU teacher.
    (0:32)

51 CU 2 shot boy and girl, tilt down   same as above
    to knees of girl, patterned stock-
    ings. (0:06)

52 ECU boy with sideburns and beard,   same as above
    focus on girl BG. (0:12)

53 MS BV same teacher, students   same as above
    BG, posters bulletin board BG.
    (0:20)

54 CU boy with his head down in his   same as above
    arms. (0:02)

55 ECU girl, finger in mouth, puts   same as above
    pen in mouth. (0:15)

56 ECU teacher, students BG, PR to   same as above
    CU girl in desk, teacher's book in
    FG, girl looks behind her, ZO to
    MS teacher and students, a boy
    gestures that the girl should smile,
    she nods and looks back at
    teacher. (0:45)

57 LS girl in gym class, swings bat at   echo of gym noise
    ball held up by flexible stick.
    (0:04)

58 ZI ECU ball on stick, girl in BG   gym noise
    swings. (0:08)

Part 4: Socialization for Girls

59 ECU hands chopping nuts with   chopping
    knife, PL to CU hands putting   Woman talks about ingredients.
    flour into measuring cup, PR to
    chopping. (0:28)

60 CU boy left, home economics   Woman home economics teacher:
    teacher right, they are dressed in   "What about this brown sugar,
    white coats, ZO to MS, PL to ZI   how's he going to measure it?"
    to boy's hand sifting flour, CU   Boy: "Packed."

of high school ring on finger. (0:25)

Teacher: "Packed, absolutely right."

61 CU ZI to ECU same home economics teacher in theater, chairs BG, she holds paper. ZO to CU, she gestures to stage. (0:06)

Teacher: "What's your number doll?" "She sure is it, isn't she a beauty, just look at that."

62 MS LA girl crossing stage left to right, ZO to LS, PR as she walks to end of stage. (0:03)

Off camera: Teacher: "She's a vision for, ah, sure."

63 ECU home economics teacher, steps forward, PL as she turns and faces camera, girls seated in chairs, BG (0:22)

Teacher: she talks about culotte costumes as dress for school.

64 CU waist, ZO to LS LA girl on stage, PR as she walks off. (0:20)

Teacher: "On someone with skinny legs I think it would look good. Could you find someone to model it Friday with real thin legs honey? And girls, don't wear culottes to school, you'll look just like that."

65 MS LA girl in skirt, ZO to LS LA, PL to teacher MS, girls seated BG, PL as teacher walks left. (0:54)

Teacher: "She's got a leg problem too. If she did something about those stockings she might look better. All right, now let's see our last one and I think this young lady did a lovely job . . ."

66 MS 4 shot girls in first row of chairs, watching stage. (0:03)

Teacher: . . . of really putting some style into this particular garment."

67 LS heavy girl, LA, PR as she walks off stage quickly, down steps on right, walks over to row of seats, PR across row of seated girls (shot 66). (0:03)

Teacher: "She's done a nice job, she's got a weight problem and she knows it and she's doing everything to cut it down. She's designed this garment herself with the idea of making it graceful and gracious and she handles herself beautifully and this is what you do with fashion and design."

68 LA CU teacher on stage demonstrating correct posture, walks toward camera, ZO to LS, tilt down ZI to CU legs and feet stage level, she walks toward camera, tilt up to MS LA. (1:20)

Teacher: "This is the important thing girls, to walk with shoulders high." She demonstrates typical Northeast High School walk, "You've just got to do something to conquer it." "Are there any questions?"

69	ECU young male teacher's face, tilt down to CU hands setting timer, school ring on hand. (0:22)	Man: "Any questions, everyone ready, anyone not ready?" "All right, begin." noise of type-writers
70	ECU hand adjusting carriage, rack focus on carriages in a line into the BG. (0:13)	typewriter noise
71	CU chart of typewriter keys. (0:02)	same as above
72	ECU hand typing, "steady" ring on finger. (0:07)	same as above
73	CU BV hands on keys, hesitating. (0:13)	same as above
74	MS BV typing teacher, rows of students BG. Track right to side view teacher. (0:13)	timer goes off "Stop typing please. As I read the paragraph from the book, let's follow on what we have typed."
75	ECU girl looking down. (0:03)	Teacher reads paragraph.
76= end 74	(0:05)	same as above
77	ECU teacher, mouth, nose, eyes, reading. (1:17)	same as above
78	LS new male teacher standing right, male students seated FG left. (0:45)	He talks about the dominance of women in the Jewish family. "This is natural." He compares it to the behavior of the "lower animals."
79	CU boy's face, he looks at book. (0:04)	same as above
80	MS BV teacher, boys seated BG, track down to knee height, MS LA student in front row, smirks at teacher's jokes. (0:32)	Teacher: "Moses was the big shot, women got in by accident. That's not true in the modern Jewish family. You know who runs your household pretty well."
81	ECU boy (shot 80). (0:06)	same as above
82=	beginning of 80. (0:06)	Teacher: "It tends to be that way in a great many of our families."
83	CU woman talking into micro-phone, gesturing. (0:18)	"Why if a man and woman live together does society say you're married? I think that's great be-

cause society does have a way to take care of regular, responsible, stable unions. I think promiscuity . . .

84   CU hands of girl fingering "steady" ring on finger, tilt down to second girl looking at ring on her own hand. (0:04)

Teacher: . . . is what any society cannot tolerate."

85   LS crowd, all girls, PR along rows of girls to stage. (0:08)

woman at microphone

86   CU woman talking into microphone, points finger at girls. ZO to LS, podium in front of woman. Poster on podium reads: Whatever thy hand findith to do, do it with thy might. (0:50)

She talks about use of birth control pills. "You take it you see according to doctor's orders. You don't just pop these things into your mouth . . . it's a medicine." (Laughter)

87   LS down front row of girls in audience. (0:12)

Teacher: "You have had practice at controlling your . . .

88   ZI LS to MS LA woman, behind podium. (0:42)

. . . impulses every since you were a baby. By the time you're a high school senior, you don't eat chocolate cake because you get fat, you do homework, you don't steal dresses. You have learned you can't have what you want when you want it. Girls and boys who haven't learned that are impulsive and they never connect what they're doing today with what happens tomorrow."

89   CU older man with glasses, PR to ECU girl standing, tilt down to her knee, up to boy on left, ZO to LS boy and girl, woman gym teacher BG, ZI to MS man behind desk, PR to girl CU, ZO to MS girl, boy, woman gym teacher (she looks impatient, disgusted), PL to older man behind desk. (1:55)

They argue about the definition of "formal" dress for the prom. Girl: "What's a cocktail length, here?" Woman gym teacher: "Above the knee is not the knee." Man: "It's nice to be individualistic, but there are certain places to be individualistic." Girl: "I didn't mean to be individualistic."

90   ECU girl, PL to ECU woman gym teacher, PL to ECU man. (0:45)

They say she was offensive to the whole class, the Sheraton ballroom was very formal. Man: "It's the one time in your life when the class looks so different you don't recognize them." It's their first chance . . .

91 CU girl. (0:04)

. . . to be young ladies and young gentlemen. Women gym teacher: "I had a boy ask and a girl come up to say . . .

92 ECU boy. (0:03)

. . . can my boy friend wear a dark suit because he can't afford the money for the tux."

93 ECU woman gym teacher. (0:29)

"I said no he can't because my husband has the right to wear the beautiful suit he just bought but he had to spend $10–$15 to rent a tux. He's honoring the youngsters by coming dressed properly. I have to wear a long gown and I can't walk in it, I can't get into the car comfortably!"

94 LS Charlie Brown poster on bulletin board, bodies swing FG, ZO to LS, focus on girls hanging from rings in gym, FG. (0:17)

Woman gym teacher (shot 93) counts seconds that girls are hanging. As one drops out, she says: "Oh boy, we're feminine!" As she counts higher, she calls out: "Tarzan!"

95 ECU woman gym teacher. (0:08)

She counts: "Super Tarzan!" and laughs.

96 CU her hand holding stop watch. (0:07)

She counts.

97= Some girls drop out and walk away.
end (0:04)
94

She counts.

98 Hallway, MS janitor walking away from camera, pushing broom, PR as he goes by. (0:04)

hall noise

Part 5: Another Teacher's Way

99 LS students seated, teacher standing BG, holding Simon and Garfunkel record jacket. ZI to ECU record jacket, tilt up to CU teacher, PL to blackboard: "thematic words," "figurative language," "setting," PR to MS teacher, ZI to ECU. (1:04)

Teacher: "The poet is Simon, and if doubt he's a poet now, wait until you hear his poetry." She says the best way to start is to look at one of their best, "Dangling Conversation." She begins to read the lyrics.

100 MS front row of students. (0:08)

lyrics

101 MS LA teacher reading, students FG, ZI to CU teacher, ZO PR to students in rows, stop on a boy and girl. (0:48)

lyrics

102 ECU first student in row, PL and bring into focus each student, one at a time. (0:18)

lyrics
She begins to tell them what to listen for in record.

103 LS teacher, windows left, tape recorder BG, ZI to CU recorder, she starts it and moves off left. (0:28)

She finishes telling them what to listen for.

104 ECU left reel, PR to right reel, turning. (0:10)

Lyrics and music: "It's a still life watercolor . . .

105 ECU reel, PL to second reel, LA. (0:13)

. . . of a now late afternoon, as the sunshine through the curtain lace, and the shadows wash the room . . .

106 ECU LA teacher, windows behind her, quietly listening. (0:23)

. . . and we sit and drink our coffee, couched in our indifference, like shells upon the shore, you can hear the ocean roar, in the dangling conversation, and superficial sighs, the . . .

107 LS classroom, quiet. (0:03)

. . . borders of our . . .

108 ECU eyes girl. (0:02)

. . . lives . . .

109 CU two girls, one chews gum. (0:04)

. . . And you read your Emily Dickenson . . .

110 ECU boy and girl. (0:05)

. . . and I my Robert Frost . . .

111 ECU girl. (0:07)

. . . and we note our place with bookmarkers, that measure what we lost . . .

112 ECU boy, tilt down to ECU wristwatch on arm of neighbor. (0:08)

. . . like a poem poorly written, we are verses out of rhythm . . .

113 ECU two girls, PR to ECU boy with chin on hand, leans hand against cheek. (0:18)

. . . couplets out of rhyme, in syncopated time, and the dangling conversation and superficial sighs, are the borders of our . . .

113   ECU two girls, PR to ECU boy
      with chin on hand, leans hand
      against cheek. (0:18)

... couplets out of rhyme, in
syncopated time, and the dangling
conversation and superficial sighs,
are the borders of our ...

114   MS woman leaning against door
      in hallway, looks thoughtful, ZO
      to ELS of hall, she is alone.
      (0:15)

... lives. Yes we speak the words
that must be said, can analysis ...

115   LS HA cleaning woman, PR as she
      drags box by a rope down the hall.
      (0:10)

... be worthwhile, is the theater
really dead. And now the room is
softly shaded ... (fade out)

Part 6: Control

116   Coach (from gym suit and Michael
      scenes) seated FG, CU, two stu-
      dents BG across his desk, tilt up
      to MS "bully" and "victim."
      Track in to CU "bully," PR to CU
      HA Coach as he writes. PL to
      "victim" and "bully" MS. (1:00)

Coach: "Hey you, turn around
pal."
"Bully": "Sir."
Coach: "Don't you 'sir' me, don't
feed me that 'sir' business. You
punched this guy in the mouth on
what basis."
Bully explains they had an argument.

117   ECU "bully," scar on nose, ZO to
      CU. (0:16)

Coach tells him he is suspended for
throwing the first punch. "Bully":
"Yes sir." Coach: "Don't give me
that 'sir' business. I don't like the
'sir' business. You know why?
Because there is no sincerity."

118   ECU mother, ZO to Eileen and
      mother CU, ZI to ECU mother's
      hand on purse, tilt up ECU
      mother's mouth, ZO to ECU face,
      ZO to CU mother and daughter,
      PR to woman with glasses seated
      behind desk, MS, ZI, to ECU, ZO
      to CU, PL to ECU mother and
      daughter, ZO to CU. (4:45)

Eileen is accused by mother of
locking someone in closet. Eileen
says they were just "messing
around." She admits she "talked
back a lot." Woman: "No doubt
the teacher was holding class
poorly, but who breaks the circle?
Someone mature enough. You're
intelligent and mature ... why
don't you offer positive leader-
ship?"
Mother: "To me I think one of the
worse offenses is disrespect for an
older person ... I told her eventually it would hurt you outside,
and finally it happened."

Part 7: Socialization

119   HA MS college counselor center,

Counselor asks Eileen if she wants

Eileen and father right, mother left. (0:24)

to go to an easy school and be at top of the class or harder school and be at bottom. Eileen: "I think I would gain more by being in middle or top than to have trouble keeping up."

120 ECU mother. (0:02)

Counselor: "Do you want a college . . .

121 ECU counselor, PR to ECU Eileen. (0:40)

. . . where at the end of four years education is complete, or go on to graduate school?" Eileen: "I'm not sure right now. I don't think I want to go more than five or six years — or more than five."

122 MS group, BV mother and father, counselor and Eileen across desk. (0:10)

Counselor: "And then I would like to ask you sir, the hard, hard question . . .

123 CU father. (0:02)

. . . of how much you could contribute to your daughter's education."

124 ECU mother's eyes. (0:02)

Father: "Well, ah, that's . . .

125 ECU counselor. (0:04)

. . . a hard question to say, because if she lives away from home . . .

126 MS group reverse angle shot 122. (0:37)

. . . it's a different story . . . So I would say about $1,000–$1,500 a year to go away to college." Counselor advises that Eileen see where she can go for that amount, then apply for scholarships at other colleges.

127 LA CU counselor, books FG obscuring counselor. (0:24)

Counselor advises Eileen to find a "dream school" and a bottom college "of last resort where you could be sure to go if none of your dreams come true."

128 CU Rona's mother (shot 24). (0:18)

Mother: "Rona is the recipient of a $10,000 scholarship to any college anywhere in the country she wants to go . . . she can go to any college and do whatever she wanted . . .

129 MS Rona and teacher (shot 24), PR track right to Rona, father

Teacher: "Tell me, did you say, you want to go to college."

BG, PL to Rona, ZI to CU.
(1:20)

Father: "You're lying to the man now, you really don't want to go to college."
Rona: "Well I want to but not to the kind of college you want me to." She tells teacher she wants to go to beauty culture school. He asks if she feels she's disappointing her parents by not going to college; she says she's disappointing her father but doesn't feel guilty because it's her life.

130 CU Rona, father BG, PR to mother and teacher, father stands, mother stands, PL to LS Rona and father, PR to mother, father, and Rona LS. The walk to door BG, teacher enters right, LS. (1:18)

Teacher: says they can't undo the past, that Rona should work as hard as she can to do her best. He asks about her gym credits for graduation.
Father: "I wish she was as smart as she is strong."
Teacher: asks how Rona felt about father's remark.
Rona: "I liked it."
Teacher: "You liked it?"
Rona: "Yes."
intercom from shot 131

131 Hallway, janitor walks away from camera with broom over shoulder. (0:04)

intercom announcement

Part 8: Control

132 MS three teachers eating at table in cafeteria. ZI to one teacher, ECU. (0:18)

They talk about giving under-developed countries so much that they don't appreciate it.

133=beginning 132. (0:45)

One teacher: "I don't think anyone appreciates anything — look at your children, when you give things to them, do they appreciate it? Sometimes when they work for it a little bit they appreciate it."

134 CU ape-to-man chart, posters on wall, ZO LS PL over rows of students, Coach is in front of class, ZI to CU Coach between two students in FG. (0:30)

He talks about organizing of labor unions in America.

135 CU boy, PL to two girls. (0:14)

Coach: "What existed that forced labor to turn to collective bargaining — what was there a lack of?"
Off camera: "Communication."

136	ECU "Our Troubled World" collage on bulletin board, includes pictures of Vietnam, CO to MS, students FG. (0:03)	Coach: "Communication and lack of security."
137	MS Coach over student's shoulder, ZO to LS. (0:25)	He lists reasons for labor organization: lack of security, lack of communication, attitude of employer to employees in regard to working conditions, living conditions.
138	New classroom. MS two girls, PR to CU girl, ZI to ECU, PL to CU LA male teacher in front of classroom. (1:05)	He talks about "other America" of poverty, and Martin Luther King's attempt to "uplift this other America."
139	ECU student, PL to ECU eye of student next to him. (0:10)	He talks about attitudes: "Let's determine some of the attitudes in this class."
140	LS same teacher, students BG. (0:34)	He asks how many students would be members of organizations in which the minority of members were "Negro," the majority? "There's no right or wrong answer, we're just trying to determine what attitudes are."
141	LS two rows of choir students, piano FG, PR to LS leader pointing to notes on blackboard. (0:18)	They sing: "Do, mi . . .
142	CU blackboard with notes written on it. (0:02)	. . . mi, so . . .
143	ECU girl singing. (0:02)	singing, two notes
144	ECU girl's mouth (0:02)	singing, two notes
145= end 141	(0:01)	singing, two notes
146	ECU girl's mouth. (0:03)	singing, two notes
147	ECU girl. (0:01)	singing, one note
148	Pointer and notes on blackboard, ECU. (0:01)	singing, one note

149 ECU young woman teacher, leans against wall, bites lip. (0:04)

Off camera: students (shot 150) describes Northeast High School as a cloister, a secluded place.

150 ECU boy with sunglasses, tilt down to his necklace, up to his face. (0:36)

He says the building is fine, but its social consciousness and most of its people stink.

151 ECU second boy. (0:04)

Off camera: boy with sunglasses: "Now I'm not qualified to make gigantic judgments about this . . .

152 ECU girl. (0:03)

. . . school, but I think its attitude toward . . .

153 ECU second girl. (0:03)

. . . education and its relationship with the world . . .

154 ECU boy. (0:04)

. . . today this school is miserable . . ."

155= (0:10)
150

Boy with sunglasses: "It's cloistered, secluded, and completely sheltered, from everything that's going on in the world. I think . . .it has to be changed and I think that is our purpose here . . ."

156 CU black male student, students BG. (0:07)

Teacher off camera: she says they're so negative.

157 ECU LA teacher, ZO to CU, door BG opens and two students enter. (0:23)

Off camera: student from shot 156: "I think one thing has to be changed around . . .

158 ECU boy with necklace, ZO to MS, ZO to LS group. (0:13)

. . . the thing that makes us so alien . . .

159 CU black student (shot 156), students BG. (0:35)

. . . you have to conform to these ideas of people like Mr. Simon, Dr. Alan . . ." Interrupted by teacher.

160 CU boy with sunglasses, kisses girl leaning on his shoulder. (0:06)

Teacher says the views of Mr. Simon are consistent with other members of the faculty.

161 CU teacher, LA, PL as she steps back, ZO to LS, PR to black student, others in BG. (0:50)

Black student (shot 156): "Scientifically and technically, Northeast High School is an advanced school apart from other high schools in the country and possibly in the world. But as Mark has said, morally,

socially, this school's a garbage can."

162   ECU teacher who read "Casey at the Bat," shot 47. (0:40)

"Now boys and girls we have a very new plaque outside in the hall with a special thought for today. 'The dictionary is the only place where success comes before work.' "

163   LS LA students from shot 162, not listening to teacher. (0:02)

Teacher continues to read bulletin.

164=   (0:20)
162

Teacher continues to read bulletin: "The spectators club will discuss Martin Luther King's assassination today . . ."

165   MS police office in hallway holding club, students file out of door BG, he checks watch. (0:12)

hallway noise

Part 9: Socialization for Boys

166   CU students filing past in hallway. (0:04)

hallway noise

167   Gymnasium and stage, track up the aisle to the stage, students fill seats. On stage boys dressed as cheerleaders get lined up to do cheers, LS LA, track to MS boys with wigs, skirts. (0:32)

whistle, band, drums

168   MS boys on stage. (0:15)

They begin cheer.

169   MS LA two boys on stage. (0:15)

They chant cheer.

170   MS LA of man (gynecologist) on stage at microphone, he reaches for written question from audience, ZI to CU, zip left to audience (all male), one boy stands and carries question to stage, MS PR, ZI to CU doctor. (1:30)

Doctor: "The more intercourse a boy or girl has prior to marriage, the less likely they are to be successful marriage partners, the higher divorce rate, greater sexual incompatibility and failure of compatibility. The real pros keep it to themselves." He reads question: "Is it possible to impregnate a girl by rubbing the surface of the vagina?" He answers: "With what, your nose?" Laughter. He says virginity is a state of mind. "I've seen girls whose hymens were so small I couldn't pass a finger through them." Laughter. "I happen to be a gynecologist and get paid for it." Laughter. "Many a girl has become pregnant through spray."

171 MS LA audience. (0:04)

Doctor: "If you're not prepared . . .

172 ECU boy. (0:02)

. . . to handle your responsibility . . .

173 ECU boy. (0:03)

. . . for that girl becoming pregnant and having a baby . . .

174 CU LA doctor, microphone in front of mouth, ZI to finger pointing, PR to ECU face, ZO to CU, ZI to ECU. (0:30)

. . . you've got two choices. One, make sure you have adequate protection to prevent having a baby. You are just as much responsibile, if not a little more than the girl if a pregnancy occurs. Nature has set us up that the male is the aggressive and the . . .

175 LS doctor BV, crowd BG. (0:15)

. . . female is the passive."

176 LS movie screen in dark room, students' heads FG, ZI to ECU screen. (0:55)

Film explains the effects of venereal disease.

177 MS soldier and coach, boys play volleyball on playground BG, ZI to CU soldier, ZO to MS him and coach, ZI to CU soldier, PR to MS coach. (1:30)

Coach: "You didn't get hit, huh?" Soldier: "No." Coach: "Good, good to see you." They talk about Peppi who was hit pretty bad in the foot by an automatic rifle. Coach: "He turned around and killed the guy. He's through with soccer forever." Soldier: "Too bad, he was pretty good." Soldier says he doesn't have to go back to Vietnam. They talk about where another boy was hit.

178 LS boys running away from camera in gym, PL and PR, tilt up to follow large inflated ball, ZI to CU ball above their head, PL to coach, PR to action. (0:25).

whistle, shouting, footsteps

179 CU pile of boys grabbing for ball, PR as coach steps in and picks up ball and carries it over head. (0:15)

One boy: "I've got it!"

gym noise

180 MS BV boy in suit standing in front of television set and digital clock, ZI to CU, PR as he reaches to console, ZO to MS, PL as he steps back. We realize we are watching a mock space flight. (0:20)

Boy in suit: "Almost there!" "Fourteen seconds — countdown." He counts down to zero. "That's it!" applause

181 LS reverse angle of people watching, women in white dresses, boys dressed in navy uniforms. (0:04)

applause

182 CU of "astronauts" on television screen. (0:04)

applause

183 Teacher, BV MS, boy with suit opens hatch BG, three student "astronauts" step out with space suits and helmets, PL to friends as they shake hands, PR to "astronauts" and teacher. Teacher reaches to help take off helmet. ZI to CU one "astronaut" while boy with suit gestures to beard in BG. (0:55)

Boy with suit: "Is the hatch clear? All right, pull." Applause. "Astronaut": "Good to be out here again." Friends: "Look at that beard man, ho, ho, ho!"

184 CU one "astronaut" ZI to ECU mouth, takes off helmet, smiles. (0:13)

He's teased about his beard.

185 MS "astronauts" walk out doorway, shake hands, PR as they walk onto stage PR to teacher at microphone, ZI to ECU, ZO PL to "astronauts" standing on stage. They begin to walk off stage. Camera tracks back, people shake their hands, one "astronaut" leans to kiss a woman, CU. (1:30)

applause

Teacher reads telegram received from Gordon Cooper, NASA astronaut, congratulating Northeast High School's "Project Spark," and the boys' successful 193 hours of simulated flight. applause

186 LS LA Drum major prancing onto empty stage, PR, he comes toward camera and stops, gives order, tilt down to head of drummer ECU FG. ZO to LS, flag carriers cross behind drum major BG. (0:40)

Noise of drum major's feet. "Drums, roll off!" Band plays "Hey Look Me Over."

187 ECU, LA drum major's face, tilt down to chest and uniform, hand

Noise of drum major's feet. Band plays "Hey Look Me Over."

pumping the baton up and down.
(0:06)

188 ECU hand holding white gun
stock, tilt up to ECU girl's face,
LA. (0:08)

"Hey Look Me Over"

189 MS cymbalists FG, drum major
and flag carriers on stage LS, PR
along row of cymbalists, track
right around cymbalists to side
view of drum major on stage.
(0:15)

"Hey Look Me Over"

190 ECU LA woman (Dr. Howard)
behind podium. (0:30)

She says she is about to read a
letter from a recent graduate, a boy
without parents, average or sub-
average academically.

191 ELS, LA teachers seated in gym.
(0:02)

same as above

192 MS two teacher, one is teacher
from Simon and Garfunkel scene.
(0:04)

Dr. Howard: "But a few teachers
who cared . . .

193 ECU teacher from shot 89. (0:01)

. . . made a great difference in this
boy's life."

194 LS from behind audience of
teachers, podium and Dr. Howard
on stage BG. (0:03)

She begins to read letter.

195 CU LA Dr. Howard behind podium,
letter FG. As she turns page of
letter, camera focuses on hand-
writing, then on Dr. Howard. She
smiles at close of letter. (2:15)

The writer is on his way to a Vietnam combat zone. He writes because his insurance money will go
to a scholarship fund at Northeast
High School in case of his death.
He is trying to become a big
brother in Vietnam.
"I really pray that the young men
in your cooking classes will use this
chance of learning very well. Thank
you Dr. Howard for helping these
men become very fine cooks." He
says he "values the lives of South
Vietnamese and the free world, so
that they and all of us can live in
peace." He asks: "Am I wrong, Dr.
Howard?" He says he's not worth
any worry, "I'm only a body doing
a job. I thank everyone for what

they all have done for me."
Dr. Howard: "When you get a letter
like this, to me it means we are very
successful at Northeast High
School. I think you can agree with
me."

196 Produced and Directed by
Frederick Wiseman. Photography
by Richard Leiterman, Editor
Frederick Wiseman, Associate
editor Carter Howard, Assistant
cameraman, David Eames. This
film is indebted to Katherine
Tyler and The New World Foundation whose interest, encouragement
and support made it possible.

CREDITS AND NOTES

Producer:	Frederick Wiseman
Director:	Frederick Wiseman
Photography:	Richard Leiterman
Editor:	Frederick Wiseman
Associate Editor:	Carter Howard
Assistant Cameraman:	David Eames

Copyright 1968 OSTI Inc.
Filmed on location at Northeast High School, Philadelphia, Pennsylvania.

Distribution:	Zipporah Films
Running Time:	75 minutes
Released:	October, 1968.

3 LAW AND ORDER (1969)

The setting is Kansas City, the institution is the Kansas City Police Department, and the subject remains the interactions between the institution and its clients, the people of Kansas City. Officers arbitrate family problems, pick up drunks, arrest suspects, take an elderly woman to the hospital, question suspects, guard a presidential candidate, picks up an abandoned child. An officer forcefully arrests a prostitute, a suspect boasts about shooting a policeman. Citizens refuse to co-operate but are quick to criticize. The film is a distillation of six weeks of shooting. *Law and Order* was financed by the Ford Foundation and Public Broadcasting Laboratory, and aired on NET. NET insisted that Wiseman delete some of Howard's expletives from the arrest scene, and Wiseman agreed on the condition that NET broadcast his objection to the deletion along with the film. *Law and Order* received an Emmy for Best News Documentary of 1968-1969. (81 minutes)

SYNOPSIS

Part 1: Introduction

Part 1 is an introduction to the institution and a prologue to the first film day. Eight mug shots slide in and out of the frame with the sound and motion of a slide projector. We cut to a mug shot-like close-up of a suspect seated before an officer who accuses him of assaulting and sexually molesting a small boy. In another office, a citizen threatens that unless police catch the man who sexually assaulted a nine-year-old girl, he'll find the man himself. In a third office, a woman complains to someone on the phone that officers threw her into a paddy wagon and brought her to the station like an animal. In a fourth office, an interviewer asks an applicant why he wants to be a police officer, and whether he could shoot someone. We cut to the swollen face of a beaten black man, who describes how he was assaulted and robbed. Shot 2-12, (4:31).

Part 2: Family Quarrel

Film day one starts with a roll call and squad cars pulling away from the station. From there we accompany police on a series of "cases." Periodic returns to moving squad cars break up the day's events. In case one, a landlord describes a violent fight between a husband and wife, charging that they have neglected their infant. Shots 13-31, (4:42).

Part 3: Jessie

In part 3 an officer retrieves a woman's snatched purse — minus money and house keys. We return to shots from the moving squad car. Shots 32-51, (4:19).

Part 4: LeRoy

An officer questions drunk, uncooperative LeRoy on a city street. LeRoy tries to walk away, and the officer pulls him to the ground, beside the squad car, while passersby look on. Shot 52, (1:45).

Part 5: Howard

In parked squads, two officers discuss a recent riot. The same officers struggle in the next set of shots with a black youth, Howard, accused of hit and run. Howard resists arrest, cursing the officers, and threatens the bystanders who turned him in, saying he'll be back to "do them in." The officers load Howard into a paddy wagon. After shots from the moving squad car, the wagon arrives at the station where officers question Howard. He is arrogant and defiant, boasting about his criminal record. Shots 53-73, (11:16).

Part 6: Accident

Once again we return to the moving squad car. An officer arrives at the scene of an accident and gives the victim first aid while waiting for the ambulance. Shots 74-77, (1:30).

Part 7: Howard

In a phone booth, one of the officers who arrested Howard calls in to find out whether Howard will be held or released. Shots 78-79, (0:38).

Part 8: Bagsby

The officer from part 7 calls for a paddy wagon to pick up a drunken, semiconscious man, Bagsby. A woman passerby comments: "What is his aim in life?" Shots 80-90, (3:12).

Part 9: Howard

In parked squad cars, the officer who called in about Howard warns his partner, Charlie, to look over his shoulder — Howard may be released. Day one ends in a moving squad car as the sun, low in the sky, reflects off windows of a building. Shots 91-99, (2:12).

Part 10: Prostitute

The night begins in a cheap hotel where officers arrest a prostitute. It's her first arrest, and the officers say they're handling her roughly to teach her the "game." Shots 100-113, (6:51).

Part 11: Night at the Station

At the station, the prostitute (part 10) is among other suspects just brought in, including a comical, drunken fat woman arrested for disturbing the peace. Shots 114-123, (2:18).

Part 12: Night Guard

In an unidentified building, an officer and his dog patrol a dark corridor. Shots 124-128, (1:07).

Part 13: Suspect

Back at the station, an officer questions a suspect accused of striking a woman and possessing a gun. The suspect is cooperative but denies the charges, and the officer turns away, frustrated. Shots 129-132, (3:40).

Part 14: Soldier

The night ends as a soldier on leave accuses the officers of sitting around and doing nothing — he has been robbed at gun point and wants to know where he'll sleep that night. Shots 132-133, (1:45).

Part 15: Men Behind the Uniforms

Film day two begins with roll call. Superiors remind the patrolmen not to call citizens nàmes like "buddy," or "bub" — nobody takes offense at "sir" or "lady." Two squad cars pull along side each other on a street and the officers talk about police pay and benefits. Shots 134-142, (5:48).

Part 16: Cab Fare

On another street, an officer tries to straighten out a fare dispute between a cab-driver and a passenger. Shots 143-149, (3:16).

Part 17: Ambulance Service

Officers arrive at a home to prepare an elderly woman for the ride to the hospital in an ambulance. Shots 150-159, (2:14).

Part 18: Young People

Part 18 is made up of sets of shots that show officers interacting with young people, progressing from their protection of an abandoned child to their arrest of gun-carrying youths. An officer picks up a small, abandoned child, drives her to the station, buys her candy, and puts her in a playpen. Back in a parked squad car, an officer talks out of the window to a group of curious young boys. Two other officers deliver a young boy to his father — they caught him playing hookey. With gun drawn, a lone officer enters a clothing shop, searches several youths, and finds two handguns in their pockets. Shots 160-192, (11:54).

Part 19: Presidential Candidate

Guarded by officers at a rally, then candidate for president, Richard Nixon, delivers a speech on law and order. He says it's about time that people in government work to reestablish respect for law and order. We return to a moving squad car. Shots 193-202, (1:33).

Part 20: Raymond

Officers mediate a family quarrel. A worried distraught father wants custody of his baby because he feels his wife isn't caring for it properly. The officers tell him they can do nothing about it, he has to get a lawyer and file for divorce. Frustrated, the man runs away from the camera, down the street. The final image is the long shadow of a moving squad car. The credits move into the frame like the slides from shot one. Shots 203–214, (5:24).

CREDITS AND NOTES

Producer:	Frederick Wiseman
Director:	Frederick Wiseman
Photography:	William Brayne
Editor:	Frederick Wiseman
Associate Editor:	Carter Howard
Camera Assistant:	David Martin
Editing Assistant:	Andrea Green
Production Assistant:	Robbin Mason
	Susan Primm

Copyright OSTI Inc., 1969.
Funding provided by the Ford Foundation.
Filmed on location in Kansas City, Missouri.

Distribution:	Zipporah Films
Running Time:	81 minutes
Released:	March, 1969.

4   HOSPITAL (1970)

Wiseman filmed *Hospital* at Metropolitan Hospital in New York City. Again, he focuses on routine tasks of the institution. Its employees admit patients, examine them, give them medication, operate on them, counsel them, sympathize with them, Patients arrive critically ill, knifed, with no money, frightened, alone, intoxicated, overdosed.

Hospital's parts are made up of related "services" separated by returns to waiting rooms and hallways (with one exception). Dr. Schwartz appears regularly throughout the film as do interinstitution confrontations. Except for these and the opening and closing shots, the order of the parts in the film seems to be random, like the events within the hospital itself. There is no chronological or thematic superstructure.

NET first broadcast *Hospital* in February 1970. It received Emmys for Best Documentary, 1969-70, and Best Director, 1970; the Catholic Film Workers Award, Mannheim Film Festival, 1970; Columbia School of Journalism, Du Pont Award Best Documentary, 1970. The Corporation of Public Broadcasting funded the film through a grant to NET. (84 minutes)

SYNOPSIS

Part 1: Introduction

Doctors prepare a patient, and themselves, for an operation. As the surgeon makes his incision, we cut to people entering a building we assume to be a hospital. Inside, we see people waiting, in line, in waiting rooms, on hospital carts. (2:33)

Part 2: Emergency

A frightened woman describes the symptoms of a patient she just brought to the hospital, a doctor questions an alcoholic man, Dr. Schwartz tries to get information from a drug user, and a police officer helps a woman into the emergency room. Dr. Schwartz calls New York Hospital to protest the way it transferred a patient to Metropolitan — they jeopardized the patient's life, and "this kind of thing happens all the time." The part ends with shots of patients in the waiting room. Shots 1-9, (4:13).

Part 3: Admission, Diagnosis

An elderly woman, hard of hearing, applies for financial aid to help pay hospital bills. In the following shots, patients go through the first stages of admittance. One man weighs in, and a second has his first interview with a doctor. He is frightened, ashamed to be examined by a female doctor, and fears he has cancer. The doctor reassures him and schedules diagnostic tests. In the next shot, a patient undergoes a diagnostic test, drinking liquid while a technician takes X-rays. Finally, doctors examine an admitted patient in his room. The part ends with scenes of janitors at work in the hospital's hallways and washrooms. Shots 10-35, (11:48).

Part 4: Medicine as Science

A nurse wheels medication into patients' rooms, and assists an elderly woman and a male patient to drink. In the autopsy room a doctor holds a human brain and explains its characteristics to an audience of doctors. In another room, a lecturer explains the bone structure of man, using a woman as an illustration. Wiseman cuts to an operation, and a nurse relays the laboratory's report that the tissue samples are nonmalignant. Finally, a doctor makes a pelvic examination of a young woman. We return to shots of the waiting room. Shots 36-76, (10:22).

Part 5: Trauma

Nurses care for and worry about a small boy who fell 15 feet from a window — his grandmother refuses to come to the hospital and the social worker can't locate his parents. One nurse offers to take him home for the night, but her supervisor warns her not to get "involved in something like that." We cut to Lewis. Police brought him into the hospital after an accident, but he refuses to stay because he is worried about the welfare of his children home alone. The officers finally insist that he remain at the hospital overnight and usher him to a room. We return to a hallway. Shots 77-97, (8:05).

Part 6: Psychosocial Problems

A homosexual tells a psychiatrist about how he hasn't been able to get welfare. He asks for help — he considers himself ". . . a freak of nature." We cut to shots of the waiting room. In the last one, the homosexual sits in the hallway, lighting a cigarette. We hear the psychiatrist and cut back to his office where he talks on the phone to Miss Hightower from the welfare department, demanding that his patient (the homosexual) receive assistance so that he can stay out of the hospital and get his own job. Two welfare agents give the psychiatrist the run around and finally one hangs up on him. Shots 98-115, (10:22).

Part 7: Drug Abuse

Orderlies pick. an intoxicated man up off the floor, put him into a wheelchair, and strap him in. In the next shot, a doctor tries to get information from an incoherent woman drug user. In another room, Schwartz examines a young man who took an unknown drug. The boy is frightened and bewildered. Schwarz gives him medication to make him vomit, and tells him he'll be all right. Messengers take the boy down the hall to a bare room, where he waits, frightened and nervous, for a psychiatrist. He vomits again, and asks messengers to play music so he can relax. The part ends with a return to the hallway. Shots 116-131, (13:07).

Part 8: Violence

Doctors and officers wheel a blood-soaked black man down a hallway to an emergency room where doctors bandage his neck wound. Afterward, the woman he arrived with comes in, kisses him, and holds his hand. A doctor examines an older man with a broken jaw, and we return to the waiting room, hallways, and janitor. Shots 132-148, (6:05).

Part 9: Limits of Service

Ambulance attendants talk in the hallway while their elderly patient lies on a cart. They've driven her from hospital to hospital trying to find an empty bed. They say that if she could only afford a private hospital she would have had a bed. They leave to drive her to another hospital. In the next shots, an ambulance arrives in the dark and attendants rush an elderly, seriously ill woman into the emergency room. Doctors work on her and ask her friend for a medical history, frustrated that they can't pin down her problem. In one of the final shots, Schwartz talks to an elderly man (Fields) who is waiting for an opening in a nursing home. Fields wants to stay at the hospital, he's afraid to walk the streets because an old man in his neighborhood was beaten. Schwartz explains that Fields has to wait for social welfare to place him in a nursing home. Fields turns and walks slowly away (reminiscent of the last scene of *Law and Order*), balancing against the wall. We return to the hallway. Shots 149-180, (10:46).

Part 10: God

The final part takes place in the hospital chapel. The priest tells patients and employees that everything comes from God. He reminds them of their total dependence upon God for everything and of their inadequacy to offer Him anything in return. As the patients sing, the camera focuses on a close-up of the hospital building, and zooms out slowly to an extreme long shot. Cars speed along a freeway in the foreground. Shots 181-end, (4:02).

SHOT LIST

Shot No.	Visual	Sound
1	HOSPITAL (0:05)	rhythmic machine noise (continues through shot 16)

Part 1: Introduction

2	LS HA operating room, patient lies spread eagle on operating table in center frame, two doctors work BG right. (0:05)	
3	ECU SV female patient's face, electronic monitor BG. (0:03)	
4	ECU SV masked surgeon looking right. (0:03)	
5	ECU HA patient (shot 3) with oxygen mask covering her face, doctor's hand holds mask. (0:03)	

6   ECU from foot of table, patient center, surgeon inserts tube into patient's mouth. (0:05)

7   ECU patient, surgeon holds instrument in her mouth. (0:04)

8   MS SV doctor in same room, arranging instruments on table. (0:03)

9   ECU SV instrument tray filled with scissors, doctor's hand arranges instruments FG. (0:07)

10   LS five doctors in same room, one opens surgical gown and helps another to put it on. (0:07)

11   MS neck to knees of surgeons suiting up, wrapping waistbands around gowns. (0:07)

12   LS six surgeons around operating table, patient center, one walks past left to right FG. (0:04)

13   MS two doctors open drape cloth and place it over patient. (0:06)

14   HS HA patient's exposed skin draped with cloths. (0:05)

15   MS HA over surgeon's shoulder, he makes a long incision, ZI to CU, second doctor places absorbent cloths over incision. (0:15)

16   MS BV people in street clothes walk toward the entrance of a building. (0:04)

17   LS BV people seated in chairs in waiting room, reception desk BG. (0:04)   corridor noise

18   LS BV more people seated in chairs, waiting, person walks past left to right FG. (0:04)

19   LS SV larger group of people waiting in chairs. (0:03)

20   LS people waiting in line along
      bare wall. (0:03)

21   LS down corridor, orderlies push
      patient on cart toward camera,
      LS to CU, track back, tilt down to
      CU of elderly female patient lying
      on cart, it passes left to right, PR
      as they enter room, doctors wait
      inside, door closes. Hand lettered
      sign on door reads: Cardiacs only.
      (0:17)

22   CU two patients lying on carts FG,
      one wears bandage on head, PR
      slowly along his body to two shot
      of other patients lying on carts
      along wall. (0:06)

23   MS elderly man lying on his
      stomach on cart against wall, SV,
      his body shakes. (0:03)

24   MS from head of woman lying on   intercoms page doctors
      cart, she's tied on. (0:02)   corridor noise

25   LS people waiting in corridor,
      elderly woman seated center in
      wheel chair, she talks to woman
      standing beside her. (0:04)

26   LS man strapped into wheel chair
      against wall, he slumps in chair.
      (0:04)

27   LS line of people waiting seated
      in chairs. (0:04)

Part 2: Emergency

28   LS doctor standing left against   Doctor asks woman about the
      wall, black woman seated right,   medical history of a woman just
      ZI to ECU woman looking up   admitted to the hospital. Woman:
      at doctor, she begins to cry, he   "I shook her and shook her but
      touches her shoulder. (1:52)   she wouldn't wake up." Off
                                            camera: "You come inside in a
                                            little while, we'll give you a tran-
                                            quilizer."

29   MS over doctor's shoulder, black   Doctor asks him if he has been
      man left, looking at doctor.   vomiting, if his stools were black.
      (0:50)   Man answers he had an operation
                                            for "alcohol."

30	MS young doctor (Dr. Schwartz) who will reappear several times in the film. He leans over a young man sitting in chair. Doctor pats the man's face to make him respond. (0:35)	Doctor says it's very important that he know whether "it was a pill or did you shoot up? How much did you take?" Young man asks about "cops." Doctor: "No cops, no cops."
31	LS police officer helping black woman up hall toward camera, PR as they walk by, BV as they walk to room, woman cries and has difficulty walking. (0:20)	Woman crying, in pain.
32	LS BV police officer as he lifts woman to carry her into room (same woman shot 31). (0:05)	We hear voice of Schwartz (shot 33): "Yes, this is Dr. Schwartz calling from Metropolitan Hospital emergency room . . .
33	CU Dr. Schwartz (shot 30) on telephone, seated at desk, patients seated BG. ZI to ECU, ZO to CU, PR as he hangs phone up, he sighs, stands and walks off left. (2:05)	Schwartz complains to New York Hospital employee that the conditions under which a patient was transferred to Metropolitan from New York were "absurd." "Now, I think this patient's life was put into some sort of jeopardy, this is the sort of thing that we see all the time." He listens, then says: "No, this is Metropolitan."
34	LS dark hallway, people walk up to counters on right. (0:08)	hallway noise
35	LS waiting room, patients seated FG, others lined up at windows, BG. (0:05)	room noise
36	MS one row of chairs in waiting room, elderly woman, child, BG. (0:05)	room noise

Part 3: Admission, Diagnosis

37	CU hand holding microphone, tilt up to CU elderly woman with hearing aide. (0:25)	Off camera: "How long have you been hard of hearing?" Woman answers about 40 years. Interviewer: "Since about 1929?"
38	MS interviewer and same woman seated at desk. (0:03)	Woman: "No, since 1919."
39	ECU same woman, ZI to ECU eyes, ZO to ECU. (1:45)	She tells how it's been "a very hard pull." She talks about medical costs, that she doesn't like to take

government aid because she wants to be self-supporting. Interviewer: "Oh yeah, yeah, I know."

40   MS same woman, holds micro-phone of her hearing aide, puts on glasses, ZI to ECU, tilt down to CU hands signing paper. (0:45)

Interviewer: "You're not a veter-an?" Woman: "no, but I did work for the UNRA overseas once, and I had an UNRA uniform." Inter-viewer asks her to sign form. Woman: "Well I thank you very, very much."

41   CU hands on imprinting machine, ZO to BV MS employee at desk, people BG. (0:10)

room noise

42   CU man on scale, hand adjusts scale, he steps off, PR to CU him and nurse, hallway and desks BG. (0:35)

Nurse: "OK, 152½, right?" "You keep that, that's for you. Over here, sit down there."

43   ECU elderly male patient, ther-mometer in mouth, he looks around. (0:05)

room noise

44   MS HA waist down of woman doctor left, two legs dangling right, she tries to get reflex re-actions by hitting knees. (0:20)

Doctor: "Just relax your legs, let them hang loose, like they're in water."

45   ECU same man shot 43, woman doctor crosses in FG, (0:35)

She tells him to stop drinking, she looks at his teeth and asks if he would like to have them fixed. He says yes.

46   CU same man, seated on exami-nation table. (0:10)

Doctor: "Are your eyes blurry?" Man: "No." Doctor: "What hap-pens to your eyes?" Man: "They get dark, completely dark for minute."

47   ECU man's eye, woman doctor left looking into eyes with light, ZO to CU, BG is completely dark. (0:15)

Doctor: "Let me look inside your eyes."

48   ECU same man, ZO to MS doctor left, ZI to ECU man, rubs away tear. (2:05)

She asks if he has any trouble pass-ing urine. He says: "It itches and bleeds, not inside, outside. I'm ashamed to talk to you, because ..." Doctor: "No, no, I want to know because I have to fix this up." He starts to cry: "I think I have cancer." She says they have to check him up. "Do you want me to check it or do you want a man doctor?" She says there's nothing to be ashamed of.

49   CU BV woman doctor, same man BG, he nods agreement. (0:20)

She says she'll give him pills for diabetes and have his teeth fixed. He'll be sent to the GU clinic to be checked out, and a counseling nurse will try to find him work where he won't have to be on his feet all day.

50   ECU man lying down, drinking from cup FG through straw, ZO to MS, he's under X-ray machine, operator left. (0:20)

Operator: "Drink it all down please. Stop breathing. Breathe. Now stop breathing. Swallow some more."

51   CU fluoroscope, movement. (0:15)

Operator: "Stop breathing, breathe."

52   MS over doctor's shoulder, patient lying on bed BG, second doctor leans over patient left. (0:50)

They talk about X-rays, his blood tests, heart murmur.

53   MS second doctor shot 52, listening to patient's heart, ZI to ECU patient's face. (0:17)

room noise

54   ECU doctor, tilt down to patient, he sits up, tilt up to doctor, tilt down to doctor's hands tapping on patient's back, tilt up to doctor. (0:27)

Doctor: "Could you sit up?"

55   MS LA patient sitting, doctor BG listening through stethoscope, another doctor BG. (0:15)

Doctor: "Say 99."
Patient: "Ninty-nine."
Doctor: "Now whisper, 'light.' "
Patient repeats.

56   CU doctor left, patient right, doctor feels patient's neck. (0:55)

Doctor: "Whisper, 'what.' "
Patient repeats.

57   MS same patient, lying in bed, observing doctors walk away from side of bed past camera. PL as examining doctor starts to cover him with blanket. He walks off left. (0:18)

Examining doctor: "OK all right. Oh, you're tied up here, huh? You feel cold?" Patient: "No." Doctor: "OK."

58	MS BV man walking down hall-way, camera follows, tilt down to HA of plastic jug he's carry-ing. (0:07)	hallway noise
59	Camera moves down long hall-way, on right we see a ward of patients lying in beds, LS. (0:07)	hallway noise
60	LS man from shot 58 walks into room, toward camera, patient is in bed FG, PL as he turns corner to spray liquid from the jug into sink and waste can. (0:12)	room noise
61	CU same man's hand holding spray nozzle, sprays waste can and closes lid. (0:05)	room noise, spray
62	LS hallway, woman pushes cart with linens past, PR with her, LS. (0:07)	intercom

Part 4: Medicine as Science

63	LS door of room, nurse wheels in medication cart, PR as she passes CU, tilt down as she stoops to cart. (0:05)	Nurse: "Good evening ladies, how are you?" Off camera: "Good even-ing." Nurse: "I have a little medica-tion for you here."
64	ECU elderly patient, nurse helps her sit up, she shakes and strains. ZO to MS woman and nurse. Nurse helps her to drink, ZI to ECU hand and cup, woman lies back, mouth shaking. (1:05)	Nurse: "Sit up, take it easy." Woman: "My back." Nurse: "I know you're in pain . . . now it's good to the last drop." Woman: "Thank you very much."
65	ECU male patient's mouth, he drinks from syringe of liquid. ZO to MS nurse shot 64 behind bed, patient FG, she refills syringe, ZI to CU mouth of patient. (0:40)	Nurse: "Was that good, you want a little more juice?"
66	CU hands pouring liquid into funnel, tilt down to ECU new male patient with tube in nose, tilt up to CU same nurse shot 65, down to ECU man. (0:25)	He tries to speak. Nurse: "That's your medication now."
67	CU doctor looking down, tilt down to the brain he's holding, ZI to ECU brain. (0:15)	Doctor: "Let's get to the brain proper and we do see the very marked flattening." He says he'll weigh it.

68	MS scale upper right, two doctors lower left, tilt down to brains both are holding, CU. (0:20)	He says the brain is small, "one of the reasons her symptoms were not so alarming and progressed so slowly."
69	MS 4 shot line of doctors working, standing along table, holding brains. Scale upper center. (0:03)	Doctor continues to describe brain.
70	MS 4 shot other side of work table, examining doctor holds brain and probes it. (0:12)	Doctor continues to describe brain.
71	ECU one of the observing doctors. (0:03)	Doctor continues to describe brain.
72	ECU brain held by examining doctor, he probes it and spreads it apart. (0:04)	Doctor continues to describe brain.
73	MS LA 4 shot doctors along worktable, several hold brains, CU FG brain. (0:35)	Doctor says he will take a sample of the brain he is holding.
74	ECU brain held by examining doctor, ZO to CU, PL to brain held by second doctor, ZI to ECU first brain as examining doctor gestures to it. (0:50)	Doctor continues to describe brain.
75	MS woman lying on table, head in FG, man stands beside her, BV, pointing to her uncovered feet while talking to people seated BG. (0:08)	He talks to audience about the characteristics of human leg and foot structure.
76	MS two men with suits, seated in audience. (0:06)	same as above
77	ECU LA young man in audience. (0:04)	same as above
78	ECU older man with bow tie, LA. (0:02)	same as above
79	LS from behind audience, lecturer and woman BG. (0:16)	Lecturer: "Only man can rotate the leg inward and outward."
80= 75	(0:06)	Lecturer: "Only man can develop cerebral palsy, because only man has a wine-glass geometry."

81 CU HA two members of the audience, seated. (0:02)	Lecturer: "So when they try to imitate cerebral palsy . . .
82 ECU man in audience, hand over mouth. (0:04)	. . . in the experimental animals, it's a waste of time."
83 ECU man in audience. (0:03)	Lecturer continues to talk about experiments with animals.
84 MS reverse angle shot 75, woman's feet FG, FV lecturer standing right. (0:28)	Lecturer: "Man acquires these disorders when he tries to adapt to a certain level of civilization."
85 ECU gloved hands and surgical instruments. (0:04)	rhythmic noise of a machine
86 CU two doctors with surgical masks and caps. (0:03)	same as above
87 ECU incision. (0:07)	same as above
88 ECU doctor with mask, PR as he turns and leans right. (0:02)	same as above
89 CU doctor's arm as he reaches into incision. (0:05)	same as above
90 CU over doctor's shoulder of incision and hands. (0:05)	same as above
91 ECU incision held open with clamp, doctor's hands and instruments. (0:24)	same as above
92 CU over doctor's shoulder of incision, hands, ZI to ECU incision. (0:09)	same as above
93 CU LA doctor looking down, framed by arms of other doctors, a hand moves in with sciessors. (0:04)	same as above
94 HA CU hands around wide open incision. (0:20)	same as above
95 CU wide open incision, movement of organ. (0:08)	same as above
96 ECU wide open incision, movement of second organ (heart). (0:06)	same as above

97 CU woman in surgical gown on telephone, PR as she crosses to shout . . .

Same rhythm as above in BG. Woman: "Can you give me the report?" She shouts . . .

98 . . . into operating room, PR to LS operating room, table, doctors, PL to woman, zip right to nurse in operating room. (0:45)

. . . to doctors in operating room: "He has a report of no malignancy whatsoever." The doctor asks whether it's true of all of the samples, she asks the person on the phone, and shouts back: "All of them."

99 MS woman right, curtain left in examining room. Doctor walks out from behind curtain and walks left to a woman patient on examining table, PL. ZI on ECU his face as he makes pelvic examination, tilt down to CU of slide as he wipes on a sample, ZO to MS doctor at foot of table, PL to CU woman patient, PR to MS doctor, turns out light, PR as he gets something from nurse, PL to CU woman patient, PR to doctor, ZI to ECU doctor, PR as he walks off. (1:40)

Doctor: "Relax, relax, take a deep breath. OK, good, everything's all right."

100 Waiting room, MS pregnant woman and children seated on bench. (0:03)

room noise

101 LS waiting room, people seated at desk, PL to two women MS holding babies, seated against wall. (0:04)

room noise

102 MS waiting room, woman with child lying across lap seated in chair. (0:02)

room noise

103 LS three children in waiting room, seated in chairs. (0:04)

room noise

104 CU two women left, baby right, nurse picks him up, tilt up to CU nurse and baby. (0:11)

room noise

Part 5: Trauma

105 ECU woman on phone. (0:24)

Woman, sounding impatient: she says that the child should not be sent home because his grandmother is intoxicated and unable to care for the two children. "She didn't even know the child was gone."

106 ECU police officer on phone, sunglasses. (0:15)

He talks about the same child: "Well, I think the child was left with a grandmother that was completely intoxicated and incapacitated and refused to come down here. The parents, I don't know, we can't locate them. I don't know, I think something should be done about it, I don't know."

107 LA MS nurse, same officer, child right. (0:20)

They say that the child's grandmother refuses to come down.

108 CU small black boy. (length of shot unavailable)

room noise

109 MS same officer left, woman on phone right (shot 104). (0:06)

To someone off camera: "Will you fill out a neglect form?" To phone: "All right, she's going to fill out a form."

110 CU child (shot 107), eating ice cream, dirty mouth. (0:15)

Off camera: "Nina, this is Kathy, now I know the old goat is there so just answer yes or no, do you have a bed on the ward?"

111 CU nurse (Kathy) on phone. (0:25)

Kathy: "Well, for really nothing, there's no disease, but I need a bed . . . a bed for a little boy that doesn't have any place to go."

112 CU woman. (0:23)

She asks if there are any other siblings in the home. Off camera: someone tells her no one knows, that the boy fell out of a 15-foot-high window and the police were called.

113 CU two nurses, same boy on table BG being cleaned up by a third nurse, older nurse crosses FG left to right, track left to CU of young nurse (Kathy shot 111) older nurse track right to beginning of shot. (0:47)

Two nurses: they say that by law they can't keep the boy, but by common sense they can't discharge him either. Kathy: "If I took him home tonight what would I do with him in the morning?" Older nurse: "Oh now, don't you get involved in something like that Kathy." Kathy: "Well what am I gonna do with the kid?" Older nurse: "Well he'll be

placed, don't worry about it."
Kathy: "Do you think I could get
something for him to eat from the
kitchen?"

114   CU two police officers. (0:10)

Talking to someone off camera:
"Don't worry about anything. You
have to go upstairs though, the
doctors want to take a look at you
tomorrow morning."

115   MS man with bandage on head
      seated left, nurse talks to him
      right. (0:07)

She tells him they'll make sure his
children are taken care of.

116= (0:16)
114

Officer: "That isn't a long time to
wait Lewis, it's very important
to your children." Lewis: "I'll be
all right now."

117   Lewis (shot 115) ECU. (0:03)

Officer says if he was all right the
doctors would have let him go
home.

118   Doctor and officer, ECU, officer
      crosses FG right to left. (0:16)

They discuss how to keep Lewis
there, officer suggests "action,"
doctor hesitates.

119   ECU doctor, and officer, officer
      walks off right, doctor walks back
      to CU and turns to face camera
      again. (0:23)

Officer says it's up to the doctor,
Doctor: "I say let's wait for the
social worker, after all he has young
children."

120   MS social worker bending over
      desk, talking to Lewis seated left
      FG, BV. (0:45)

She asks who is with the children,
Lewis says they're waiting for him.
She asks who gives them lunch, he
says he gave it to them this morning.

121   ECU social worker. (0:04)

Social worker: "Where is their
mother?"

122   ECU Lewis, ZO to MS Lewis, CU
      social worker right FG, ZI to ECU
      Lewis. (2:15)

Lewis: "I gotta go now." Social
worker: "But you're going to end
up in the hospital even sicker."
Lewis: "I buy some medication."
She asks if he gets money from the
welfare department, and he answers
that he works in a bar from 6:00
P.M. to 3:00 A.M. She asks who is
with the children at night, and he
answers that the bar is close to his

123 MS Lewis, social worker right FG, HA. (0:15)

home, and he walks over to check on them. Lewis insists that he feels all right, that he must go, and he'll buy some medicine some place.

She asks if there is any other reason he will not come into the hospital. Lewis: "I don't want to stay here." Social worker: "No one wants to stay here, no one wants to be in a hospital."

124 MS Lewis right, officer left. Officer puts hat on Lewis' head, stands him up, second officer crosses FG to stand at Lewis' other side, PL and track back as they pass camera and walk to hallway. (0:28)

Officer: "Come on Lewis, you have to go up now. Come on Lewis, we ain't gonna hurt ya."

125 Hallway, orderly pushes cart with patient toward camera, PR as he goes by, turns corner and continues down second hall, LS to CU to LS. (0:08)

hallway noise

Part 6: Psychosocial Problems

126 ECU young black man, ZO to CU, tilt down to CU waist and lap, ZO to MS, tilt up. His speech and gestures are feminine. (0:45)

Man: "In homosexuality you experience a lot, where there is a man who looks like an average Wall Street worker and he has a suit on and a tie and his hair combed to the side looking like a million dollars . . ."

127 ECU same man with head resting on hand. (1:20)

Off camera: "Mr. B_____, I want to establish one thing with you. There are lots of people who have this problem — who can go along very well, and if somebody couldn't do anything about it, I wouldn't try to change it, but I might try to help him get along with it." Man: "I recognize I'm not normal . . . I'm a freak of nature, so any kind of help that would be given to me here . . .

128 ECU psychiatrist (speaker from shot 127) seated at desk. (0:05)

. . . I assure you it would do me a heck of a lot of good."

| 129 | CU same homosexual, Lindsay campaign poster on wall behind his head. (0:16) | He says he's been having difficulty obtaining social welfare. |

129 CU same homosexual, Lindsay campaign poster on wall behind his head. (0:16)

He says he's been having difficulty obtaining social welfare.

130 CU psychiatrist writing, ZI to ECU. (0:08)

He continues to talk about welfare difficulty.

131= (0:22)
129

One welfare center has denied him service because he's a minor.

132= (0:50)
127

He says he's been supporting himself by male prostitution, "at times female because I get confused." He laughs.

133 MS psychiatrist at desk, leans toward homosexual seated FG right. (0:20)

Psychiatrist says he should not feel guilty if he tries as hard as he can to do the best he can.

134= (0:30)
127

Psychiatrist says the first couple of weeks will be the hardest, that he will try to get him on welfare.

135 Hallway, patient on cart wheeled past left to right, people follow the cart, MS to LS. (0:10)

intercom

136 Waiting room, rows of seats filled with people, LS. (0:05)

intercom

137 LS people seated along wall on right. (0:04)

intercom

138 Two elderly people seated on bench along wall, people cross FG left to right, MS. (0:04)

intercom

139 MS woman sitting, reading book in waiting room. (0:05)

intercom

140 MS man lies on bench, a second sits on opposite side of bench. (0:03)

intercom

141 LS small boy sitting on the far corner of an otherwise empty bench. (0:07)

intercom

142 LS homosexual (shot 134) seated on bench in waiting room, lights cigarette. (0:15)

We hear psychiatrist's voice from shot 134: "He needs some welfare assistance, because clearly he's not in a position . . .

143 Psychiatrist (speaker shot 142) on phone, CU. ZI to ECU eyes, ZO to ECU face, eyes wide open. ZO to CU, ZI to ECU, he leans over desk, ZO to CU. End of shot he looks up in amazement and says "she up on me!" (4:53)

... to work for himself." He says the patient should be ready to work in about a month. If he is sent to a hospital, he'll never be ready, and at least this way there's a good chance to straighten him out enough to be able to work. "There's a what! Miss Hightower, I can't help what his mother does. Miss Hightower, I don't wish to direct any conversation to his mother." He says this is an emergency situation and he can keep the man out of the hospital only if he gets assistance. "Is this a welfare center? Are you concerned with your clients and the possibility of keeping them out of the hospital? Why don't you answer? Miss Hightower, I as a psychiatrist am asking your assistance of welfare which you have in your hands to help this person so he has a chance to stay out of the hospital and get back to work." He says the patient's family threw him out because of his difficulty, that the mother has shown no interest or assistance. Hightower puts Stevis on the phone. "Miss Stevis, this is an emergency situation . . . will he get money regardless of what the worker finds at home. I wish an answer and if you can't give it I want to talk to somebody who can give it. Miss Hightower, are you going to give him assistance regardless of what the worker finds at home? I wish a commitment, I don't wish that you tell me you don't know what you're going to do! She hung up on me!"

Part 7: Drug Abuse

144 MS disheveled man on floor, orderly bending over him on left, second orderly bends over him on right, they lift him by his arms, woman enters right BV. (0:16)

Orderly: "Come on now, come on get up, wake up, get up."

145 CU HA same man, orderlies' hands on his arms, tilt up as they

Orderlies: "Hold on." "Come on" "Let's go, that's a boy." "Stand lift him up and turn him toward wheelchair BG. (0:37)

up." "Stand up."

146 ECU patient's backside, his pants are on backwards, orderly's arms try to guide him into chair, tilt up as he sits, CU of patient with orderly on either side. Left orderly leaves, right orderly crosses FG and leaves. (0:33)

Orderlies: "Turn around." "Come on." "Don't you know how to sit down yet." "Turn around." "That's wonderful." "Let's tie him to the chair." Off camera doctor: "What was it, wine or whiskey?"

147 MS two doctors standing beside man, orderly enters with strap to tie him in, doctors leave, patient holds up arms, orderly walks to back of chair and when he touches the patient on the head, patient puts hand to head and looks angrily at the orderly. (0:27)

Patient answers doctor: "I don't know." Orderly: "OK, both hands up." "Relax back forward." Patient protests and sobs. Orderly: "Nothing wrong with that." (*impatiently*)

148 MS woman patient in wheelchair left, doctor leans over her from right, he leaves right, he enters right and pushes wheelchair off right. Woman sits slumped in chair, head resting on hand. (0:32)

Doctor: "You inject a needle? When did you inject, what, heroin?" She's incoherent, she nods.

149 MS doctor left, patient sitting on table right (young man), doctor takes him by the shoulders and lays him back onto table, puts strap over his knees, turns right and calls off camera. Doctor is Schwartz from earlier scenes (shots 30 and 33). (0:47)

Doctor asks what the young man thinks he was given, mescaline? The boy says he thinks he's going to die. Schwartz assures him he won't. He orders medication and says no to a stomach pump. Schwartz: "How long ago did you take it?" Boy: "It was in the park, let's see, during the day."

150 CU Schwartz left, boy lying right, puts his head up, Schwartz makes him lie down again, puts strap over chest, holds the boy's forehead, boy breathes hard.

Boy: "I been trying to puke it out and trying to shit it out but it doesn't come out."
Schwartz: "You're going to be all right . . . now lie down for a minute." Boy: "What am I gonna do?" Schwartz: "There's no serious poison you could have taken at 7:00." Boy: "No, somebody in the park gave it to me." He becomes panicky. Schwartz: "If it was really serious it would have done you in by now." Boy: "No, it was a pill, a pill."

151 ECU boy, lying on table, ZO to
CU Schwartz and boy, Schwartz
prepares to give him medication
in a cup. (0:40)

Schwartz: "We're going to give you
some medication that will counter-
act the pill." Boy: "Doc, can I call
my friend Patricia? Oh shit, I don't
want to die." Schwartz: "You're
not going to die, try to relax. Now
I want you to swallow this." Boy:
"OK, I will."

152 MS Schwartz left, boy lying on
table right with pan on lap,
Schwartz helps him to sit up,
gives him medication to drink,
gives him second cup of medication, boy grabs for water, ZI to
CU boy, he vomits, Schwartz
holds his head, takes cup and
pan, boy looks around be-
wildered, frightened, ZI to ECU
Schwartz, ZO to MS as he helps
boy lay back and he puts strap
around his chest. Schwartz takes
blood pressure. (2:17)

The boy gags and tries to vomit.
Schwartz: "Drink this, all the way
down, go ahead, OK, a little
water." After the boy vomits,
Schwartz asks: "How you doin'?"
Boy: "I don't want to die."
Schwartz: "It all came up — you're
not gonna die, you're doing very
well." Boy: "What am I gonna do,
I'm so lost." Schwartz: "OK now, I
want you to lie down . . . that was
excellent, it all came up." Boy:
"Oh doctor, do I need a psychiatrist?" Schwartz: "Yes you do and
you're going to have one very
shortly."

153 CU boy lying on table, looking at
doctor, doctor crosses FG, ZO to
MS as boy gags, doctor puts his
hand on boy's shoulder and brings
pan back. The boy looks frightened and bewildered. (1:00)

Boy: "Maybe it was a real trip he
gave me. Oh shit, I'm so afraid of
life now." Schwartz: "Let's go
down the hall." Boy gags. Schwartz:
"Oops, let's leave this with you.
Relax, relax, we're gonna send you
down the hall with the messenger
to talk to the psychiatrist."

154 Hallway, PL as cart with same boy
goes by and down the hall, LS to
ELS, boy sits up and looks around,
scared, bewildered, he's strapped
in, messenger pulls cart from front.
(0:10)

hallway noise

155 MS two messengers left, boy sitting on table right, holds head in
hands, turns to sit on edge of
table, MS messenger takes "sheet"
from someone behind camera,
ZI to ECU hands as boy grabs his
hair, ZO to ECU face, runs hands
through hair, ZI to ECU hands,
ZO to ECU face. (1:08)

Boy: "I'm so afraid. Am I gonna
die?" Messenger: "No, you're just
gonna talk to a psychiatrist." Boy:
"I don't wanna lie down, I'm afraid
if I do . . ." Messenger: "Just relax."
Boy: "I don't wanna die."

156 MS boy standing in same room leans against wall, vomits, falls to knees in vomit, tilt down, doubles up and vomits, stands up, tilt up CU face, vomits again, doubles up and vomits again. Messenger enters right and turns him toward bed, crosses FG, MS. Messenger leaves right, boy doubles up again and vomits, LS, puts hands to head, ZI to ECU, he walks around and looks at floor, wipes mouth, ZO to LS through door, messenger right, ZI over his shoulder to boy CU, he walks around, runs hands through hair, tilt down to vomit on floor. (1:40)

Boy vomits. Messenger: "That's all right, lay on your bed Steve, go ahead." Steve: "No, no, I don't wanna die." He shouts: "Please!" He gags and vomits.

He calls: "Doctor?" "Oh shit. Am I all right?" Messenger: "Yeah, you're all right." Steve: "I'm so sorry, I'm so sorry." Messenger: "No, that's all right. Just lie down on the bed." Steve: "Wait, I don't wanna lie down, I'm afraid to lie down. Can you play music or something. Anybody who knows how to sing or something, or play music. I don't know. Oh shit."

157 ECU boy standing. (0:37)

"I think I should go back to my family." Messenger: "Where you from?" Boy: "Minnesota. Yeah, it's pretty hard making it here on my own." Steve says he's going to school, but he didn't even know why. Now he's studying art. "You can't do anything with art, you can't do anything with anything in life, you know that, just get a job someplace, that's about it."

158 Hallway, LS black man lying on cart along wall. People walk past, patient is wheeled by in wheelchair. (0:17)

hallway noise

159 LS another hallway, messengers guide two Spanish-speaking people up hallway, the woman has blood on face and blouse, ECU as they pass and go by camera left. (0:15)

hallway noise, Spanish.

Part 8: Violence

160 Hallway, LS to CU as black man is wheeled in by messenger, shirt is soaked in blood, tilt down to lap as he passes up to black woman following behind. Messenger holds cloth to victim's neck. (0:12)

hallway noise

161 MS same black man in wheelchair, FV. Doctors group around him, ZI over shoulder of one doctor to CU man, they take off his blood-soaked shirt, ZI to ECU man's face, tilt down to doctor's hands cutting away shirt, ZO to MS, they take off shirt, doctor walks around with hands covered with blood, doctor puts gauze to man's neck. They take him by the arms and lift him out of chair, PR as they help him up to table, lay him down, lift his legs onto table. (1:30)

Doctors: "Get an IV." "Oh, there's a cut there, see?"

siren in background
Doctors: "Let's get him up on the table." "Can you stand up?"

162 ECU doctor with stethoscope in ears, looking up, mouth open, concentrating. (0:03)

room noise

163 ECU blood pressure gauge. (0:03)

room noise

164= Doctor stands up, PL tilt up. (0:04)
162

Doctor: "One twenty over seventy."

165 CU hand opening cloth bag containing surgical instruments. (0:03)

room noise

166 CU man's neck, HA, clamps around edges of wounds, ZO to CU, he swallows. (0:06)

room noise

167 MS doctor left, man lying right, second doctor enters right, PR to CU two police officers nearby. (0:34)

Doctor: "Where was it, on 12th Street?" "You know the guys who did it?" "Don't move George." George murmurs answer.

168 CU George and doctor's hands stuffing cotton into wound in neck, George grimaces. (0:16)

Doctor: "Move the light over here." George groans.

169 MS BV two police officers in doorway of same room, wheelchair goes by in hallway outside. (0:04)

room noise

170 MS BV same woman shot 132, doctor behind her, George lying right. ZI to CU of them holding hands, George puts his hand on hers, ZO to CU as she leans to kiss him, ZO to MS, his neck is bandaged. (0:53)

Doctor: "But he's gonna be all right. Good thing it wasn't any deeper. It looked like a lot of bleeding, but it wasn't all that bad." He tells her she can see George again tomorrow.

silence

171 CU new black man BG, doctor right FG, ZI as he checks eyes, ECU over doctor's shoulder, man opens mouth slightly and doctor tries to look in. Tilt down to CU hands and chest as man unbuttons shirt slowly. (1:30)

Doctor asks if he's been losing weight in the last month. "Look up here, I want to look in your eyes." He asks him to open his mouth wide, but the man tells him his jaw has been broken. Doctor tells him to take his shirt off.

172 MS patient, lying on table, chest bare, CU hands FG working with machine. (0:13)

intercom

173 LS patient lying on side, arm bandaged. (0:04)

intercom, room noise

174 LS patient lying on table in hall-way, covered with blanket. (0:04)

intercom

175 LS man filling out forms in waiting room. (0:03)

room noise

176 LS janitor, sink BG, he empties plastic container, woman enters right, walks to purse near sink, MS of janitor picking up broom, crosses left to right, PR CU, tilt down to waste can, janitor turns right. (0:27)

intercom

Part 9: Limits of Service

177 CU two ambulance men leaning against wall. (0:05)

They talk to someone off camera.

178 LS cart with patient lying on it, elderly woman. Two men shot 177 BG. (0:02)

Off camera: someone says "It don't make sense."

179 CU two men leaning against wall across hall from shot 178, zip left to - shot 177, zip right to second pair of men (messengers). (0:37)

They talk in sad, unbelieving voices about how they have been forced to drive the elderly woman (shot 178) for three or four hours looking for a hospital with an available bed. One messenger: "Don't make sense!"

180 ECU one of the ambulance drivers. (0:04)

Black messenger off camera across hall: "And maybe she'll end up back here."

181 CU woman on table, head FG, upside down, she lifts head, looks around. (0:10)

Black messenger: "That's what happens when you don't have no money."

182 ECU black messenger. (0:24)

"If she had money she'd be staying at a private hospital." He asks about relatives; ambulance drivers across hall say she has no relatives. He says that's another bad thing.

183= Track forward as she's pushed
181 down hall, ZO to LS as they walk away from camera, door to outside at end of hall, nurse walks in right and laughs. (0:17)

Black messenger: "Well, take it easy."

siren overlap with shot 156

184 Outside, night, LS PR as ambulance goes by, lights flashing. (0:03)

siren

185 Outside, night, flashing lights on ambulance, MS BV ambulance and attendants, unloading stretcher zip left as another ambulance pulls up. (0:04)

siren

186 Inside attendant crosses right to left, moves table out of the way. Two men wheel in elderly woman patient in night clothes, doctor enters left, MS, doctor takes pulse, other attendants BG. (0:16)

patient gasps
Attendant: "We just got this patient. She's bad too."

187 CU attendant attaching tubes to suspended bottle. (0:04)

Doctor: "Ok, where's the nurse, I need her help." Attendant: Nurse!"

188 ECU hands tying tube tightly around woman's upper leg. (0:02)

room noise

189 MS patient, doctor behind table. (0:14)

Woman gasps and coughs. Doctor asks for morphine.

190 LS woman lying center, doctors grouped around table, working on her legs and breathing. (0:25)

room noise

191 MS from foot of table, two doctors at head, third FG left. One assists breathing, other listens to heart with stethoscope. (0:12)

Doctor: "Sounds good."

192= Door opens BG and attendant
191   wheels in electronic equipment.   suction noise
    (0:25)

193   View from foot of table, slightly   room noise, machines
    left of shot 192. (0:24)

194   CU head doctor. (0:03)   His diagnosis is "pulmonary
    edema."

195   MS, five attendants around table,   Doctor: "Is there an anesthetist
    arms working on patient. (0:15)   here?"

196   MS head doctor, second doctor   Doctor: "Want to get another IV
    left, equipment BG, priest enters   going." "What happened to the
    room BG, PR to doctor left,   anesthesiologist?"
    priest right. (0:17)

197   CU priest, he looks down, side to   Off camera: "You don't think she's
    side, reaches forward, back away,   on overdose?"
    walks left, PL, stops, walks right,   "No." "Do you have the cardio-
    PR, moves lips. (0:20)   gram ready?"

198   CU two doctors, priest right BG,   Doctor: "Run it for awhile."
    first doctor leaves left, equipment
    BG. (0:05)

199   CU readout from equipment,   Off camera: (*surprised*) "She's got a
    stylus. (0:06)   good pulse?" "Yeah, she has a
    pulse. I don't know how long she
    can hold it."

200   MS woman's head, doctor assists   Head doctor asks question.
    breathing BG, head doctor right
    FG leaning over woman. (0:04)

201   CU woman, tubes in mouth, doc-   room noise
    tor's hands holding instrument,
    tilt up and right to CU doctor,
    down as he puts ear to instrument,
    her mouth works. (0:10)

202   MS doctor from emergency room   Friend: "Yes, she has been taking
    in office, patient's friend seated   medication for her high blood pres-
    right, ZI to ECU friend, ZO to   sure." The friend says the patient
    CU as she looks in purse for name   lives alone, that they had a birthday
    of patient's doctor, ZO to MS doc-   party today and maybe the work was
    tor and friend, stamps fall out of   too much. Friend (*impatient*):
    her purse, doctor bends to pick   "The only thing I'm interested in is
    them up. Friend gives him card   what is her condition?" Doctor:
    with doctor's name, he puts it in   "Grave, critical." Doctor asks if
    his pocket, backs away from desk,   she's diabetic. Friend says no. Doc-

stands up and walks off left.
(2:45)

tor asks if she's under anyone's
care, friend looks for card with
doctor's name. Friend looks at doctor. "She's all right?" Doctor: She's
not all right." Friend: "She *is* critical?" Doctor: "Yes."

203 LS in emergency room from foot
of patient's table, attendants
left, friend (shot 202) right at
side of patient. Speaks to her in
foreign language, kisses her on
cheek. Looks up to answer question of attendant. Looks back to
friend, holds back tears. Patient
seems to recognize her friend.
(0:55)

Friend speaks to patient in foreign
language, tells her not to worry.
Attendant: "Excuse me, was she
ever here before as a patient?"
Friend: "No, I don't believe so."

204 New angle, camera tracked left,
MS. Doctor enters right, takes
friend out, friend kisses patient,
patient looks toward friend as
she leaves through door BG.
(0:43)

Friend speaks foreign language,
patient nods. Attendant: "Let's go
outside, OK?"

205 New setting, Dr. Schwartz (from
previous parts) BG, black man left
FG. (0:30)

Schwartz: "Mr. Fields, I gotta get
back to work. I understand your
problem. There's no question about
it, you're too old to live alone.
Social welfare is trying to find a
place for you to stay, but the hospital is not the place for you now."

206 ECU elderly black man, ZO to
MS him and Schwartz on right.
Fields shakes Schwartz's hand.
Schwartz walks away from
camera to right, sits at desk BG
and taps his fingers on desk top.
(0:40)

Fields tells about being beaten, tells
about another man who was shot in
his own home. "This is a tough
country." Schwartz: "You're not
the only one in this position, and
there are many people everyday
placed into appropriate nursing
homes. If you call the number
tomorrow, the lady will take care
of you." He tells Fields he will get
his new glasses tomorrow "for sure,
for sure." Fields: "Yes, that would
be a great boost to me, 'cause I
can't read." Schwartz: "You
definitely should have glasses."

207 LS Fields walking away from
camera, down corridor, balancing
against wall. (0:05)

intercom

208 CU hand holding disinfectant jug   intercom, footsteps
(same man shot 58), camera
tracks forward with him down
hallway, tilt up to CU, stop and
watch as he walks to LS. (0:14)

Part 10: God

209 Patients seated in wheelchairs   silence
facing camera, others walking in
bed clothes up aisle in chapel, LS
to CU. (0:07)

210 Patients in hallway file past camera   Overlap voice of priest from shot
on right, LS to CU, turn into   183. "Today especially we con-
chapel door. (0:14)   front the mystery of God."

211 CU LA priest, crucifix upper right,   "Forgetting ourselves we approach
flowers BG. (0:23)   reverently with awe, with wonder.
Realizing our own insufficiency and
nothingness before our God."

212 CU to LS down row of seated   "Who of us humans could ever
patients, listening, some in wheel-   know the mind of God?"
chairs. (0:08)

213 CU two women listening. (0:03)   "Who of us could give Him anything He has not already?"

214 ECU old woman. (0:03)   "Or lend Him . . .

215 CU two women, one with man-   . . . anything He would need. For
tilla. (0:04)   everything that . . .

216 CU three women, white uniforms.   . . . exists comes from Him, every-
(0:05)   thing is by Him."

217 ECU woman. (0:04)   "Everything is from Him."

218 ECU woman, rosary in hand.   "To Him be glory forever,
(0:03)   hallelujah."

219 ECU priest, crucifix BG. (0:40)   "Glory to God in the highest, we
praise you, we worship you, we
glorify you. Today let us thank
God for God."

220 CU to LS down row of singing   singing
patients. (0:10)

221 CU woman with scarf, hands   singing
folded in front of her. (0:15)

222 ECU woman. (0:15)   singing

223 CU two women, mantilla covers   singing
    head of one. (0:04)

224 ECU old woman, hands to mouth.   singing
    (0:05)

225 LA CU to MS down row of   singing
    patients in chairs. (0:04)

226 Man takes collection, walks down   singing
    aisle, patients FG and BG, male
    patient seems to be looking for
    money in his pocket or coin
    purse, collection passes him by,
    MS. (0:45)

227 CU exterior shot of two floors of   Singing fades out to noise of cars.
    large building (hospital), ZO to
    ELS of building from freeway, cars
    drive by FG, right to left. (0:30)

228 Directed and Produced by
    Frederick Wiseman, Photography
    by William Brayne, Edited by
    Frederick Wiseman, Associate
    Editor Carter Stanton-Abbot,
    Sound Mixer Richard Vorsek,   Sound of cars from shot 227.
    Camera Assistant David Martin,
    Assistant Editor Susan Primm,
    Production Assistant Robbin
    Mason and Margaret Anderson.
    An OSTI Film. Copyright OSTI
    Inc. 1969, All rights reserved.
    Hospital was made at Metro-
    politan Hospital Center in New
    York through the cooperation
    of the Department of Hospital
    administration, staff, and
    patients.

CREDITS AND NOTES

Producer:	Frederick Wiseman
Director:	Frederick Wiseman
Photography:	William Brayne
Editor:	Frederick Wiseman
Associate Editor:	Carter Stanton-Abbot
Sound Mixer:	Richard Vorsek
Camera Assistant:	David Martin
Assistant Editor:	Susan Primm
Production Assistant:	Robbin Mason
	Margaret Anderson

Copyright OSTI Inc. 1969
Filmed on location at Metropolitan Hospital Center in New York

Distribution:	Zipporah Films
Running Time:	84 minutes
Released:	February, 1970.

linked more natural — as expect progressive

5 BASIC TRAINING (1971)

Wiseman filmed *Basic Training* at the U.S. Army Training Center at Fort Knox, Kentucky. He follows recruits through training from their arrival as civilians to their graduation as soldiers. Each part of the film is a "lesson" in basic training. Instructors drill recruits in personal hygiene, use of weapons, hand-to-hand combat, patriotism. Officers hand out penalties for disobedience. The film progresses toward the large-scale day and night war games in which recruits apply what they've learned. The film ends with a commencement ceremony. NET aired *Basic Training* for the first time in October 1971. (89 minutes)

SYNOPSIS

Part 1: Processing

Recruits shed their identities as civilians and individuals, and take on the look of soldiers. They arrive by bus in civilian clothes, a sergeant assigns them bunks, some one measures their chests for uniforms, barbers shave their heads, and photographers take their pictures for ID cards. Recruits line up for vaccinations and pose inside a globe and American flag for formal portraits. As they stand in formation, a sergeant tells them to address him with, "yes or no sir." They listen to a welcome speech by an officer (who was ushered in by a band playing "Caissons"). Later, a company commander warns them to do as they're told, to "just go along." Shots 1–46, (6:38).

Part 2: Physical and Mental Fitness

Part 2 begins with day one of elementary physical and attitudinal training. A sergeant walks into a dark barracks and awakens recruits. They wash and shave, and an instructor shows a recruit how to clean the urinals. A televised instructor demonstrates the right way to brush teeth, while recruits imitate him from their seats. Outside, recruits exercise, crawl along the ground, and swing from an overhead ladder. Finally, the recruits gather in a supply room to get their first rifles. Their sergeant summarizes his view of why they shouldn't balk at learning how to use their weapons: in Vietnam it will boil down to kill or be killed. Part 2 ends with a shot of marching, chanting recruits. Shots 47–84 (7:19).

Part 3: Skills for War

Weapons training begins in part 3. A sergeant dramatically demonstrates an automatic rifle and recruits throw grenades. A drill sergeant tries to teach a misfit (Hickman) to march in formation and recruits stand on bleachers while a photographer takes their "class" picture. Recruits practice bayonet thrusts in an open field. In the final shots, two recruits jousting with cudgels ignore the sergeant's whistle and continue to lunge at each other. Shots 85–131, (9:53).

Part 4: Misfits

In part 4 the training center deals with its misfits. An officer sentences Booker to seven days in correctional custody for striking a fellow recruit. We hear that

Hickman, the out-of-step recruit from part 3, tried to commit suicide and a sergeant refers him to a chaplain. The chaplain gives him a pep talk, telling him life has its ups and downs and we have to pick ourselves up out of the mud when we fall. Shots 132–148, (8:16).

Part 5: Men Behind the Uniforms

In part 5, recruits and sergeants take a break in the field. First, recruits practice hand-to-hand combat, and then relax and eat an outdoor lunch. A sergeant disciplines a recruit for sneaking a can of soda onto the training field. Recruits rest under trees and one relates his sexual exploits to his friends. The sequence ends as a sergeant tells a friend about reincarnation, referring to General Patton's beliefs and the possibility that prejudiced men could be punished in the next life by coming back as "Negroes." We return to shots of marching men. Shots 149–171, (8:44).

Part 6: Conformity

Part 6 contrasts men who accept and fit into the army's mold with a man who, rejecting the premise that everyone must give up his individuality, declares he is a man without a country. The part opens as a young recruit proudly displays his rifle to his family. They praise his performance and his coming to manhood through the army. In the next set of shots an officer disciplines Johnson for wanting to take care only of himself. Johnson rejects the officer's premise that the army "isn't only one man, it's millions of people." The setting changes to a back room, where Johnson talks to a sergeant and other recruits. He says that doing what you're told could get you killed, and he has no feelings of loyalty to the army or the country. Wiseman cuts to a lieutenant's promotion to captain. His wife proudly pins the insignia onto his uniform. Finally, a "lifer" tells recruits that he has been in Vietnam once, is in the states to learn a "new technique," and is going back again to get "some of this squared away by the time you young men get over there," and if he doesn't, it'll be their job to carry on the tradition of their forefathers. We return to men chanting and jogging in time along a road. Shots 172–191, (13:37).

Part 7: Baptism

Part 7 returns briefly to another training exercise. Recruits wearing gas masks line up in a small cement block building. A sergeant orders them one by one to take off their masks and breathe in the tear gas, not letting them leave the building until he gives the order. We return to marching, chanting recruits. Shots 192–201, (3:52).

Part 8: Indoctrination

Part 8 is made up of two "sermons." The first is from a sergeant who introduces films on the achievements and traditions of the United States Army and why we're fighting in Vietnam. He tells recruits they are part of an undefeated army, and it's up to them to carry on that tradition. Recruits march to chapel, where the chaplain tells them that God can give them the strength and power to get them through "these two to three years that now face you." We return to marching, chanting men. Shots 202–221, (6:26).

Part 9: Practice for Vietnam

Part 9 gives recruits previews of what many of them might be doing in the next couple of years. An instructor displays an antipersonnel mine and explains that it's responsible for eight percent of the casualties in Vietnam. Another instructor shows recruits how to use "VC" helmets' leather straps and buckles to strangle a man in hand-to-hand combat. Hickman (parts 3 and 4) plays the role of the "VC" soldier. Recruits march to maneuvers chanting: "Mr. Nixon drop the bomb, I don't want to go to 'Nam." The war games are geared to jungle fighting. For the night maneuvers, the men blacken their faces. In the field, they move silently and in deliberate slow motion. All we hear is crickets. They slide face up under barbed wire and search for land minds in the dark. Suddenly, machine guns open fire and men crawl out of trenches and under barbed wire. Wiseman cuts to men marching, silhouetted against the dawn sky — they're off to daytime maneuvers. They don jungle camouflage and attack thatched huts, giggling when they find their friends in the huts. Shots 222–283, (11:50).

Part 10: Confirmation

Part 10 is the commencement. A band marches onto a large field, recruits follow in formation. An officer presents a recruit with the American Spirit of Honor Award. In his acceptance speech, the recruit outlines the results of basic training: men from widely different backgrounds come to Fort Knox and leave as fighting men of the U.S. Army. He conjures up the ghosts of Gettysburg and San Juan Hill and calls upon the men to take up the banner of their forefathers. The band plays again, and the camera tracks back as the drum major leads the band forward. Shots 284–313, (5:48).

CREDITS AND NOTES

Producer:	Frederick Wiseman
Director:	Frederick Wiseman
Photography:	William Brayne
Editor:	Frederick Wiseman
Associate Editor:	Pat Thomson

Copyright Basic Training Co., Inc., 1971.
Filmed on location at Fort Knox, Kentucky.

Distribution:	Zipporah Films
Running Time:	89 minutes
Released:	October, 1971.

6   ESSENE (1972)

Wiseman filmed *Essene* at an Anglican monastery in rural Michigan. He never identifies the location or denomination of the monastery in the film. Wiseman named the film after a second century *B.C.* brotherhood dedicated to practicing poverty and seeking high degrees of holiness. Some of the monastery's brothers apparently have lived there for decades. But others seem to be there on shorter retreats. The buildings are a mixture of rustic log structures and a modern chapel. Wiseman follows the monks in their worship and in their search for fulfilling relationships with their God and other members of the monastic community. The brothers attempt to heal psychological and spiritual wounds though community life and prayer. Even the monastery isn't free from the misfits that challenge institutional values in Wiseman's other films. Through comparisons and contrasts among characters, the film's parts reveal the monastery's purpose, its need for community, its view of the virtues of asceticism, its worship, and the healing of several members. PBS first broadcast *Essene* in November 1972, and the Ford Foundation and Corporation for Public Broadcasting provided funding. The Catholic Broadcasters' Association gave the film the Gabriel Award in 1972. (86 minutes)

SYNOPSIS

Part 1: Community

Part 1 reveals one of the monastery's goals: to worship God as a community. We see a young man raking leaves in the park-like surroundings of the monastery, and somewhere inside, men kneel before a crucifix and a monk (whom brothers later refer to as the abbot) reads in his study. We meet several monks in closeups as they listen to the abbot read the rules for the observation of Lent. He sees the need for a sense of community, a "corporate consciousness," and "corporate approval" of actions. In a community prayer session, monks request prayers for people and causes that are important to them. Finally, the abbot talks informally to a small group of monks about how little everyday annoyances within the community should be resolved by listening to the Spirit, not the ego. A monk relaxes on a porch, another dusts the furniture in a study, and a third monk, wearing a sun hat, picks vegetables from a garden. The same monk from shot 1 continues to rake leaves outside. Shots 1–40, (9:55).

Part 2: Ego

A misfit stands in the way of the sense of community that the abbot was trying to build in part 1. The abbot asks an older monk (whom the shopkeeper later calls "Herb") why he refuses to allow other brothers to call him by his first name. Herb is stubborn and defensive. He becomes short with the abbot and refuses to concede that the monastery's sense of Christian community is grounds for first-name relationships. The part ends outside as a monk stands silhouetted against a bright sky, a brother and a nun talk in a hollow, a young monk rests against a tree, and the sun sets behind a hill. Shots 41–53, (6:47).

Part 3: Worship and Healing

Day one has ended, and the monks gather in the chapel for a night vigil. A guitarist accompanies their song, they chant in Latin and pray with the abbot. In a series of short shots, monks and a nun pray silently before a small altar. In a meeting room, the brothers dedicate a vigil to Father Anthony. Anthony kneels in the center of the room while brothers and lay people cluster around him, laying their hands on his head and body. Chanting in harmony, they ask Jesus to "heal him," and "make him whole." Shots 54-69, (8:30).

Part 4: Ego

Herb (part 2) goes into a small town to pick up necessities and we follow him down a sidewalk and into a grocery and hardware store. Unlike his earlier encounter with the abbot (part 2), Herb is cheerful and even lets the hardware salesman call him "Herb" and "Herbert," a nickname the salesman applies to the brothers in general. The storekeeper goes on to kid Herb about making "muster" that morning. Herb drives back to the monastery, past farm fields, and pulls onto the monastery grounds. The young monk from part 1 is still there, cutting grass. Shots 70-76.

Part 5: Discipline

Brothers continue to define the institution in terms of community and asceticism. Anthony (part 3) asks a young monk how well he's fitting into the community. They agree that things are going better this week, and the young monk won't have to think about leaving the monastery early. He asks Anthony for a theological rationale for discipline. Anthony says asceticism makes a man more receptive to God's messages and graces. In the next set of shots, the abbot stands in front of a blackboard and lectures on the tension between the Law and the Spirit — and on the mystery of God that's so big, it's almost "meaningless." The part ends with a shot of the young monk raking leaves outside. Shots 77-83, (5:54).

Part 6: Healing

In part 6, we meet a sensitive monk whose healing we'll witness in part 9. Here he walks on the grounds with a nun and tearfully describes the hurt he has experienced from laying himself open to the brothers during the last few weeks. The sister comforts him and assures him that the process of growth is not easy, but he'll be "OK." They walk into a chapel and Wiseman cuts to the same monk singing "Deep River" at a piano. Again, the part ends outside, as several monks walk along a path to the chapel. Shots 84-88, (7:30).

Part 7: Community

In the chapel, the abbot celebrates Mass. His sermon is about Brother Joseph, who found faith after a breakdown 16 years ago — now people "come to the monastery and see nothing else but Brother Joseph." After the sermon, the monks take turns offering personal prayers for people and causes. They receive Communion, and as they pass on the liturgical kiss of peace, the camera tracks back along a row of monks, to a lay family in the back of the chapel, where a father passes the kiss on to his son. In the dining room, the brothers eat without talking, accompanied by the peaceful background music of a guitar. Shots 89–131, (10:20).

Part 8: Community vs. Ego

In part 8, the elders take up the problem of a misfit, Brother Wilfred. (From their description of Wilfred, it seems likely he is actually Herb.) The abbot, Joseph (part 7) and Anthony (parts 3 and 5) try to decide what they should do about Wilfred's divisive behavior. Anthony and Joseph insist that Wilfred never liked anyone in the community "from the abbot straight down." Joseph concludes it's simply the man's personality. The abbot says he can't take action without specifics, but Anthony claims they've been giving him specifics for 18 years. Anthony declares that the divisive people in the community "have got to start loving the brothers, that's all there is to it." The part ends outdoors, as the abbot and other brothers load grain onto a tractor-pulled wagon. Shots 132–144, (5:17).

Part 9: Healing

In contrast to the description of Wilfred's divisiveness, part 9 returns to the "healed" monk's (part 6) anguished efforts to integrate into the community. In a group prayer meeting, he tells an allegorical story of his struggle to fit into the community. He feels he has let his ego take over and as a result, he's lost sight of his God. He stands and implores his brothers to pray for him. He kneels, and they gather around him to pray and sing. Several monks embrace him, and they continue to sing as he returns to his chair. The part ends with a shot of the abbot in his study, a monk making his bed, another monk cleaning vegetables outside, and Herb, sitting alone outside, writing in the breeze. Shots 145–184, (13:48).

Part 10: Healing

In a meeting of the same brothers from the Wilfred scene (part 8), the abbot says he wants to help them understand him better so they can "get more mileage out of him." He tells of the alienation he felt from his father and how he tends to recoil into himself when he comes up against "powerful passion." It's this tendency that he must heal within himself before he can deal successfully with the brethren in their "various needs and delinquencies." We go outside, where the "healed" monk and the nun from part 6 walk and talk along the path to the chapel. They turn and go inside. Shots 185-192, (3:51).

Part 11: Ego vs. Spirit

Inside the chapel, the abbot delivers a sermon that summarizes the monastery's reason for existence. He contrasts the concerns of Mary and Martha, one for the Spirit, the other for earthly matters, or the ego. He describes the conflicts that arise within the community when two egos meet, leading to arguments like "who left the rake out overnight." He says they must imitate Mary's concern for spiritual matters. He ends the sermon speaking for Christ asking, "Will you listen, really deeply, like Mary, sitting at the feet of Truth, that you may be happy? Will you listen, that the Father, the Spirit, and I may come to dwell within you?" Shots 193-205, (11:29).

CREDITS AND NOTES

Producer:	Frederick Wiseman
Director:	Frederick Wiseman
Photography:	William Brayne
Editor:	Frederick Wiseman
Associate Editor:	Spencer Bruskin
Camera Assistant:	Oliver Kool

Copyright, Zipporah Films, 1972
Funding provided by the Ford Foundation
and the Corporation for Public Broadcasting.
Filmed on location at Three Rivers, Michigan.

Distribution:	Zipporah Films
Running Time:	86 minutes
Released:	November, 1972.

7 JUVENILE COURT (1973)

Juvenile Court actually has no title. Wiseman reduced his "narration" in this film to zero by eliminating the title shot. Instead, he intercuts a shot of a large building with a closeup of the sign: JUVENILE COURT 616. The court is in Memphis, Tennessee. Again, Wiseman records the daily interactions between the institution's agents and its clients. Like *Law and Order*, the film breaks down into parts made up of individual cases. PBS broadcast *Juvenile Court* in 1973. It received the Silver Phoenix Award from the Atlanta International Film Festival, 1974; an Emmy nomination for Best News Documentary, 1974; and the Cine Golden Eagle Award, 1974. The Ford Foundation provided funding. (144 minutes)

SYNOPSIS

Part 1: Introducton

Part 1 is a 10-minute version of the whole film. In this introduction, we meet several major characters, and see the entire process of juvenile court that will be repeated and varied throughout the rest of the film. Part 1 opens with shots of a city street, a large building, and a sign: JUVENILE COURT 616. A squad car pulls into a parking lot. Inside a waiting area, officers take handcuffs off a boy; a second boy is on the phone, asking his parents to come and get him; a third boy sobs: "Mama, don't let me go," as officers lead him to a bench. At a table, an officer dictates the details of an arrest into the telephone. In a hallway, an officer displays the switchblade he took from a youth. A man reads a young girl her rights, a photographer takes a mug shot of a tearstained face. Officers search a young boy, barbers give short haircuts to three boys, and a psychiatrist shows a boy ink blots and analyzes a girl's drawing with a social worker. A boy visits with his mother, then walks to the television room to join a group of boys watching a program. Boys exercise in a courtyard and secretaries work with computer files. We meet Judge Turner in his courtroom, where he places a boy on probation and chides his parents for keeping a gun where their son could get at it. The part ends in a hallway, where adults and children sit along walls on benches and a secretary answers the phone with, "Good morning, Juvenile Court." Shots 1–49, (10:14).

Part 2: Diane

Part 2 is the case of Diane Minor, an 11 year old who violated probation by running away from home. Miss A. (we can't make out the rest of her name), who is probably a social worker (part 1), walks Diane to the courtroom. Miss A. tells Diane the judge probably won't let her go home because her mother doesn't give her enough supervision. In the courtroom, Judge Turner orders that Diane be placed in a foster home. We follow Diane, her mother, and Miss A. to an office, where Miss A. tells Diane that this is the best thing for her, and she should do her best in her new home. Diane's mother looks on from the background with a bitter expression, as Miss A. tells her to have Diane's clothes at the juvenile court at 1:00 p.m. The part ends with shots of the hallway, where Diane and her parents sit in silence on benches. Shots 50–81.

Part 3: Child Abuse

Part 3 is a case of child abuse. In his chambers, Judge Turner hears how a three-year-old boy was severely beaten by his mother's fiancee. The lawyer claims that the man just got carried away; that according to the psychiatrist's report, he was just unaccustomed to disciplining a child. Turner decides not to prosecute and sends the boy back to his mother, adding that "hopefully everyone's learned a lesson from this experience." We return to shots of the hallway and waiting rooms. Shots 82-92, (9:20).

Part 4: Tommy

In part 4, we meet Tommy, whose case we'll pick up again later. A psychiatrist asks the 15-year-old boy about charges that he fondled a small girl when he was babysitting for her. Tommy denies that he did it. Shots 93-99, (3:29).

Part 5: Counseling

In an office, a woman social worker firmly tells a young girl: "Come hell or high water, you say to yourself you're going to be somebody!" Shots 100-101, (4:57).

Part 6: Bobby

In another room, men from Teen Challenge urge Robert Young to accept Christ, turn away from drugs, and lead a Christian life. Robert says he does accept Christ and joins the men in prayer. Shots 102-107, (5:40).

Part 7: Counseling

A psychiatrist holds ink blots for a young man to see, and we return to hallways, waiting rooms, and photographers taking mug shots. Shots 108-114, (1:05).

Part 8: Bobby

We return to Robert Young (part 6) as he tells his mother about the bad drug trip that landed him in juvenile court. He says he's accepted Christ and is changing his ways. His mother says he's told her that before, and even though she always believes in him, he just turns around and pulls the same thing again. Shots 115-118, (2:47).

Part 9: Patricia Jones

A mother, in tears, stands at an officer's desk. He tells her he picked her daughter up for shoplifting, but the girl denies the charge. Shots 119-122, (1:15).

Part 10: Robert Humphrey

A mother brings her son into juvenile court after she found out he stole money from a golf course. She hopes juvenile court can straighten him out so he can get into the army. The officer says she's done the right thing. Shots 123-127, (2:40).

Part 11: Anita

Miss A. meets with Anita's parents and tells them that their daughter probably needs more restrictions, that Anita attempted suicide just to get more attention. When Anita walks in, she tearfully tells her parents she wants to go home. Miss A. asks her why she thinks her parents don't care about her, and whether she still claims that her stepfather made sexual advances. Anita says he did. Her mother says maybe Anita was jumpy because she knew about charges of incest against her natural father. Back in the hallway, the secretary answers the phone with: "Good morning, Juvenile Court." Shots 128-143, (8:08).

Part 12: Lisa

A minister talks to a young girl at the request of her parents. She tells how she and her parents grew apart little by little. The minister says this is a part of growing up, and it isn't going to be easy. Shots 144-146, (2:20).

Part 13: Bobby

In a long series of shots Robert Young (parts 6 and 7) faces Judge Turner. A narcotics bureau officer says Robert sold LSD to an undercover agent. Robert denies the charge. The minister from Teen Challenge, who himself had a long criminal record, tells how Robert has accepted Christ, and asks Turner to let Robert come into the Teen Challenge program. The probation officer says Robert can stay straight only as long as someone is working closely with him. Turner agrees that Robert should be tried before a jury. The court officer announces the next case. Shots 147-186, (13:38).

Part 14: Cynthia and Craig

In an office, a motherly woman who participates in the court's shelter program helps two small children into their coats before taking them to her home. Shots 187-191, (2:27).

Part 15: Joseph

An officer calls a mother to tell her that police found her son on the Highland Strip, an area notorious for drugs. They charged him with being a runaway, and they're sending him home on a bus. Shot 192, (0:50).

Part 16: Shoplifter

In an office, a boy sits down next to his father, and the officer says: "Tell your father what happened today." The boy says: "I got caught stealing a shirt," and the father looks away, disgusted. We return to shots of hallways and a photographer taking mug shots. Shots 193-196, (0:37).

Part 17: Tommy

Tommy's case (part 4) reaches Judge Turner. In his chambers, Turner questions the mother about the incident, and then calls Tommy in. Tommy denies the charges, and Turner agrees to have him take a lie detector test. The psychiatrist recommends that Tommy receive treatment. Shots 197-229, (20:25).

Part 18: Child Abuse

In an office, the man from the shelter program (part 13), asks a small boy (who wears bandages covering his head and neck) how he was burned. The boy says his uncle poured hot grease on him. The man tells him he can have lunch and watch television until his grandmother picks-him up. Shots 230-231. (1:44).

Part 19: Foster Boy

A foster father turns his boy in for stealing money from a dresser. He tells the boy he'll take him back home after the weekend if he promises to behave and forget "all the places you been." Shots 232-234, (2:53).

Part 20: Disinterested Mother

In contrast with the foster father's concern, Turner talks on the phone with a mother who refused to show up for her son's hearing because "there was no reason for juvenile court to take the child in the first place." Turner tells her she has no argument because she didn't show up for the hearing. Shots 235-236, (0:52).

Part 21: Pam

Miss A. tells Pam she has to follow rules and regulations, even if they don't make sense. Pam can't understand why 18 is the magic age of freedom and responsibility — "nothing matters if you're a kid." We return to hallways and waiting areas. Shots 237-243, (2:54).

Part 22: Robert Singleton

Part 22 is a lengthy record of the case of Robert Singleton, a young man (17 years old) who insists that he was threatened into driving a getaway car, but now finds himself charged with robbery with a deadly weapon. The camera follows Turner and the lawyers into chambers where they try to decide what action would be in the boy's best interests. Should they send his case to criminal court, or keep it in juvenile? The attorney general agrees that if Robert pleads guilty and goes to the state training school, juvenile court can retain jurisdiction. The lawyer tries to talk Robert into pleading guilty, but Robert dreads the training school, believes he's innocent, and wants to "fight it out" in court. The lawyer pleads guilty anyway, and tries to convince Robert that they performed a miracle: he'll only have to serve several months in the training school. Robert says this isn't justice, and as he leaves the room he calls the attorney general a liar. The attorney general tells one of the lawyers: "He accused me of lying!" The lawyer answers: "Don't they all?" Wiseman returns to the first two shots of the film: the large building and the street. This time young girls walk down the sidewalk, away from the camera. Shots 244-304, (33:20).

CREDITS AND NOTES

Producer:	Frederick Wiseman
Director:	Frederick Wiseman
Photography:	William Brayne
Editor:	Frederick Wiseman
Camera Assistant:	Oliver Kool
Production Assistant:	James Medalla
	Rene Koopman

Copyright 1973, UDOC Films, Inc
Funding provided by the Ford Foundation.
Filmed on location in Memphis, Tennessee.

Distribution:	Zipporah Films
Running Time:	144 minutes
Released:	October, 1973.

8 PRIMATE (1974)

Primate was filmed in the Yerkes Primate Research Center in Atlanta. Its account of the seemingly routine investigations of primate life and behavior is without narration and has less verbal information than the other films. *Primate* raised a storm of controversy from animal lovers, high school science teachers, and Yerkes scientists. The night that the film premiered on WNET in New York and most PBS stations nationwide, WNET received 150 phone calls, one bomb scare, and one threat on Wiseman's life. Some stations refused to air the film.

Much of the controversy seemed to result from Wiseman's refusal to verbally explain the events we see. *Primate* has more than twice the number of shots as the other films and much less dialogue. The meanings we assign to what we see must come from the ambiguous images and whatever snatches of conversation Wiseman allows us to hear. Some critics argued that the complex, abstract nature of scientific research is unsuited to Wiseman's technique. Others said that his almost mundane style ironically extracts profundity. (105 minutes)

SYNOPSIS

Part 1: Introduction

Part 1 is an introduction to the institution that reveals its research function and the relationship of the employees to the inmates. The film begins with silent shots of photographs of famous scientists, a shot of the sign: "Yerkes Regional Primate Research Center," of the center's exterior, and of gorillas, orangutans, and chimps in cages. From here, the part becomes a progression from conception through adolescence. A reproduction researcher explains to a visiting researcher how he observes and records the copulation habits of the apes. The visitor replies: "I don't think it ever is the whole story, that's what makes it so good, complexity." We watch an employee hand food through cage doors to apes. We return to the reproduction researcher who observes an orangutan mother and her newborn and dictates his observations into a tape recorder. We visit the "newborn reception" room where a woman diapers and bottle feeds newborn chimps, then performs an experiment on an infant chimp: how long will he hang onto a bar by one hand before he lets go. We watch women minister to a number of young chimps in cages, take temperatures, give them drinks from cups. Finally, we see an adolescent chimp playing in an outdoor playground complete with jungle gym, as a researcher sits and observes in the background. The introduction ends with a researcher drawing a blood sample from a monkey and feeding the sample to an electronic analysis machine. Shots 1–99, (18:12).

Part 2: Artificial Insemination

Part 2 introduces the first experiment which we'll pick up again later in the film. Researchers prepare electronic equipment that will stimulate a chimp to ejaculate. The chimp is brought into the room, given a sedative, attached to the machine, and stimulated to ejaculate into a test tube held by researchers. The semen is sent to a refrigerator and we return to the cages and faces of baboons, orangutans. An observer, surrounded by cages, watches their behavior. Shots 100-143, (7:40).

Part 3: Intelligence

The experiments in part 3 test three animals' intelligence and language capacity. They progress from what seems to be a simple stimulus-response experiment with a monkey, to a more complicated experiment with a chimp who selects objects displayed before him by a researcher, to a highly sophisticated language system between a chimp, Lana, and a young researcher, Tim. Lana and Tim communicate via symbols displayed on a computer keyboard. Lana requests food and services from Tim by combining symbols into sentences. Lana lives in a comfortable, apartment-like room and plays with Tim and an orangutan. Shots 144-176, (3:44).

Part 4: Behavior Control

A woman researcher implants electrodes into a monkey's brain. The monkey wears a wired box that is attached to its head. Once the electrode is implanted, we watch the woman and a male researcher stimulate the monkey electrically to have erections. Shots 177-188, (2:39).

Part 5: Aritifcal Insemination

The artificial insemination researcher from part 2 returns to address a group of researchers seated around a table. They talk about the timing of the artificial insemination experiment. They discuss the procedure, which animals to use, whether the semen should be frozen or fresh, and end with the statement: "I guess all we can do now is assume our artificial insemination will go and we'll let nature take its course." Shots 189-211, (3:45).

Part 6: Behavior Control

We return to the monkey and woman researcher from part 4. The woman adjusts the control box attached to the monkey's head and takes him to a cage with a large window. Inside the cage are two female monkeys. The male researcher from part 4 joins the woman researcher and they sit before an electronic console where they can watch the three monkeys. Their experiment begins. They electronically stimulate the male monkey to mount and copulate with the females. They try various electronic frequencies and comment on the results. Shots 212-238, (5:18).

Part 7: Medicine

In part 7, a woman analyzes the contents of a small monkey's stomach, a man drills on a monkey's tooth, and surgeons operate on a large chimp. The long surgery part looks like any human surgery scene. The chimp's stomach is shaved, he is anesthetized, "nurses" slip gloves onto "doctors" hands, we watch the operation, doctors sew the incision closed and bring the chimp back to its cage. The part ends with a researcher feeding grape juice to a chimp who clings to the bars of its cage, at the same time the researcher takes a semen sample from the chimp by milking its penis with a lubricated tube. Shots 239-301, (9:13).

Part 8: Evolution

A researcher carries an orangutan down a corridor and into an examination room. Much of the orangutan's hair on its shoulder and back has been shaved off. The researcher explains to a coworker that he is implanting electrodes into the orangutan's shoulder muscle. The orangutan seems to be sedated and his bare skin makes him look the most "human" of all the animals so far. The researcher carries the orangutan to an outdoor mobile van where the orangutan, with electrodes and wires attached to its shoulder muscles, swings from bars and reaches for suspended food. The researcher observes and at one point he swings from the trapeze himself, trying to get the orangutan to imitate him. Then the researcher from the mobile van stands before electronic equipment and explains to the camera that his muscle experiments with the orangutan are intended to "illustrate human and great ape evolution" and establish when men began to walk bipedally. This is the only time in any of Wiseman's films that someone addresses the camera directly. His explanation is intercut with shots from inside the van of the same researcher modeling behavior for a gorilla who is attached to wires like the orangutan. Shots 302-337 (8:05).

Part 9: Reproduction

The reproduction researcher from part 1 returns to watch two gorillas copulate. He discusses their behavior with a young woman who records their actions on a checklist. We see shots of the gorillas copulating, intercut with shots of the woman observer seated very still in front of the outdoor cage. The part ends with shots of gorilla faces, orangutans, and other apes in outdoor cages. Shots 338-355, (37:04).

Part 10: Flight Experiment

We meet the flight monkey and flight researcher who we will see again in part 14. The researcher prepares the monkey for an experiment. The monkey wears a box on its head that houses electrodes implanted in its brain. The researcher explains what he is doing to a woman who seems to be a lay person and is curious about the experiment. The monkey's electrodes are adjusted, he is placed in a box that revolves. We watch his reactions via television screen. We see images of the spinning monkey intercut with researchers taking notes, electronic equipment, graphs. Shots 356-381, (6:34).

Part 11: Vivisection

In this part we watch researchers anesthetize a small gibbon, drill a hole in its skull, and insert a needle. They return the gibbon to his cage for "25 minutes," and while we wait out the time, we see custodians empty garbage cans and the faces and eyes of gorillas, baboons, and orangutans in their cages. We return to watch a "surgeon" open the same gibbon's chest cavity, inject what we assume to be a dye into its artery, behead the gibbon while its heart continues to beat, crack the skull open, remove the brain, section the brain and place slices on a microscope slide, look at the slides through the microscope and compare the results to photographs in a large book. The part ends as two researchers look at the slides and comment: "I think we're on our way. Yeah, that's sort of interesting." Shots 382–490, (21:55).

Part 12: Medicine

In part 12, we watch researchers, including the artificial insemination researcher, attempt to save the life of a chimp whose temperature has risen to 109 degrees. They hose her down and place ice packs on her chest. The chimp vomits, shivers, and moans. The researchers look on and comment: "Poor gal, there's a wonderful animal there." Shots 491–513, (3:33).

Part 13: Pure Research

We get an idea of the institution's purpose and self-image while listening to ten researchers seated around a table lament the government's attitude toward basic research. "The amount of basic research is being whittled further and further down 'til the time will come that you won't have anything to apply, and what it will mean of course is that our place will be taken by the laboratories in Europe." Shots 514–533, (2:43).

Part 14: Flight Experiment

We watch a van drive away from the research center, carrying the flight monkey aboard. From inside the van we watch as it pulls up to a huge USAF jet. A forklift raises the flight monkey to the jet. Researchers place him in a box and we watch him via a television screen. The jet takes off, climbs upward, and dives to simulate zero gravity. The researchers float above the floor of the jet as does the cameraman. One researcher dictates information into his headset. The jet climbs and dives again as we watch it through the crosshairs of a telescope. We watch the monkey and researchers react. The final images are of the monkey on the television screen, cut with the jet seen through the telescope as it climbs almost vertically. Noise of the jet's engines overlaps onto the credits. Shots 534–569, (4:44).

SHOT LIST

Shot No.	Visual	Sound
Part 1: Introduction		
1	PRIMATE (0:04)	silence
2	MS collage of scientists' portraits. (0:02)	
3	CU portrait of one of the scientists from shot 2. (0:02)	

4   CU second portrait from shot 2.
     (0:02)

5   CU third portrait from shot 2.
     (0:02)

6   CU fourth portrait from shot 2.
     (0:02)

7   CU fifth portrait from shot 2.
     (0:02)

8   CU sixth portrait from shot 2.
     (0:02)

9   CU seventh portrait from shot 2.
     (0:02)

10   CU eighth portrait from shot 2.
     (0:02)

11   MS sign on wall: Yerkes Regional
     Primate Research Center. (0:02)

12   MS bust of man, on pedestal.
     (0:02)

13   LS exterior of large, factory-like
     building, taken from a hilltop,
     trees surround low, new building.
     (0:02)

14   LS gorilla in cage, standing against
     wall, he swings off camera left
     from bar overhead. Walls are
     white. (0:04)

15   LS orangutan in cage, on floor   sound of cage door
     near small trap door in corner of
     cage, he stands up and walks on   orangutan grunts
     all fours slowly toward the cam-
     era, he passes on right, staring into
     camera. (0:12)

16   MS large chimpanzee with infant   sound of cage doors
     seated between its legs, chimp
     eats something. (0:07)

17   MS two gorillas sitting against cage   Off camera: reproduction research-
     wall right, one fingers the small   er from shot 18: ". . . very playful.
     door BG. (0:05)   Actually for her age she's too . . ."
                                              Second researcher from shot 18:

"... and they're in there for a purpose ..."

18   MS speakers shot 17, reproduction researcher has bushy beard, smokes a pipe, other researcher stands right, looks into cage left, steps off right, bars BG. (0:35)

Reproduction researcher: "... just as cage mates, they're not involved in any particular research projects. The animals we do the sex testing on we keep sexually isolated ... no males and females together. We don't want them doing anything sexually when we're not in a position to see them or evaluate them." Second researcher: "Do you have any in a cage together for the purpose today?" Reproduction researcher: "Well they're tested everyday, there's no test going on this minute." Sound of metal against metal.

19   LS same gorilla from shot 17, one stand against door BG, other crosses FG. (0:06)

Second researcher: "What kind of observation technique to you use?" Reproduction researcher: "Mostly we use check sheets, you see that young man sitting over ...

20   LS through cage bars, man in white shirt sits on folding chair, in corridor between cages, LA. (0:03)

... there, he works for me ...

21   MS over man's shoulder (shot 20) as he writes on note pad. (0:03)

... at the moment he's making observations on a ...

22   MS rang mother and infant, mother crouches, grooms infant who rests against her chest. (0:10)

... mother/infant pair, but he would be doing essentially the same kind of thing if he were observing the male/female gorilla pair."

23=   (0:05)
21

Reproduction researcher: "Mainly he has a timer, the clock sitting on the ground."

24   Same two researchers, new angle, second researcher SV left, reproduction researcher FV, cage BG. (0:36)

Reproduction researcher: "He has the check sheet and the check sheet is divided into time intervals, and every time the clock turns a minute he moves to a new column and in that column are represented 20 categories of behavior ... when the clock changes he moves to the next column again and we have a frequency of responses per unit of time. But . . .

25   LS same two researchers they walk down corridor of wire fence and cages to ELS, one side of corridor is open to outdoors. (0:08)

. . . this kind of thing, mainly observing small groups or pairs of animals there's no problem in getting down just about everything . . .

26   MS mother chimp with infant at her breast, she is seated. (0:03)

. . . we believe that's going on."

27   MS rang hanging by feet from overhead bars in cage. (0:05)

New voice: "Amy Goodall observed what she called a 'rain dance' . . .

28   LS gorilla in cage, standing against small door, drops to all fours. (0:06)

. . . like when the rain would first start, the most dominant of males would start running up into the trees and ripping branches off and running up and down the vines with them . . .

29   LS gorilla in cage, on all fours raising and lowering hips rhythmically. (0:06)

. . . and then kakatoid activity would start . . .

30   MS gorilla in cage, eating banana, seated. (0:04)

. . . of course the knowledge is enhanced by the individual observation of other pairs."

31   MS same two researchers shot 25 in room, reproduction researcher left, second researcher right, picture hanging center on wall, picture is of gorilla copulating. (0:30)

Reproduction researcher: "This is one of the most common positions . . . let's see, in the wild I'm not sure whether Schaller saw ventral-ventral copulation in the wild or not." Second researcher: "He did." Reproduction researcher: "Much less frequently than the dorsal-ventral. In captivity you see both, and we've seen dorsal-ventral as well as ventral-ventral . . .

32   CU photograph, shot 31, of copulating gorillas. (0:30)

. . . we've also seen animals standing in different positions, dorsal-ventral when they copulate . . .

33   CU reproduction researcher left, picture shot 32 right. (1:10)

. . . so that in one case the female presented to the male while he was in a standing position, and backed into him and he attempted copulation while in that position, and was

not successful. We've seen it with males squatting sort of on their haunches, back like this, with the female having backed into him."
Second researcher: "What about information from the wild, did Schaller say anything about that?" Reproduction researcher: "He only saw about two or three copulations during the whole year he was in the wild, so I don't think on the basis of that he could make any decision as to who preferred who. See, the gorillas aren't nearly as sexy as chimps or rangs, or most other animals."
Second researcher: "I wonder if it has anything to do with population control 'cause they're big animals."

34 MS same two researchers. (0:20)

Reproduction researcher: "Orangutans are pretty big, well, it's a possibility, except I don't think it's the whole story."
Second researcher: "I don't think it ever is — the whole story — that's what makes it so good, complexity."

35 LS, Center employee cutting up food on a large table, refrigerator BG. (0:06)

corridor noise

36 CU HA food in small wagon, PR as it goes by left to right, tilt up to LS employee shot 35 handling food from wagon to animals behind wire fence left. (0:24)

corridor noise

37 CU employee's hand pushing food through wire fence, ape's hand reaches for food from behind fence. (0:06)

corridor noise

38 MS HA same employee and wagon, tilt up as he picks up food and pushes it through wire fence right, he smokes a pipe, tilt down to wagon as he reaches for handle and pulls wagon toward camera. (0:20)

corridor noise

39 MS reproduction researcher squatting in corridor outside of cages. Young woman with white coat seated BG, writing. He looks right, into cage, and dictates into tape recorder, he looks at watch. (0:10)

Reproduction researcher: "She is kneeling with her elbow on the ground, she is licking the blood from the floor. The time: 4:13."

40 CU face of rang, licking her fingers, patting her newborn infant on head, rang lies down. (0:30)

Reproduction researcher: "Its eyes are open. She now hovers over it, vocalizes, she lifts it to her chest."

41= (0:07)
39

Reproduction researhcer: "Stops vocalizing, she now lies down on side, rolls to back."

42 CU mother rang, she lies back, infant on chest, she gently pats its back. (0:12)

Reproduction researcher: "Supports the infant."
screaming of apes in background

43= He looks at his watch. (0:20)
41

"The mother appears to be sucking the contents out of the outer membrane. She's not supporting the infant, the infant is clinging . . .

44= (0:30)
41

. . . time: 4:17, mother continues to suck the placenta, shifts briefly, the infant moved a bit, she provided support with the left hand. She continues to suck on the placenta . . .

45 CU mother rang, infant clings to her head, she lies on the cage floor. (0:20)

. . . the mother shifts position, doubles over again, apparently the mother is . . . from the floor. Time is 4:23."

46 CU reproduction researcher takes photograph of rang pair through wire fence, PL as he sits back and talks into microphone. (0:17)

"Mother resting onto her back, again patted the infant that now clings to her ventrum . . . patted the infant on the back."

47 LS framed by wire fence, mother rang standing, she places infant on her head, placenta hangs from umbilical cord. (0:15)

Reproduction researcher: "It continues to cling with minimum and occasional support by the the mother . . .

48 ELS down long corridor, cages right and left, reproduction researcher kneels in BG, looking into cage. (0:04)

. . . got up briefly, then rolled to her back."

49	CU door and its window, sign on door, "Newborn Reception." Door opens, woman enters from right and walks into room, she wears a mask and gown. Door closes, she walks across room to cage inside, seen through door window. (0:10)	room noise
50	CU tiny infant chimp, woman wearing gloves puts diaper on it. (0:10)	room noise
51	CU tiny infant chimp in small cage, looking up, cage door closes, woman locks it. (0:04)	room noise
52	CU tiny infant chimp lying on table, woman's hand enters right and offers him a plastic toy. (0:09)	room noise Woman: "Here, take it, come on."
53	CU infant chimp in incubator, woman's hands lower cover of incubator. (0:06)	room noise
54	MS hands open incubator, lift infant out, tilt up as the woman walks right and sits in chair. She offers the infant a baby bottle. (0:20)	room noise
55	CU infant as he drinks from bottle. (0:03)	sucking sound
56	MS three older chimps, lying on their backs, holding baby bottles, drinking inside cage. (0:06)	sucking sound
57	CU LA woman holding and petting an infant. (0:07)	room noise
58	MS second woman in same room, she cuddles an infant that drinks from babybottle, she rocks in rocking chair. (0:06)	room noise
59	CU infant in diaper, lying face down, woman gives him something to play with, he grasps it, she turns him over, he crawls to wall behind counter, and turns over. (0:20)	infant screams

60	CU clipboard, woman's hand writes on clipboard. (0:02)	infant noise
61	CU back end of diapered infant, woman's hands reach in and turn him onto his stomach, facing camera, she places towel under his chin so he can rest his head. (0:12)	voices in room
62	MS BV woman left, she lifts infant chimp to horizontal bar over countertop, he grasps bar and she leaves him suspended by one arm, he wears diaper. (0:20)	infant noise
63	CU stop watch, woman's hand starts it. (0:03)	room noise
64	MS same chimp (shot 62) hanging by one arm. (0:04)	
65	Stopwatch, running to 6 seconds, CU. (0:04)	
66	MS same chimp, his movements are jerky, she hands him a cloth to hold with free hand. (0:12)	
67	CU stopwatch running to 30 seconds. (0:02)	
68	MS infant lets go of bar, woman catches him and lays him down, she holds him with one hand and makes notes with other. (0:12)	
69	New room, MS of its door, woman walks in, wearing face mask, takes clipboard from wall, PL as she goes to desk, sits, and begins to write, cages with young chimps BG, ZI to CU clipboard and writing. (0:30)	room noise, chimps Woman: "Good morning, good morning. Going to . . . for mommy?"
70	MS as same woman opens cage, reaches in and hugs young chimp, lays him down, ZI as she hugs him, PL ZI to CU as she inserts thermometer into his rectum, he lies back, chimp's cage mate walks over and she talks to him. (0:45)	Woman: "Come on, I'll take your temperature. Mommy's here."

71   CU same woman left, chimp   room noise
right, lying on back, she hugs
him, leaves left, he looks around.
(0:04)

72   MS same woman, she shakes ther-   room noise
mometer, reads it, takes clipboard,
PL ECU as she walks past camera
to hang up clipboard. (0:15)

73   Inside new room, LS its door, man   room noise
enters, PL, PR as he carries tray
of metal cups to table. (0:07)

74   MS young chimp standing in cage,   room noise
arm reaches in and hands him a
metal cup (shot 73), he takes it
and drinks. (0:07)

75   MS two chimps in cage, arm   room noise
reaches in and gives them each a
cup, they drink. (0:04)

76   MS two young rangs huddled in   room noise
corner of their cage, arm reaches
in and gives them cups, they
drink, one holds his arm around
the shoulder of the other, they
look into the camera. (0:11)

77   MS BV man (shot 73) as he walks   room noise
slowly past cages, PL, he turns to
second row of cages, PL, he pulls
out tray from bottom of small
cage and examines contents, PL
as he walks to clipboards hang-
in on wall, he flips through a
couple pages, glances out of window in room door. (0:36)

78   LS LA chimp outdoors in fenced   clatter from jungle gym
play yard, jungle gym, he
climbs down from jungle gym,
tilt down, he walks to ELS seen
through jungle gym, researcher
sits and observes in BG. (0:20)

79   LS LA second chimp on gym, he   outdoor noise
climbs down, tilt down. (0:04)

80   LS LA two men leaning out of   outdoor noise
building window two stories

above play yard, they are eating, one throws a paper cup to
a chimp below. (0:04)

81 CU cup on ground, ZO to LS as
small chimp looks up to window, then plays with cup. Second
chimp enters left, they push cup   corridor noise overlap from shot
off left. (0:10)   82

82 LS down long corridor, researcher   corridor noise
carries three small rangs, clinging
to his body, up corridor to CU,
tilt down to rangs, tilt up to man,
tilt down to rangs, PR as researcher
turns into room right, MS as he
walks to cage in room and puts
the three rangs in cages, tilt down
as the cage door shuts, ZI to HA
CU as he places lock on cage door.
(0:50)

83 MS SV man as he opens cage and
pulls out small monkey, man
wears gloves, he holds monkey's
arms behind its back, holds its
neck securely, and walks toward
camera to ECU monkey's face, it   screams of monkey
grins, camera tracks back, PR as
man walks to table BG, second
man reaches out to hold monkey's
legs. (0:40)

84 CU man's hands as he draws blood   Man: "OK."
sample from monkey, tilt up to
CU man, sideburns. (0:07)

85 ECU same monkey, he grins, a   Off camera: "Yeah, he's OK."
hand holds him by the neck.   monkey screams
(0:08)

86 CU machine with test tubes,   rhythmic machine noise
machine rocks samples back and
forth, hand reaches in and removes a test tube (0:06)

87 ECU spout suspended, hand   running fluid, machine noise
reaches in and places test tube
under spout, fills test tube, removes it, hand wipes spout clean,
places second test tube under
spout, fills it, wipes spout. (0:15)

88	CU second machine with test tubes attached, hands reach in and place new test tube on machine. (0:08)	new machine noise
89	ECU lighted digital counter, clicking off numbers. (0:04)	rhythmic clicking of counter
90	HA CU same machine shot 88, hands reach in and add a test tube. (0:07)	clicking rhythm
91	Digital readout on machine, CU, it records "hemoglobin: 16.8." (0:04)	machine noise
92	CU hand pouring fluid from test tube into hemoglobin counter, shot 91, hand closes lid of machine. (0:04)	machine rhythm
93	ECU eyepiece of microscope, woman enters left and peers into eyepiece. (0:02)	machine rhythm
94	View through microscope: magnified cells. (0:02)	machine rhythm
95	ECU microscope lenses and drop of liquid on slide, lenses descend on drop. (0:02)	machine rhythm
96	ECU woman's fingers on mechanical counter, she works counter. (0:01)	machine rhythm
97=closer shot of 95. (0:02)		machine rhythm
98=94 (0:02)		machine rhythm
99=93 (0:02)		machine rhythm

Part 2: Artificial Insemination

100	MS artificial insemination researcher and bald researcher both leaning over electronic equipment, oscilloscope. (0:12)	Bald researcher: "Now what we're doing, we're using a frequency generator where we can vary the frequency from around 18 cycles to around 100 cycles, I don't think you want to go more than that anyway." Artificial insemination researcher: "and on the oscilloscope here I have the signal . . .

101 ECU oscilloscope screen, sinu-
soidal wave. (0:12)

... here we're going down to about
20, go back to 100. Perfect sinu-
soidal wave all the way through."

102 Reverse angle shot 100, researchers look up at equipment, bald researcher reaches
over and picks up mug, drinks,
puts it down. (0:45)

Bald: "Just use 60 cycles to see if
we can get the same ejaculate from
John." Artificial insemination
researcher: "Using the same stimu-
lation parameters we gave the
others . . ." Bald: "And then once
we succeed on that, on future animals we can vary the frequency and
we know . . ." Artificial insemination researcher: "Right, because
obviously we're not certain whether
it's 60 cycles or 40 cycles or any
other particular frequency that's
the optimum frequency for obtaining seminal fluid." Bald: "And remember we have some indication
that at 20 to 30 cycles we were
getting better erection." Artificial
insemination researcher: "Right,
we'd get erection at one frequency
but ejaculation from another frequency." Bald: "So, we're going
to be exploring the entire spec-
trum to see where these physio-
logical phenomena take place."

103 MS large cage, chimp climbs up
wire of cage door, man pushing car enters left, crosses to
right, PR CU as he passes.
(0:06)

corridor noise

104 LS large cage, three chimps hang
on bars of cage. (0:02)

corridor noise

105 LS cage, gorilla sits BG. (0:02)

corridor noise

106 MS BV man, chimps in cage, man
walks to portable cage, PR, he
pushes portable cage against large
cage door, PL. (0:22)

corridor noise

107 CU HA same man's legs, chimp
in large cage enters portable
cage through trapdoor, PR.
(0:05)

corridor noise

108 LS corridor, man walking away
from camera, man shot 107

corridor noise

enters right with portable cage, pushs it down corridor away from camera, track forward to CU scale where man stops to weigh portable cage, PL to CU scale. (0:15)

109	MS portable cage standing alone in corridor, rocking on its casters as chimp moves. (0:07)	corridor noise
110	MS as man enters right and places second portable cage next to first. (0:03)	corridor noise
111	MS two men either side of two portable cages, they transfer the chimp from the first to the second cage. (0:06)	room noise, chimp screams
112	CU hand turning crank attached to gear. (0:02)	crank noise
113	CU HA gears, belts, attached to second cage with chimp, who is being cornered in one part of the cage, next to the bars. Tilt up to two men turning gears, MS. (0:08)	gears
114	ECU hand with hypodermic needle, PR as man walks by to cage BG, he squats and tries to stick needle through cage bars into chimp, chimp's hand reaches out to keep man away. (0:17)	chimp screams
115	CU cage, tilt down to man's hand with needle, chimp brushes man's hand away and needle breaks, researcher sticks second needle into chimp. (0:10)	chimp screams
116	MS two men open cage, tilt down as one pulls unconscious chimp from cage, they lay him on floor, LS HA chimp sprawled on floor. (0:20)	chimp screams
117	ELS corridor, cages right, two men with cart filled with electronic equipment come up corri-	footsteps, voices

dor, pass on right, PR CU HA
equipment as they pass. (0:16)

118　MS same chimp shot 116 sprawled
out on table, face down, head FG,
men spray animal's teeth, turn
head to left, other men grouped
around table BG, artificial insemination researcher and bald researcher (shot 102) set up electronic equipment, PL as they
look at equipment. (0:16)

sound of water on chimp's
teeth

119　ECU hand reaches to withdraw
rectal thermometer from chimp.
(0:03)

room noise, chatter

120　LA MS man reading thermometer,
man in BG walks off right. (0:04)

"Ninety-nine."

121　MS two men shot 102 setting electronic equipment, bald researcher
puts lubricant on tube attached
to wire, hands tube to man shot
120, PR tilt down, track right as
man inserts tube into chimp's
rectum, ZI to ECU tube with
wire. (0:34)

chatter
"OK"

122　MS bald man seen over other
researcher's shoulder, bald researcher is at equipment. (0:04)

Bald researcher: "We've got 29,
2 . . .

123　ECU as bald researcher manipu-
lates switch on instrument.
(0:03)

. . . 3 . . . 4 . . .

124　ECU chimp's penis, hand of researcher holds test tube that
collects semen. (0:08)

. . . 5 . . . 6 . . . 7 . . .

125　ECU artificial insemination researcher, tilt down as he writes
on clipboard. (0:03)

room noises

126　ECU bald researcher, zip right
to artificial insemination researcher, zip left to bald
researcher, zip right to second
researcher, he grins and looks
left. (0:22)

Bald researcher: "5 . . . 2 . . . 3 . . .
4 . . . 5 . . . 6 . . ." Artificial insemination researcher: "Forty, doin'
fine, doin' fine." Chimp purrs BG.

127=124 (0:08)　　　　　　　　room noise

128　MS two researchers shot 126 at　　room noise
　　　head of chimp. (0:07)

129=127 (0:18)　　　　　　　　Bald researcher: "8 ... 9 ... 10 ...
　　　　　　　　　　　　　　　11 ... 12 ... 13."

130　Five men grouped around chimp,　　Bald researcher: "About as much
　　　chimp center. (0:19)　　　　　as last time." Artificial insemina-
　　　　　　　　　　　　　　　tion researcher: "Oh, that's quite
　　　　　　　　　　　　　　　nice."

131　MS two researchers shot 121, look-　Artificial insemination researcher:
　　　ing at test tube. (0:05)　　　"There's no urine contamination
　　　　　　　　　　　　　　　that I can see, it's just that strong
　　　　　　　　　　　　　　　color that . . .

132　ECU black researcher listening.　　. . . we're getting from the rangs . . .
　　　(0:02)

133　ECU researcher with moustache　　. . . oh, I'd say a good 1 mm . . .
　　　listening. (0:02)

134　ECU artificial insemination re-　　. . . it's enough to get some to
　　　searcher, ZO to MS as he gives　　freeze. Why don't you take that
　　　young researcher with long hair　　down to (*unintelligible*) and let it
　　　the collection tube, PL as young　　cool to body temperature."
　　　researcher leaves room through
　　　door, LS. (0:20)

135　LS man in corridor between cages,　water
　　　rinsing cells with water from a
　　　hose, tilt down to coiled hose.
　　　(0:10)

136　MS gorilla in cell, hanging from　　water
　　　ceiling bars, he swings off left.
　　　(0:10)

137　MS baboon, sitting, looking, in　　water
　　　cage. (0:05)

138　CU baboon face. (0:04)　　　　　water

139　CU baboon, purses lips. (0:04)　　water

140　CU baboon, sitting. (0:04)　　　　water

141　MS rang mother and infant hang-　　water
　　　ing from ceiling bars in cage,　　ape noises
　　　mother lowers herself and pulls

infant until it lets go of bars.
(0:16)

142	MS SV man with white shirt, shot 21, same position as shot 21, writing on clipboard. (0:10)	water
143	LS same man shot 142, same position, surrounded by cages. (0:10)	corridor noise

Part 3: Intelligence

144	MS doorway, man with long hair enters carrying a monkey, Lana, in plastic restrainer from hips down, he walks toward camera, ECU Lana, he passes to right, PR (0:06)	room noise
145	CU as same man places Lana in chamber and closes door. (0:05)	room noise
146	LA MS television screen SV, other electronic equipment surrounds TV screen. (0:05)	tapping sound, beep
147	CU Lana's image on TV screen, she taps on something right. (0:06)	tapping sound, beep
148	LA CU computer equipment, lights. (0:05)	tapping sound, beep
149= 147	(0:05)	tapping sound, beep
150	CU stylus printing out information. (0:04)	tapping sound, beep (shots 146–150 ended with the sound of a beep)
151	MS woman researcher left, small chimp in cage right. Barrier separates them, objects hang inside barrier in view of chimp and woman. (0:08)	room noise
152	CU objects suspended in barrier for chimp to see, objects are spotlighted from above. (0:03)	room noise
153= 151	Woman changes objects on barrier from her side. (0:02)	room noise, object noise

154 CU trap door in barrier opens, chimp's hand reaches in. (0:03)	same as above
155 CU chimp's hand grabbing suspended shell and pulling on it, seen from woman's side of barrier, spotlight lights. (0:03)	same as above
156 CU chimp takes arm out of trap door and door closes. (0:03)	same as above
157 CU woman's hands exchanging shell for button in trap door window. Light goes out. (0:08)	same as above
158= Light goes on. (0:02) 152	same as above
159 MS door on woman's side she opens door. (0:02)	same as above
160 CU door opens. (0:02)	same as above
161 CU door from woman's side, chimp's hand reaches in and pulls object, light goes on. (0:04)	same as above
162 CU chimp's hand pulls out of trap door, seen from his side, door closes. (0:04)	
163 Young man and Lana, a chimp, sit before display board in Lana's special room, MS, Lana pushes buttons on display board of computer. (0:15)	Young man: "Lana, get some juice, that's right, what a good girl, come on, get some more juice, go ahead."
164 CU Lana BV, board BG, she pushes buttons. (0:08)	sound of computer
165 ECU computer display board, symbols light up. (0:02)	Young man calls out what Lana is punching into computer: "Please, Tim . . .
166 MS Lana pushing buttons. (0:04)	. . . give juice period."
167 MS computer typewriter working automatically. (0:02)	typing
168 ECU typewriter. (0:02)	typing

169	CU computer, panel of lights. (0:02)	typing
170= 163	Lana pushes buttons, tilt up to young rang swinging from ceiling bar, it swings down, tilt down, rang jumps down, Lana follows. (0:30)	Tim: "Push the button." computer
171	ECU Tim's hands pushing buttons on computer, in room with Lana. (0:08)	Tim: "Please Tim give M&M period."
172	Tim watches from outside of Lana's room through window, computer FG, PR as he leans right, electronic equipment BG. (0:08)	computer
173	CU Lana on TV monitor, pushing buttons on panel, she jumps down from platform, swings from bars overhead, pushing buttons with free hand. (0:30)	room noise
174	ECU Tim pushing buttons on computer panel. (0:03)	room noise
175	Lana and rang sit together in small cage inside Lana's room, PR to Tim pushing computer buttons in BG, he watches the two apes. (0:15)	moog music BG
176=	beginning 175, the two play with each other. (0:15)	Tim calls to Lana

Part 4: Behavior Control

177	LS girl with ponytails and glasses pushes monkey in plastic re- strainer toward camera to ECU monkey, camera tracks back, PR as they pass, MS HA.	
178	LS hallway, stairs, BG, man enters hallway carrying bunch of bananas and large knife in one hand, he walks toward camera LS to CU, CU HA of bananas and knife as he passes to right, and walks away down hall to LS (0:20)	corridor noise Overlap from shot 179: Man: "Seems to be very sensitive . . ."

179 LA CU monkey with electrodes implanted in brain, he wears protective box around electrodes, on his head. Woman researcher tries to implant electrode in monkey's brain, but he will not remain still. She steps back, male researcher enters right, LA MS as he holds the monkey's head steady. (0:40)

Woman: "One thing that seems to happen is each time the electrodes seem to get the blood around them." Man: "You want me to hold him? It looks like that's difficult to do. (To monkey:) You bite this real hard, bite this real hard."

180 ECU woman's hands, box on monkey's head, ECU eye of monkey, woman slips with the needle and monkey jerks. (0:10)

When woman slips and the needle jabs monkey: "Oh shit."

181 ECU woman's fingers with electrode needle. (0:15)

Man: "There you are." He starts to read numbers.

182 MS woman behind plastic monkey restrainer, monkey left, BV man right, PL to instruments, man tries to get monkey's attention. (0:22)

Woman: "Come boy, come baby, be still just a minute. Just need a half a millimeter." Man: "Just tap it. All right, good, that's good maybe a slight erection."

183 Both researchers from shot 182 are at desk in new room, MS HA. Instruments before them, woman writes. (0:15)

Man: "Oh, very slight, OK, 0.5."

184 ECU same electrode monkey, he smacks his mouth, opens mouth, smacks. (0:08)

Man: "Now there's smacking, yeah, good, boy now the erection's a little bigger. Off!"

185=beginning 183, PL to electrode monkey in plastic restrainer behind instruments. (0:08)

Man: "OK, now let's look at it at point 'A'. Oh now he's more eager, fast smacking."

186=beginning 185, man looks to left to MS monkey. (0:09)

Man: "And a fast after smacking and grinding, and there was a slight erection and all that . . .

187 LS monkey left, man and woman researchers seated right at desk, they watch monkey. (0:15)

. . . oh, look at that, 1.8, that's a lower threshold. That's nice, and there's an erection. Off."

188 ELS corridor, wire screen left, open to outdoors, man walks ELS to CU and passes left, he walks through wire door and closes it. (0:12)

corridor noise

Part 5: Artificial Insemination

189 MS artificial insemination researcher (shot 100) seated behind
desk, talking, holding pencil.
(0:28)

He says he wanted to get together
with the artificial insemination
grant people and plan "logistics for
the first artificial insemination . . .
using either Banana, Sherri, or
Flora, which are the three females
that we reserved for this artificial
insemination." He has checked
their menstrual cycles.

190 Reverse angle shot 189 over
shoulder of artifical insemination researcher, table is surrounded by researchers. (0:20)

Artificial insemination researcher:
"We've frozen sperm. We've got
John which we could electro-ejacu-
late that day, or the day before and
get fresh sperm. The safest thing
would be to get an ejaculate . . .

191 CU three researchers, one is
seated on table, all are listening.
(0:20) One is bald researcher from
previous shots.

. . . use that fresh ejaculate and
transfer it into the animal, because
if for some reason or other we have
problems with adequate volume we
can always go to the frozen sperm
for backup."

192 ECU artificial insemination researcher. (0:40)

"If we could knock Flora down
Tuesday or Wednesday − do we use
fresh semen on Tuesday or Wednesday? Off camera: "I think you
really need to use fresh semen both
days." Artificial insemination researcher: "I think the best procedure would be to ejaculate on the
day we transfer it, and then ejaculate John on Wednesday and use
fresh semen that day."

193=two researchers from shot 191,
including bald researcher, MS.
(0:15)

Bald researcher: "What day would
be the best day to use the fresh
sperm from John, Tuesday or Wednesday?" Artificial insemination researcher off camera: "I think we're
going to . . .

194 ECU bald researcher, hand on
chin. (0:04)

. .. . use fresh semen . . .

195 MS artificial insemination researcher. (0:04)

. . . the perfect ejaculate . . .

196 ECU researcher with beard. (He is copulation researcher from previous shots.) (0:03)

. . . we have to assume . . .

197 ECU researcher with pencil, hand on chin. (0:04)

. . . that we're going to get the maximum ejaculate . . .

198 ECU young researcher with long hair and beard. (0:04)

. . . volume and total number of sperm the . . .

199 ECU SV artificial insemination researcher. (0:17)

. . . first time we do John. I don't have any information . . . to what degree seminal volume is to be replaced in 24 hour period, particularly if . . .

200=190 (0:10)

. . . I guess all we can do now is assume our artificial insemination will go . . .

201=199 (0:04)

. . . and we'll let nature take its course."

202 LS down hall, man pushes electrode monkey shot 187 up long corridor, in plastic restrainer. Tilt down as he passes, MS to right, PR as he passes, tilt up and watch man push monkey down corridor to LS, they turn corner. (0:20)

corridor noise

203 LS laboratory, through doorway, from corridor, two men work inside. (0:08)

glass against glass

204 MS SV man with white shirt shot 143, sitting at desk in small office, reading. (0:05)

room noise

205 MS artificial insemination researcher seated at desk, SV, looking into microscope. (0:04)

room noise

206 View through microscope, magnified sperm. (0:02)

room noise

207=CU shot 205. (0:02)

room noise

208=206 (0:02)

room noise

209 CU hands of artificial insemina-   room noise
tion researcher focusing micro-
scope. (0:05)

210=207 (0:03)   room noise

211=206 (0:01)   room noise

Part 6: Behavior Control

212 MS woman shot 179 right, elec-   Woman: "Got him. That wasn't
trode monkey center, second woman   too bad."
researcher left. They lure monkey
into restrainer with a banana, then
fasten restrainer around his neck.
(0:42)

213 CU LA first woman, unscrews   First woman: "Give him a little
protective case on monkey's head,   more banana."
monkey chews on banana, woman
stands on stool to get better position, ZO to MS, second woman
left. (0:37)

214 ECU monkey chewing, looks into   Woman: "This is one of the new
camera, hands of first woman   ones." "We'll try it'" One asks if
work on case on monkey's head.   monkey's comfortable, or should
(0:28)   he be raised higher in restrainer?

215 MS first woman right, monkey   Women: "He's just so good."
center, second woman enters left,   "OK." "He was just so good."
first woman screws protective
case back onto monkey's head, ZI
to ECU monkey's eyes, ZO to CU
his head, second girl gives him
banana piece, they push him
down through restrainer collar
into cage, close lid. (0:42)

216 MS same two women on either   monkey's chatter
side of monkey's portable cage,
second woman lifts portable cage
to trap door in large cage, PR, she
walks to LS with portable cage.
(0:24)

217 MS from inside electrode monkey's   trap door, monkey squeeks
permanent cage, trap door opens,
monkey jumps into cage with
case on head, stops and looks
around. (0:05)

218 CU same trap door, second monkey jumps into cage and runs to corner behind first. (0:05)	room noise
219 MS BV two researchers from shot 183, seated at electronic console, looking through window of electrode monkey's cage. (0:06)	Woman says they'll stimulate the monkey, she reads off numbers. "Twenty-one left lateral one."
220 LS through window, two females and electrode monkey in cage. (0:07)	Woman: "Two A, at A 22, right lateral one . . ."
221=219. (0:03)	Woman continues to call out numbers.
222 ECU woman's finger on console button. (0:02)	same as above
223 ECU woman's finger on lighted button. (0:03)	Woman: "On."
224= Electrode monkey is stimulated 220 and attempts to mount nearest female, females begin to fight, electrode monkey retreats to perch in cage. (0:25)	Man: "Virgo, he attacks the proximal one, he stops and goes back to Virgo, the rear grab. Now he's crouching. Off. Virgo is really attacking Rebecca at this point."
225= (0:02) 219	Man: "It's point three, one millisecond."
226 LS electrode monkey and female through window. (0:02)	Man: "Track three."
227=222 (0:02)	room noise
228=223 (0:02)	room noise Woman: "On."
229= male mounts female, thrusts, end stops and sits down, yawns. 226 (0:15)	Woman: "Off. No? He always looks like he's going to ejaculate but he doesn't."
230= (0:05) 225	Woman: "Next stimulation will be between 25.50."
231 ECU woman's finger pushes console button. (0:02)	room noise
232 ECU woman's hand starts stopwatch. (0:02)	room noise

233 LS two monkeys, male mounts, thrusts, stops and dismounts. (0:13)

Man: "He's opening his mouth, a very vigorous thrusting."

234= She stops watch. (0:04)
232

Woman: "Off."

235 LS view of cage, all three monkeys pace cage. (0:06)

Man: "Stimulate 9A, 13 milliamps."

236= (0:03)
225

Man: "Fifty per second."

237 Woman's finger pushes button. (0:01)

Man: "On."

238 LS of cage, male mounts, dismounts, mounts again, after man says "Off," male dismounts. (0:30)

Man: ", , , and that ear flapping and smacking, they're really agitated. Off. Point 12."

Part 7: Medicine

239 LA ECU new monkey in new laboratory, hand enters and pushes tube down monkey's nose, woman researcher stands BG. (0:15)

Woman: "You're all right."

240 MS two women researchers, monkey center, one woman pushes tube into monkey's nose, other watches, monkey is in plastic restrainer from neck down. (0:08)

Woman: "Good girl, you're OK. Good girl." Monkey makes noise. machine noise

241 ECU FV monkey, it gags and vomits, woman's hand continues to push tube into nose. (0:08)

machine voice

242 ECU SV monkey, hand holds its head from right, tube left, woman exits left, monkey looks around. (0:12)

machine noise

243 MS same woman, one walks to electronic instrument right, inserts contents of hypodermic needle into machine, second girl sits at monitor. (0:17)

Woman: "Go."

244 ECU stylus marking on computer   Woman: "Stomach content . . ."
     printout. (0:04)

245 ECU machine agitating test   machine noise
     tubes on rocker arms. (0:04)

246 MS HA new monkey restrained   drill noise
     on table, male researcher drills
     on monkey's teeth while woman
     researcher (from shots with elec-
     trode monkey) restrains monkey.
     (0:10)

247 ECU monkey's mouth, its tongue   drill noise
     moves, male researcher drills its
     teeth. (0:10)

248 MS BV woman researcher, FV   room noise
     male researcher from across
     table, man puts drill away. (0:05)

249 LS to ECU as two men wheel   corridor noise
     large chimp on cart up corridor,
     pivot left, tilt down to chimp as
     they pass, tilt up as they walk
     away to LS down corridor. (0:12)

250 MS woman right, chimp lying on   room noise
     back on cart left. Woman
     measures chimp's abdomen with
     caliper, PL as she puts caliper
     down. (0:20)

251 ECU woman's finger pushing   button
     button on X-ray machine. (0:02)

252 CU chimp, head FG, lying on   cart rolling down corridor
     back on cart, PR and track for-
     ward as two men wheel him right,
     into room, they stop and turn
     him to his side, MS. (0:20)

253 CU woman in surgical gown   sound of paper sign
     putting sign on door: "SUR-
     GERY IN PROGRESS, GREENS
     ARE REQUIRED." (0:04)

254 CU hand with electric clippers   clippers
     shaving belly of large chimp
     (probably same chimp shot 249
     to 252). (0:06)

255   MS "nurse" watching clipping by man, she leans on a table. (0:09) — clippers

256   CU hands shaving chimp's abdomen with razor. (0:08) — room noise

257   CU hands inserting hypodermic needle in chimp. (0:03) — room noise

258   MS chimp from bottom of table, hands reach in to turn him over. (0:05) — room noise, chatter

259   CU two "doctors," standing, watching. (0:03) — room noise, chatter

260   MS man washing rectal area of chimp. (0:03) — room noise

261   CU hands putting jelly on metal plate, tilt up ZO to MS as two doctors lift chimp on top of plate face up, doctor walks off screen right. (0:15) — room noise

262   MS from foot of table, three doctors insert air tube into chimp's throat, chimp coughs. (0:08) — cough

263   ECU hand connecting air tube to machine. (0:03)

264   ECU hand adjusting what appears to be blood pressure monitor. (0:06)

265   CU HA hands squeezing air bag on breathing machine. (0:05) — sound of rushing air

266   ECU electronic monitor on desk. (0:05) — room noise, machines, chatter

267   CU BV doctors washing hands at sink. (0:04)

268   ECU hands washing, shaking. (0:07)

269   MS nurse BV putting down on doctors, FV, second nurse BG, doctor stands, nurse ties back of gown closed. (0:10)

270   BV MS nurse FG, doctor BG, she
       puts glove on his hands. (0:10)

271   MS FV doctor BG, nurse BV FG,
       helps him put on other glove.
       (0:06)

272   MS nurse holding up sterile cloths
       to place over incision, second per-
       son BG, surgical instruments right.
       (0:03)

273   MS as doctors adjust light above
       operating table. (0:04)

274   MS as nurse from 270 give doctor
       cloth, PL as he walks to operating
       table and places cloth on chimp.
       (0:06)

275   MS as they take sterile plastic and
       walk left, PL, to place it on chimp.
       (0:06)

276   ECU hands fingering surgical
       knife. (0:02)

277   CU surgery room light, rotating
       to face into camera. (0:03)

278   HA ECU hands and knife making
       incision. (0:02)

279   HA CU head of chimp, eyes closed,
       an object in its mouth. (0:02)

280   CU doctor with mask watching
       operation, he looks right. (0:02)

281   ECU second doctor looking left,   chatter
       wearing mask. (0:02)

282   ECU incision, scissors, fingers of   chatter
       doctor. (0:07)

283   BV CU three heads of doctors
       looking into incision. (0:03)

284   CU incision, hands, instruments.
       (0:07)

285   MS nurse FG, doctors BG at oper-   Doctor requests instrument.
      ating table, she cuts thread, she
      reaches back to hand doctor an
      instrument. (0:07)

286   ECU incision, doctor ties stitches
      in incision shut. (0:06)

287   MS three shot after surgery, doc-
      tors remove cloth from chimp, tilt
      down to chimp's chest, they wipe
      the chest, pull instrument out of
      the chimp's penis, fluid flows
      from penis. (0:30)

288   MS nurse wheels cart into room
      toward camera. (0:02)

289   MS as doctors lift chimp to its   gurgling sound, chatter
      side, its arms are taped with ban-
      dages, it has tube in throat, it
      gags. (0:10)

290   MS as doctors take IV out of   "What about the scissors, John?"
      chimp, PL as they go by, they
      walk out of door pushing chimp
      on cart, LS. (0:15)

291   MS in corridor, chimp jumping in-   chimps screaming
      side of cage, PR and track forward
      behind three men pushing cart
      with patient, track forward and
      PL along cages with chimps
      screaming and swinging inside, PR
      and track forward, PL, track for-
      ward and stop as doctors pick
      chimp up and lay him in cage, tilt
      down, chimp is connected to IV,
      PL to another chimp in adjacent
      cage, he screams. (0:38)

292   CU patient chimp in cage, he   chimp moans
      opens mouth and moans, ZO to
      MS, cage door slides shut (0:15)

293   MS man picking up small cages,   screaming, metal against metal
      PL as he walks down long corridor
      with cages on right of corridor, PR
      to chimp in cage. (0:20)

294   MS new man right, new chimp in   chimp screams
      cage, he runs toward bars and

clings to bars, man wiggles his
finger at chimp. (0:20)

295   In a small room, CU man's hands
on a long plastic tube, he puts
lubricant inside tube, ZO tilt up
to long haired man, MS, tilt down
and ZI as he uncaps a Welches
grape juice bottle and picks it up
along with plastic bottles, leaves
frame left. (0:24)

296   MS track forward behind long
haired man as he walks up corridor, and passes camera, PL past
cages with chimps. (0:08)

297   CU FV track back as long haired   Chimp noise, man calls chimp by
man carries plastic tube and juice,   name.
PR as he stops at cage, chimp   "Come on up here, come on."
comes to bars and clings to bars,
man gives him a drink out of
plastic bottle, tilt down as man
milks the chimp's penis with the
lubricated tube. (0:25)

298   ECU HA tube milking penis. (0:06)   "Come on."

299   CU man left, chimp right, chimp   "Come on."
drinks from plastic bottles, man
rhythmically milks penis. (0:12)

300   MS man milking penis while chimp   "That's a boy."
drinks. (0:08)

301   LS down corridor, man crouches
next to cage. (0:04)

Part 8: Evolution

302   LS down corridor, cages right, two
men walk toward camera, one
carrying a rang with half of its
hair shaved off, PR as they pass in
CU through door on right. (0:13)

303   MS muscle researcher, holding   Muscle researcher talks to someone
rang, petting its bare skin, tilt up   out of frame.
to man, tilt down to rang, the men
lay the rang on the table and pet
it. (0:40)

304 CU face of young woman watching. (0:04)

Muscle researcher: "I'm now going into the muscle which is the rotator of the scapula."

305 ECU hands pushing pin into rang's muscle, hands leave frame, rang moves arm and needle moves, man withdraws needle. (0:25)

Muscle researcher: "You can see when I rotate her scapula, the needle moves. That tells us that we're in the muscle that we want to be in. It also draws the electrode down into the muscle and pushed the needle out, as you can see."

306 LA CU man from 303 concentrating. (0:04)

307 CU face of rang, drooping eye lids, man's hand FG. (0:04)

308 HA MS two scientists from 302 leaning over rang. (0:04)

machine noise

309 ECU as man pastes electrodes on rang's skin. (0:05)

310 CU hands brushing adhesive on skin of rang, tilt up as he shakes liquid in a bottle. (0:16)

311 CU head of rang, eyelids droop, it lies on its stomach while scientists work in BG. (0:06)

chatter

312 ECU SV scientist looking down, tilt down to his hands working on rang, assistant holds hair dryer that dries adhesive. (0:13)

"Can someone hold her hand here?"

313 MS three shot of scientists standing around rang. (0:05)

hair dryer noise

314 CU hands attaching two electrodes to adhesive patch on rang's skin. (0:10)

chatter

315 MS three scientists, they sit rang up, untangle wires, rang looks around. (0:30)

"Really hold her. Where's my connector?"

316 LS two scientists carrying rang down corridor with wet pavement, rang wears a jacket, they walk toward camera, PR as they pass and go to LS. (0:20)

footsteps

317 LS outside, two scientists carry   footsteps, chatter
     rang past, PR tilt down, tilt up,
     they enter trailer, third person
     crosses left to right and goes into
     second trailer door. (0:20)

318 Inside trailer, rang LS walking on   sound of air-conditioner
     floor, muscle researcher from shot
     303 holding leash attached to
     rang, PL as rang walks left, she
     reaches for bar. (0:12)

319 LA MS same researcher, he ges-
     tures to rang. (0:03)

320 LS of rang, she grabs onto swing-
     ing bar and pulls herself up. (0:15)

321 CU same researcher looking up at
     rang. (0:03)

322 MS LA rang reaching for food
     suspended above her head. (0:07)

323 ECU rang's fingers reaching for
     suspended apple slice, she can't
     reach it. (0:13)

324 MS BV as she lowers herself to
     floor from swinging bar. (0:08)

325 LA CU of same researcher, stand-
     ing, watching. (0:03)

326 CU rang, holding onto bar, she
     lifts her legs, BV. (0:10)

327 LS same researcher, left, he swings
     the apple slices to attract her
     attention, rang right on swinging
     bar. (0:08)

328 ECU rang's hand clutching bar.
     (0:04)

329 Same researcher stands face to
     face with rang, he gestures to her.
     (0:08)

330 ECU rang looking at researcher.
     (0:04)

331 LS BV same researcher, he swings
on bar while rang watches SV
from right. (0:08)

332 CU FV same researcher standing
in front of electronic instruments,
speaking into camera. (0:08)

"We're conducting electronic
studies on the three great apes,
gorilla, chimpanzee, and orangutan
in order to understand human and
great ape evolution. When muscles
contract they produce electric
potential which the equipment that
we have can read. From these read-
ings we can infer . . .

333 LS gorilla swinging from same bar
that rang used in shot 327. (0:15)

. . . .which muscles are active during
particular movement of these animals. We hope through these
studies to find out which boney
markings are related to which particular . . .

334= (0:30)
332

. . . behavior of animals and then
trace those behaviors back into the
fossil record so we can know for instance when man began to walk bipedally, when he began to manu-
facture and use tools regularly,
when the apes began to swing
beneath branches and hang beneath
branches and engaging in other sus-
pensory behavior, when the two
African apes, chimp and gorilla,
came to the ground and engaged in
knuckle walking . . .

335 LS interior of same trailer, muscle
researcher is with gorilla, he runs
around the room with the
gorilla in and out of frame, scientist hands the wires attached to
gorilla to a black man standing
at side of room, he continues to
run around room. (0:30)

. . . which is their own particular
kind of locomotion. I do not sub-
scribe to the theory that the living
apes, chimps and gorillas closely
resemble the ancestors of man. I
believe somewhere between five
and ten million years ago, the
ancestors of man and the great ape
diverged. I believe this divergence
initiated in the trees . . .

336= (1:00)
332

. . . The African ape's ancestor was
doing something different from
man's ancestor, in the trees. This
moved the center of gravity in the
ape up into his chest. In man it
moved the center of gravity down
into the pelvis. When members of

the two lineages experimented in terrestrial locomotion and habitat, the ape tipped over and became a knuckle walker while man was predisposed to walk bipedally on his feet . . . his hands were free to carry objects and of course to carry tools once he began to make them. Then man ventured out into the open savannah country and became a hunting animal which again is rather a unique attribute of at least Pleistoscene man."

337 Hallway with cages right, two men wheel instruments past, CU to LS. (0:08)

Part 9: Reproduction

338 MS LA reproduction researcher (shot 18) and young woman seated left, man stands, smokes pipe and holds camera. (0:04)

Reproduction researcher: "How soon after the session started yesterday did she present to him?"

339 MS two gorillas in cage. (0:08)

Woman: "Uh, about five minutes."

340= He squats next to woman, she
338 wears coat, he wears raincoat, corrider is open to outside. (0:08)

Reproduction researcher: "Did you get any impression before they started that she was receptive?" Woman shakes her head "no."

341 LS gorilla shaking its hips. (0:05)

oustide noise

342=340

Reproduction researcher: "See any swelling now? It may be that this is one of her first cycles after the birth. It may be a little different than what it was before . . . shorter or whatever. This is the first time that she showed a period of receptivity after the birth." Woman: "She was with Chad once." Researcher: "Oh, see what she just did — picked up some feces. It's not uncommon for different females to smear feces around when they want the male to keep his distance."

343 ECU reproduction researcher watching gorillas. (0:34)

Researcher: "He looks very interested. You said he touched her.

Did you record that interaction?
I mean verbally?" Woman: "Yeah."

344 LS male gorilla pounding his   noise of outdoors
chest, chasing female in cage.
(0:09)

345 CU SV male gorilla, female walks
off frame, he looks around.
(0:10)

346 ELS woman (shot 340) wearing
coat, sitting in chair, holding pad
of paper, surrounded by cages.
(0:04)

347 MS SV the two gorillas copulating.
(0:08)

348 LS SV same woman seated very
still, legs crossed. (0:04)

349 MS BV male gorilla thrusting into
female, hips moving, they stop,
female stands in center of cage.
(0:10)

350=346 (0:08)

351 MS rang hanging from ceiling,
looking at camera. (0:08)

352 MS gorilla sitting in corner of cage,
eating banana. (0:06)

353 LS gorilla standing in corner of
cage on all fours. (0:05)

354 CU gorilla sitting in corner of
cage. (0:04)

355 MS BV attendant backing out of   room noise
doorway pulling rack of cages
on wheels, turns right, second
man pushes from behind, PR SV
as they push rack into cabinet,
close door, lock it, one attendant
walks off right, the other to left.
(0:16)

Part 10: Flight Experiment

356 MS FV two men, women ECU SV FG, man gestures and explains experiment to woman. (0:55)

Woman: "You work on this every day because of the next flight . . ."
Flight researcher: "Well, more or less. I mean we've got other things we're doing. What our main purpose here is to get the line data before the flight sufficiently ahead of time with enough replications so that we have a lot of runs and we can do statistics on all the data, thus making sure there isn't any habituation . . ."
Woman: "In other words you're repeating what you did before but now you know more of what you wanna get."
Flight researcher: "In addition to getting reflex eye movements now we're getting recordings from within the brain itself and correlating that activity with the eye movements. So we'll have it all within the same animal. But these flight experiments are planned to simulate different gravities, not only zero, but also one-sixth and one-nineth for moon and mars."
Woman: "So you do it once for each gravity." Flight researcher: "Yes, and another variable is turning the lights on inside the shroud, or off so he does or does not have visual references." Woman: "And each time you're at different gravities, they tell you." Flight researcher: "Oh, yeah."

357 LS flight monkey, woman with pigtails pushes him in cart up corridor toward camera to CU, tilt down HA monkey, track back to follow cart, PR as they turn right, tilt up, CU woman SV, monkey glances around. (0:12)

hallway noise

358 MS flight monkey, flight researcher and two other men holding monkey on cart, they release monkey from carrier and center man holds him by his arms, zip left to two shot, MS woman left,

Flight researcher: "OK, you ready? OK, now wait a minute." Woman (shot 356): "I want to see him, you know, restrained. Oh, he does resent this doesn't he?" Second man: "Yeah, generally he does."

(shot 356), and man in doorway, woman steps forward to look at monkey, CU, equipment BG, (0:20)

Monkey screams.

359 MS BV two men at working table; flight monkey BG, track left as they carry him left to experiment cart, tilt down to CU HA as they place monkey's neck in restrainer, screw restrainer down, tilt down to CU HA three men adjusting screws, tilt up PL to woman CU FV (shot 356) she talks to men off camera, flight researcher stands in BG. (1:00)

Monkey screams.
Flight researcher: "The screwdriver's down here Paul. That would be the right adjustment." Woman: "Why do you put the box on now?" Researcher: "Pardon me?" Woman: "Why do you put the box on now? The box, the top, no the cover, you know, the cover." Researcher: "Just while he's moving." Woman: "Oh, just while he's moving."

360 MS HA flight monkey in restrainer, it revolves to BV, man enters right carrying container with wires and switches and places it over monkey, MS HA, PL to flight researcher, PR to first man, they revolve box containing monkey and examine it. (0:30)

machine noise
Researcher: "Wait a minute. He, ah, disconnected it as he came up."

361 HA MS flight monkey, black box surrounding him from neck down, it revolves. (0:02)

machine noise

362 CU SV monkey, head on, hands work on the electronic box attached to his head. (0:03)

machine noise

363 MS same angle, box enters right and covers monkey's head, tilt up to man, joining the boxes. (0:15)

Man: "OK, all clear?" "Camera's plugged in and everything, huh?"

364 CU television screen turned off, hand reaches in right and turns on screen, flight monkey inside of box appears on screen. (0:15)

Off camera: "The switch light is over there. There he is, bigger than life, OK, now we got video."

365 MS SV flight researcher and other man, flight researcher talks into head set, electronic equipment in BG, he bends to read something. (0:12)

Flight researcher: "Our ground experiment will be using the trapezoid acceleration profile and . . ."

366 ECU display panel of electronic equipment. (0:04)

. . . there are the data changes."

367 MS flight researcher, zip left down to readout of machine, zip right tilt up to MS flight researcher. (0:20)

Flight researcher: "The vertical lines are on channel three. The left lateral geniculate is on channel four and the left cortex is on channel six. The animal is grounded . . .

368 CU television screen upper left, readout and stylus below him, control panel. (0:10)

. . . through the left of your . . ."

369 CU SV flight researcher he reaches to stylus left, tilt down PL, CU drum and graph. (0:15)

Flight researcher: "We're getting parallel recordings of the model six. It seems to have adequate signal there. We may be overdriving the cortex . . ."

370 CU SV flight researcher before control panel, he wears head set, steps back to his right to look at control panel. (0:10)

". . . the lateral geniculate rolls off with a low frequency cut of 2.5 cycles per second. We're approximately . . .

371 CU television screen upper left showing monkey, readout, and stylus below him. (0:05)

. . . five seconds in front of the acceleration profile. The lights are on."

372=end of shot (365), box holding monkey begins to rotate in BG. (0:07)

Flight researcher: "3 . . . 2 . . . 1 . . . now it's on."

373 CU television screen with monkey. (0:07)

Flight researcher: "We're holding."

374=end of shot (372), box rotating, box slows, tilt down ZI HA tape deck FG. (0:06)

Flight researcher: "Decelerating now . . . and stop."

375 CU television screen with monkey. (0:04)

Flight researcher: "Ah, we're holding the program right at this point, the animal's very alert . . .

376 ECU flight researcher looking right. (0:03)

. . . deceleration starts . . . now."

377 ECU whirling box with monkey inside. (0:03)

machine noise

378 ECU monkey on television screen. (0:03)

machine noise

379 ECU stylus on drawing graph. (0:03)

machine noise

380	ECU drum graph rotating. (0:04)	machine noise
381	CU whirling box, it slows, ZI to top of box, wires protrude, it stops. (0:05)	Flight researcher: "Decelerate now."

Part 11: Vivisection

382	LS corridor cluttered with electronic equipment, man with white coat walks LS to MS, left to right, carrying plastic gibbon restrainer. (0:05)	hall noise
383	ELS starkly bare corridor, man from last shot walks toward camera to CU, PR as he passes, carrying restrainer. (0:08)	hall noise
384	CU hand of same man placing restrainer on scale, he bends into frame to read weight, writes it down, straightens, picks restrainer up. (0:10)	hall noise
385	LA MS gibbon pacing inside its cage, man enters left, wearing gloves, reaches into cage, grabs gibbon. Gibbon clings to cage bars. PL as man carries gibbon out door, down hall left. Seen through door window. (0:50)	gibbon chirping
386	CU hand reaching in from left holding same gibbon, places gibbon in plastic collar restrainer, man from shot 385 tries to fasten collar around struggling gibbon. (0:20)	gibbon chirping
387=	CU end of shot 386, hands fasten collar around gibbon's neck. (0:20)	gibbon screams
388	ECU gibbon in restrainer, blinking eyes, looking around room. (0:06)	silence
389	LS same researcher carries gibbon by restrainer into room, PL as he walks by to CU of gibbon, man places gibbon and restrainer on scale, records weight, MS BV gibbon twisting in restrainer. (0:20)	room noise

390   Reverse angle end of shot 389,   room noise
man walks toward camera away
from scale, carrying gibbon in
restrainer, track back holding CU
of gibbon, PL as they go by in
CU, man walks down long corridor from shot 383. (0:20)

391   LS same man carrying gibbon   room noise
enters lab, sets him on table,
second man bends over instrument
panel left, first man crosses
right to left and watches second.
(0:10)

392   CU BV researcher holding elec-   Man: "OK."
tronic hair clippers, gibbon BG,
man with clippers shaves gibbon's
leg, gibbon looks around quietly,
man straightens up. (0:25)

393   CU gibbon looking around, he   room noise
bares his teeth. (0:05)

394   ECU gibbon's shaved leg, hands   Off camera: "There's a . . .
of researcher holding it. (0:07)

395   CU HA gibbon unconscious in   . . . little ointment to, ah . . .
restrainer, hands lift him out, man
on right hands him to man on left,
who carries him to table BG, MS
BV. (0:08)

396   ECU gibbon's head from top,   Sound of electric clippers, research-
gibbon lies on table, hands reach in   er chatter.
and rub ointment on each eyelid,
shaves top of head with electric
clippers. (0:40)

397   ECU hands holding scalpel, makes   room noise
incision through skin on gibbon's
skull, front to back, skull is held in
restrainer, skin splits open, hands
dab the incision. (0:15)

398   New angle ECU of gibbon head,   drill noise
hand reaches in with tiny drill,
drills hole in skull. (0:15)

399   ECU researcher looking intently at   They talk about adjusting instru-
precision instrument, ELA, he   ment.
straightens up and adjusts instrument. (0:04)

400	ECU hands turning adjustment screw on instrument. (0:04)	"It's added . . . so what we have to go is three micrometers . . .
401	ECU precision instrument implanting needle into gibbon's skull. (0:03)	. . . plus. OK, now."
402	MS SV flight researcher shot 356 and second researcher bending over table. (0:12)	Men: "You went in at eight, at lateral eight . . . OK. Which would bring us down through here, paralleling that portion of the magnosoidal layer, and we are at plus three."
403	ECU blown up photos of brain tissue, hand turns page and gestures. (0:10)	"Yeah, you see now it coulda gone a little more interior where we could have got a better shot, but you see here . . . so I decided I'd sooner play safe. I'm sure we can hit this."
404	CU LA flight researcher and other researcher looking down, one bends to write on notepad, tilt down to hand writing on pad, he stands up. (0:20)	Flight researcher: "So I would estimate we're about here." Other man: "Why don't we make notes we're doing it?" Flight researcher: "Yeah, OK . . . OK."
405	ECU precision instrument with needle rotating. (0:06)	clicking of instrument
406	ECU needle penetrating skull. (0:05)	clicking
407	ECU instrument rotating. (0:04)	clicking
408	ECU needle penetrating skull. (0:02)	clicking
409	ECU instrument rotating, next to needle is gauge showing depth of penetration. (0:03)	clicking
410	ECU needle penetrating skull. (0:03)	clicking
411	CU gibbon's head in restrainer, needle penetrating the skull. (0:04)	clicking
412	MS new angle, instrument, skull center, light shining on skull. (0:05)	clicking

413 ECU oscilloscope screen, showing   Researcher: "That's it for about
     heart beat. (0:06)   25 minutes."

414 ELS long corridor, second re-   corridor noise
     searcher from previous scene
     carries gibbon to CU, tilt down to
     gibbon, wrapped in blanket, PR as
     they pass. (0:08)

415 LS CU hand opening cage, same   gibbons chirping
     man enters left and places gibbon
     in cage, eyes closed, lying in
     blanket, slow LA PR of rows of
     gibbon cages, other gibbons jump
     around inside their cages. (0:15)

416 ELS in corridor, two women   corridor noise, rattle of trash
     push trash container toward   container
     camera, HA CU as they pass, pivot
     to see other end of corridor ELS
     of man sweeping floor with dust
     mop, hold on him. (0:30)

417 MS man opening door of refriger-   room noise
     ator, vapor inside, he walks out
     of frame. (0:10)

418 LS exterior of research building,   outside noise
     door opens, man carries gar-
     bage can out, second man helps
     him dump contents into bin, PL
     as they walk left. (0:20)

419 LS down row of large, outdoor   chimp sounds
     cages, reproduction researcher
     walks LS to CU, passes left, carry-
     ing camera, smoking pipe. (0:08)

420 ECU gorilla face. (0:10)

421 CU gorilla sitting, looks down at
     fingers resting on chest, shadow
     of cage bars across face. (0:04)

422 ECU gorilla, pinches his nose with   metal on metal
     his fingers. (0:04)

423 ECU eyes of gorilla. (0:04)   birds chirping

424 ECU rang face looking up and left,
     he bites his lip. (0:05)

425 ECU baboon face. (0:06)

426 ECU gorilla looking at camera.
(0:05)

427 CU HA cart with instruments,   corridor noise
bottles, track back along corri-
dor as woman pushes it forward,
tilt up to woman, PL as she turns
into room. (0:10)

428 MS PR as man walks into room   chatter
carrying gibbon from brain experiment shot 385, he places it on
scale, calls out weight, walks toward camera, places gibbon on
table FG, tilt down to CU gibbon
unconscious, second man wearing
surgical mask stands at table. (0:30)

429 MS LA surgeon filling hypodermic
needle. (0:08)

430 CU HA gibbon lying on table   "Hold 'em. Hold this open."
spread eagle, hands enter right and
hold gibbon's arms, hand enters
left and cuts into gibbon abdomen
with scissors, first hands reach to
hold cavity open. (0:25)

431 CU HA surgeon looking down.   "Sometimes they just come out of
(0:25)   the stomach like this."

432 CU HA reverse angle gibbon, intes-   "I cut the thorax open and then we
tines lie outside of abdomen, first   spread it."
man spreads gibbon's arms,   "Right."
stretches skin over chest, surgeon   "Ready?"
cuts into chest, opens chest, ZI   "Can you open it up some more?"
ECU incision, heart still beating,   "Lift up the head please."
surgeon cuts tissue away from
heart, heart beats, he places thread
around top of heart and ties it, in-
jects fluid dye into artery. (1:30)

433 CU LA fluid bottle hanging upside
down on hook. (0:06)

434 CU new angle gibbon, incision   Researchers chatter. "Should we
runs from abdomen to neck, hands   put in the solution?" "No, not
pick up its head, ZI ECU gibbon's   really."
face. (0:45)

435 CU as surgeon cuts the gibbon's
head off with scissors and knife.
(0:05)

436   ECU gibbon head, surgeon cuts away skin and exposes skull, surgeon movements are quick and sure. (0:08)

437   ECU surgeon hands as he cracks gibbon skull open like a nut, exposing brain. (0:20)   bone cracking

438   LA ECU eyes of surgeon. (0:08)   cracking

439   ECU as surgeon cuts away tissue around brain, second pair of hands hold head steady. (0:20)

440   ELA MS surgeon adjusting overhead light upper right. (0:04)

441   CU HA hands putting skull with exposed brain into jar, second set of hands reach in to cap jar. (0:05)

442   CU hands placing skull and jar on scale. (0:04)

443   CU row of jars. (0:04)

444   CU hands pouring fluid through funnel into jar with skull. (0:12)   sound of fluid

445   CU HA hands and vice-like instrument FG, hands remove skull from fluid, adjusts vise to grip skull, ZI ECU skull suspended in vise. (0:50)   sounds of glass, metal

446   ECU skull still attached to gibbon face, hands rotate skull on vise so we see face upside down. (0:07)

447   ECU vise, hands enter to adjust knife blade, tilt down to see blade poised above brain, knife penettrates brain between lobes. (0:10)

448   CU LA of gibbon face in vise. (0:10)

449   HA CU gibbon face, hands manipulate instrument so that knife slices into brain. (0:15)   instrument

450 ECU hands adjusting top of instrument. (0:03)

451=shot 449, knife slices brain. (0:16)

452 MS SV surgeon, he opens book of   book pages
brain section photographs that lies
on table, instruments BG. (0:15)

453 ECU book, finger points to   instruments BG
picture. (0:08)

454 HA MS jar with gibbon skull,
hands remove skull from jar and
place it on towel. (0:20)

455 ECU hands cutting away bone
attached to brain. (0:17)

456 CU SV surgeon, pan down along his
arms right to CU brain, he lifts
brain, makes incision, PL to surgeon's face, ZO to MS as he drops
brain and puts down instrument.
(0:45)

457 ECU surgeon hands and brain, tilt
up and down as he detaches brain
from skull and face, surgeon drops
brain into solution in jar, it floats
to bottom. (0:10)

458 ECU gibbon face, slumping to side   Surgeon: "OK Kathy, the brain is
on table, SO to MS, tilt up to MS   removed and we can discuss how to
LA surgeon, assistant (Kathy)   section the brain . . . the midpiece
walks behind surgeon, MS LA 2   we cut transverse, and please stain
shot, PR as she picks up pad and   every section . . ."
pencil to take notes. (1:00)

459 CU HA tray of specimens lying   room noise
in small depressions, Kathy pours
liquid over specimens. (0:10)

460 CU dial, hand adjusts dial. (0:05)   room noise

461 CU container of dry ice, Kathy
removes lid, takes out cubes, and
replaces lid. (0:08)

462 CU HA man's hands pounding bag   pounding
of dry ice with hammer. (0:15)

463   ECU hands with eyedropper re-   room noise
       moving liquid from bottle. (0:04)

464   CU eyedropper putting liquid on
       small platform atop dry ice, hands
       put brain in liquid and sprinkle
       dry ice around brain. (0:20)

465   MS HA hands removing brain from
       ice, track left as it's carried to
       instrument, placed in vise, CU HA.
       (0:20)

466   CU HA hand turning crank on in-
       strument one revolution. (0:02)

467   CU HA brain in vise, knife slices
       brain like a meat slicer. (0:04)

468   HA CU hand placing brain slice in
       container shot 459. (0:03)

469   ECU instrument moving brain
       into knife. (0:04)

470   HA CU hand placing brain slice in
       tray, shot 459. (0:02)

471=shot 466. (0:03)

472=shot 469. (0:02)

473   ECU specimen tray, hand enters
       and deposits brain slice. (0:02)

474   ECU slide box in fluid, hand
       reaches in and removes one
       slice. (0:08)

475   CU hands holding slide up to
       light. (0:05)

476   CU lens of microscope, hands
       enter right and place slide under
       microscope. (0:03)

477   ECU hands changing eye piece on
       microscope. (0:03)

478   ECU hand turning focus knob. (0:03)

479   ECU lens rotating above slide.
       (0:04)

480 ECU SV flight researcher looking at slide through microscope, he backs away and surgeon enters to look. (0:04)

Flight researcher: "Oh, here's a whole cluster of them."

481 ECU brain slice as seen through microscope. (0:08)

Surgeon: "Yeah, by gosh."
Flight researcher: "I don't know where that is, but . . ."
Surgeon: "No, no, that's all right. That is beautiful."

482=end shot 480, surgeon stands up, flight researcher bends to look. (0:06)

Flight researcher: "A whole aggregation."
Surgeon: "Yeah, you can see . . .

483 ECU brain slice seen through microscope, localized dark dots. (0:10)

. . . how localized it is . . ."
Flight researcher: "Yeah, no fuzzing out. They all look uniform in size."

484=end shot 482, flight researcher moves away from microscope, surgeon bends to look. (0:10)

Surgeon: "They're all pretty concentrated."
Flight researcher: "And here's some more down here."

485 ECU brain slice through microscope, concentrated dots. (0:10)

Flight researcher: "We'll be able to scan them a lot better . . ."
Surgeon: "I have the impression that this is a portion of the optic radiation . . .

486 CU both men, surgeon looking through microscope, he backs away. (0:07)

. . . and for sure it does not look like dirt . . ."
Flight researcher: "No . . . it's much too regular."

487 ECU brain slice through microscope, black spots. (0:04)

488 CU SV flight researcher FG, surgeon FG, surgeon BG. (0:06)

Surgeon: "Well, I think . . ."
Flight researcher: "There's just batches of it, here's a whole stream of them."

489 ECU brain slide through microscope (0:03)

Surgeon: "Yeah."

490 CU SV flight researcher, PL to surgeon seated BV at microscope. (0:07)

Surgeon: "I think we're on our way." Flight researcher: "Yeah, that's sort of interesting."

Part 12: Medicine

491 MS five men grouped around table where chimp is laying, face up, with water that pours over its abdomen, tilt down to foot of table where water runs onto floor. (0:20)

They chatter about what they're doing.

492 ECU chimp's face, hand enters and pours water over its head, its mouth opens, it looks around. (0:14)

chatter

493 ECU hand attaching bottle to hook above table. (0:03)

494 ECU hand injecting chimp with hypodermic. (0:02)

495 CU hand with water hose, he rubs the chimp's abdomen, PR. (0:12)

chimp noises
chatter

496 MS hands tying cloth restraints to chimp's wrists, they hold its arms over its head. (0:05)

Off camera: "Wanna have that door shut? In case she gets up or something and gets away from us?"

497 CU two men, one is artificial in-semination researcher, wearing white coats, PL as one leans for-ward. (0:04)

chimp noises

498 MS from head of table, chimp vomits, woman holds chimp's arms so that chimp lays on its side, attendant leans toward chimp's head and cleans its mouth. (0:15)

chimp noises

499 CU from head of table, chimp vomits, water jet in its mouth, attendant on right leans toward chimp, hand enters and wipes away vomit. (0:05)

chimp noises

500 MS=498, zip left as woman takes bowl of water from man off camera, zip right as she hands it to attendnat, attendant enters with stethoscope and listens to chimp's heart. (0:14)

chimp noises

501=shot 500, attendant lifts ice bag right and places on chimp's side. (0:10)

502   CU chimp, mouth open, it twists
head, eyes closed. (0:08)

503   ECU attendant looking at chimp, he's
quiet. (0:02)

504   CU SV chimp, ice pack on chest,
chimp shivers. (0:10)

                            Off camera: "Well, we've got an
overnight temperature on the
other animals . . ."

505=shot 497. (0:10)

                            "Well, all we can do is hope there's
no brain damage or anything . . .
109 body temperature? "That's,
that's almost critical."
"It is critical."

506   ECU LA chimp opening and
closing its mouth. (0:05)

                            silence

507=shot 497, one chews gum, the
other rubs his nose. (0:08)

                            "Did she actually have any real
seizure?" "Yeah, she did."

508=shot 506. (0:03)

                            silence

509=shot 497. (0:08)

                            "Poor gal. There's a wonderful
animal there."
'Good animal."

510   ECU HA chimp, eyes closed, it
screams, gets quieter, then groans,
shivers. (0:26)

                            chimp screams

511   LS man walking down corridor
carrying what looks like disinfectant, sprays cages, tilt down to
nozzle, CU, tilt up to baby gorilla
CU in cage, man crosses FG right
to left. (0:20)

                            gorilla noise

512   MS female rang crouched in cage
with baby to her breast, she reaches
up, grabs trapeze, swings left.
(0:04)

513   LS LA fat man sitting in chair
outside of cage, recording activity
he observes off camera to right.
(0:05)

Part 13: Pure Research

514   LS large table, 10 researchers

                            Off camera: "The situation *now*

seated around table in meeting room. (0:05)

with regard to . . .

515 MS group of five at end of table, listening, we recognize artificial insemination researcher. (0:04)

. . . medical research is geared toward practical results . . .

516 CU LA one male researcher looking left. (0:02)

. . . if basic . . .

517 CU head on female researcher we recognize. (0:04)

. . . research is eliminated for a . . .

518 CU head on male researcher. (0:04)

. . . long period of time, you'll be left with nothing to apply . . .

519 CU head on young male researcher. (0:02)

. . . If you think back a bit . . .

520 ECU SV man who is speaking, older researcher. (0:20)

. . . to some of the original studies that had been done which now became famous: for instance, Flemming's discovery of penicillin, simply consisted of his observation that there were a few spots of mold on a plate on which he was culturing bacteria . . . and you can imagine maybe what results would be if he applied for a NIH grant now to study this mold." (*Laughter*).

521 MS three shot down row of seated researchers, listening, on is reproduction researcher. (0:02)

". . . Ah, it would have gotten nowhere and yet . . .

522 CU head on of young researcher, with glasses and moustache. (0:04)

. . . this was one of the fantastic developments . . .

523 CU man looking right, resting head on hands, sideburns and moustache. (0:02)

. . . of medical . . .

524 CU researcher looking down, sideburns. (0:03)

. . . treatments you could imagine . . .

525 ECU SV artificial insemination researcher, looking left. (0:03)

. . . so this is the thing that really worries me . . .

526 CU flight researcher, looking down. (0:03)

. . . about attitudes . . .

527 MS HA researcher in shirt sleeves at end of table. (0:02)

. . . in Washington now about research and . . .

528 MS SV speaker, looking right. (0:10)

. . . the amount of basic research is being whittled further and further down till the time will come that you won't have anything to apply. And what it will mean of course is that . . .

529 LS table and researchers from behind speaker. (0:10)

. . . our place will be taken by the laboratories in Europe."

530 CU reproduction researcher, speaking. (0:20)

Reproduction researcher: "We're out to really emphasize the frontiers of research and the opportunities to be derived from them because those are the areas where we still do maintain a position and priority."
Indian researcher off camera: "We can't always look for applied values: 'What is the applied value of this research?' . . .

531 CU SV Indian researcher, speaking, second researcher BG. (0:23)

. . . and you can't find applied value in every piece of research that is done all over the world. But you can also not say that it is useless work either . . . eventually it will come to the point where it will be beneficial, in the long run."

532 LS from foot of table, first speaker is talking. (0:10)

"All research is useful, even if that usefulness is not apparent at the time it's done . . ."
". . . once addressed . . .

533 MS SV speaker, surgeon from previous scenes BG. (0:35)

. . . a meeting somewhere in New York in which the title of his address was 'The Usefulness of Useless Knowledge' . . . sometimes information isn't valuable until there is another piece of information and then the first piece of work in light of the second one takes on a completely different value, and I think this is the way discovery often works."

Part 14: Flight Experiment

534 ELS exterior of research center, pipes, etc., FG. Van drives in BG and disappears behind hill FG left. (0:15)

van noise

535	LS PL with van pulling U-Haul trailer left along road, parking lot of research center FG. (0:05)	van noise
536	ECU flight monkey from previous scenes in plastic restrainer, wearing electronic box on head, he looks around. (0:10)	van noise
537	LS out of van windshield taken from behind driver, out of window we see large USAF jet, van turns left, camera PR to stay on jet, BV of three men leaving van through side door, door of jet is open, they wear flight uniforms, and carry flight bags. (0:20)	van noise

footsteps |
538	LS jet left, forklift enters right and drives left, it carries the restrainer with flight monkey. (0:07)	forklift noise
539	CU flight monkey in restrainer, his hand grips neck collar. (0:05)	forklift noise
540	LS HA forklift, it lifts box and monkey up about 15 feet, two men stand on either side of lift, monkey twists in plastic restrainer. (0:20)	forklift noise
541	CU SV man waiting above forklift in doorway of jet, looks right. (0:04)	
542	LS lift with monkey, drives toward door of jet, PL as goes left, three men reach out of jet door and lift monkey off fork lift. (0:03)	Men: "OK, bring it forward."
543	LA LS second door in jet, shot from inside, man enters right and climbs ladder into hatch. (0:07)	
544	SV CU man inside of jet wearing head set, electronic equipment BG. (0:03)	"All right, this is April 26 . . .

545   Video screen CU of flight monkey in restrainer, similar to shot 364. (0:05)

      ". . . this is run NP 105."

546   ELS USAF jet from outside, PL as it taxies left, airport BG. (0:15)˙

      jet noise

547=shot 545, its eyes droop slowly. (0:05)

      jet noise

548   ELS to LS jet taking off on runway to ELS, right to left, long pan left. (0:15)

      jet noise

549   LS LA three men in flight suits and head sets seated in cargo area of jet, speaker kneels before equipment, adjusts equipment, others are seated. One takes pictures with still camera. (0:20)

      Speaker: "Channel three are the horizontal eyes D and C. Channel four are the vertical eyes J and P. Channel five is the one-ninth jack output analog signal. Channel six is the left lateral geniculate J and P. Channel seven is the one per second sign mark."
      jet noise

550=shot 547, monkey blinks. (0:02)

      jet noise

551   ELS telescopic view of jet in air, masked by telescope eyepiece, centered in telescope crosshairs, flying horizontally. (0:03)

      jet noise

552   MS LA electronic equipment, man adjusts it. (0:04)

      Over the headset we hear voice: "We'll be . . .

553   ECU recording tape turning slowly on reels. (0:04)

      . . . Zero G . . . 63 degrees, per second squared, counterclockwise."

554=shot551, jet angles upward, vapor trail, turns to angle downward. (0:04)

      jet noise

555=shot 549, they begin to float above the floor, man with camera takes pictures, Wiseman's camera floats as well. Man who was adjusting controls pedals his legs in the air. (0:15)

      "There you go."

556=shot 551, jet angles downward then levels off. (0:06)

      jet noise

557=MS shot 549, camera tracks in to CU as they settle to floor. (0:06)

      Voice: "His eyes are sort of droopy now."

558=shot 547. (0:04)

559 MS LA man adjusting electronic equipment, talking into headset, television screen with monkey upper. (0:10)

"The next time one will be twenty degrees per second squared, the animal's been alerted, counter-clockwise, lights off."

560=shot 551, jet climbs with vapor trail. (0:06)

"Acceleration now."

561 MS HA SV two men floating in front of equipment. (0:08)

"Hey!"
jet noise

562=shot 551, plane dives steeply, (0:02)

jet noise

563=shot 559, men float higher and touch ceiling. (0:09)

"Clockwise terminal velocity . . .

564 MS black box holding monkey rotates, we see monkey rotating on pedestal, alone. (0:04)

. . . deceleration now, lights are on."

565=shot 547, the monkey chews, looks around. (0:02)

jet noise

566=shot 551, diving jet levels off. (0:05)

jet noise

567=shot 547, monkey licks its lips. (0:05)

jet noise

568=shot 551, jet climbs nearly verti-cally. (0:03)

jet noise

569 Directed and Produced by Frederick Wiseman. Photography by William Brayne, Edited by Frederick Wiseman. Camera Assistant James Medalla. Assistant Editor Oliver Kool. Synchronization Ken Sommer. Mix Richard Vorisek. A Zipporah Films Release, © 1974. Primate Films, Inc., All Rights Reserved. Funding provided by Ford Foundation.

Jet noise runs through the credits.

CREDITS AND NOTES

Producer:	Frederick Wiseman
Director:	Frederick Wiseman
Photography:	William Brayne
Editor:	Frederick Wiseman
Camera Assistant:	James Medalla
Assistant Editor:	Oliver Kool
Synchronization:	Ken Sommer
Mix:	Richard Vorisek

Copyright 1974, Primate Films, Inc.
Funding provided by the Ford Foundation.
Filmed on location in Atlanta, Georgia.

Distribution:	Zipporah Films
Running Time:	105 minutes
Released:	October, 1974.

9 WELFARE (1975)

The welfare center is Waverly Center on 14th Street in New York City. In one of his longest films to date, Wiseman reveals the incredibly complex problems — social, bureaucratic, psychological, political — that plague the country's social welfare system. Wiseman allows long scenes to build to climaxes of verbal interactions between caseworkers and clients that reveal — in the way people talk to each other — the institution's values and problems. Through these interactions we learn that the problems of the clients are ones that go beyond poverty to medical, social, and psychological incapacities. Characters reappear throughout the film, reinforcing the impression that they are waiting interminably for appointments and assistance. (167 minutes)

SYNOPSIS

Part 1: Introduction

In opening shots reminiscent of *Law and Order*, we see quick shots of faces posing before a camera that we assume is taking pictures for identification cards. Outdoors, people wait in line against a large brick building. Indoors, workers call out numbers, people wait in lines and chairs, a Native American tells someone off camera: "I'm a human being like you, like anyone, you know," and the worker replies: "We can't give it to you, Waverly's not responsible." (6:00)

Part 2: Unmarried Couple

We meet a young couple (one of the couples we saw waiting in line in part 1) as they apply for assistance during an interview with a woman caseworker. It seems that the couple has made a pact not to tell the whole story of their circumstances. The woman slips up by telling the worker that she's married, but not to the man. Then she mentions the man's wife, and the man denies that he has one. They tell of eating in restaurants and leaving without paying the bill. The woman says that her mother refuses to help her and tells her to "Go hang yourself." The man, a former employee in "social services," doesn't explain what has happened to the "good money" he was making when he was working. Part 2 ends when the worker tells them they've been "accepted," and the two break into smiles, saying, "Now we can eat." (9:30)

Part 3: Faces

In part 3 a long series of short portraits teaches us more about the clients. Often, they talk to workers who are off camera. People wait in hallways, workers call out: "Who's next, come on people, move down." An old woman tells a worker that "they" took all her Social Security and Medicaid papers. Two old men who are hard of hearing talk to a worker off camera. The worker repeats that they're at the wrong office, they should go to the Social Security office on Broadway. More people wait in lines, in chairs, alone in hallways. An angry man is told he's at the wrong office, he belongs at Social Security. An old woman goes to a water fountain to take a pill, walks slowly to a garbage can and looks inside. A worker insists to a pregnant woman that her doctor's certification isn't enough proof of her pregnancy. When the worker consults with a supervisor, he tells her yes, they will accept the certification.

The young unmarried couple from part 1 waits in a corridor. The confused and confusing supervisor who reappears later tries to explain procedure to a woman worker. The worker walks away in the supervisor's midsentence and tells a young mother that she won't get her child back until she gets rid of the diseased dog in her apartment. We meet the "head" supervisor who we'll see several times. This time he talks with a young man who tries to get housing money. The young man's story becomes more confused as he tells it. Finally he walks away angrily.

Another angry client talks to a worker off camera, insisting that "you never sent the checks." A third frustrated client explains to a worker that she has been coming back every day for two weeks, she has all the notarized letters required, but her caseworker refuses to accept them. The part ends with shots of people — we recognize some of them — waiting in the halls. (20:10)

Part 4: Valerie Johnson

Recently out of a hospital, Valerie Johnson sits down in front of a caseworker and begins a long, confused, frustrating interchange in which the worker tries to unravel the incredible mix-up that sent her to the center. The worker's supervisor concludes, "She's obviously a conversion. We can't help her here, she's a conversion case." Valerie insists that Social Security sent her to Waverly. The worker calls the Social Security office. A loud Spanish-speaking woman walks in and out of the frame, shouting to the worker, showing him papers, speaking to no one in particular. There is a mix-up about Valerie's address and name, that's why she hasn't been receiving her checks for rent, that's why she was evicted.

After about 15 minutes of this, Wiseman cuts to shots (accompanied by Valerie's voice over) of people waiting; one woman rests her head in her arms, others sleep in the waiting areas. Valerie finally talks directly with the supervisor and explains her situation yet again. We cut to more bored, tired faces. Valerie's friends arrive and try to lobby for her. Valerie's voice quivers: "I'm gonna get put on the street." The scene ends without resolution as we return to people waiting in hallways. (24:00)

Part 5: Welfare Rights

In part 5, clients complain, discuss strategies with fellow clients, and demand assistance from workers. In a waiting area, two clients discuss their dilemmas. The woman says she has to sneak onto the train to get to the welfare office each morning — she can't afford the fare. The man says a worker told him, "I take care of two and a half million people, so if one or two thousand don't get their checks, I'm still doing a good job."

A welfare activist demands that the head supervisor (part 3) give priority to a woman who is applying for assistance. The supervisor says the client can't get any money today, come back tomorrow. The woman starts to cry and lifts her blouse to show an operation scar. The supervisor says the woman hasn't lived in a vacuum all these years, she knows grocery men, she can get credit until her check comes.

The activist says: "She's an emergency case." The supervisor replies: "Everyone's an emergency case."

We cut to shots of hallways, workers' desks piled high with papers, a typist, a computer operator, computer cards, computer room, video readouts, printouts, and finally a computer printing out "City of New York" checks. People file out of the center's doors and guards close the doors on film day one.

We return to clients talking among themselves in a waiting room. Standing in a hallway, one man fingers through papers he carries in his pockets. Talking to no one in particular, he recites a long list of places he's gone to with the papers, trying to get assistance. "Something's awful funny here. I got no carfare, I walk the streets. I've been here four times this week." Frustrated, he lets the papers drop to the floor.

At a phone booth, we overhear a woman's conversation. She describes her day at the center to her friend. "I have one dollar to my name, I'm just out of an institution for manicdepression. She told me to come back Monday. I'm writing a letter to *Village Voice*." Her friend on the phone suggests she contact Geraldo Rivera. (19:30)

Part 6: Bigot

For 17 minutes Wiseman watches as a white bigot taunts a black guard. The man tells how he was mugged by three "niggers" who got "particular sadistic delight in kicking whitey's head in. I'm gonna get a gun and blow his balls off." He talks about fighting in World War II and killing 500 men he never saw. The black guard talks about shooting men in Vietnam whom he did see. The white man says: "I'm getting a 357 magnum and blowing up every black I can." Finally the guard says: "It's been nice talking to you, I've learned a lot from you." We cut to the guard talking to a black woman, asking her to be patient about waiting for assistance. We return to the bigot, standing near an exit, threatening several black guards. Finally the guards shove him outside and slam the door behind him. A guard jams the door closed with his nightstick and we hear the bigot shouting and kicking the door from outside. (17:00)

Part 7: Cutting Red Tape

A worker leads a blind man to an elevator, down a hallway, and in front of a desk. The blind man holds out a sheet of paper and talks to someone we assume to be behind the desk. But when the camera pans right, no one is there. The worker returns to seat the blind man in a waiting area.

In another room a young caseworker walks a woman's application through channels, cutting red tape, trying to make sense of a confused supervisor (part 3). Again, the caseworker walks away in the supervisor's midsentence and tells the client she has to wait for 15 days before she can get her money. "So you're in a bind. Since welfare is really based on what clients say, they really have to do what you tell them until it's proved otherwise."

We return to hallways and waiting rooms. A worker asks a bald man about his employment experience. He answers, "I don't have too much employment experience because I was just released from prison." He's on parole. The charge was homicide. We return to offices, hallways, and workers looking through files. (13:30)

Part 8: Hightower

It seems that Wiseman's work has come full circle when we meet Miss Hightower, the same woman who hung up on the psychiatrist in *Hospital*. She complains loudly and aggressively to the head supervisor (parts 3 and 5) about being denied a promotion. She leaves and a second supervisor enters to discuss a client. (5:30)

Part 9: Faces

We return to hallways, where we see the Native American from part 1, the unmarried couple from part 2, and people who appear to be recent immigrants. A young black woman asks about what benefits she can get. Since she has a job, she will have to move to a cheaper apartment before she can get assistance. We listen to a German immigrant discuss his problems with a young long-haired man. "God is not like Social Security. He doesn't say 'this man is poor, let's give him a couple bucks.' He can do what he feels like. No, you cannot fool around with God, you have to be good all the time." The old man says sometimes he blacks out and just walks around. "I don't feel like going to a nut house but I wish I could see a doctor." We return to waiting rooms, faces, two children dueling with umbrellas, workers calling out names. (10:35)

Part 10: Power

In part 10, a young woman supervisor treats clients harshly and without understanding. Another worker reprimands her for asking personal questions of his pregnant client, but the woman supervisor refuses to admit that the questions are improper. The young Latino (part 3) makes an appointment with a caseworker, he was promised a check and never received it. On her break, the woman supervisor complains to her superior that she needs more workers — one of the personnel has to go to "disaster training" that afternoon.

An angry, insistent black woman demands help for a client who we assume is her mother. "Whose fault is it? Her husband is in the hospital, he won't support her. She went to Social Security and they sent her here. She can't wait for a fair hearing." The caseworker asks the woman supervisor for advice and they confer on the case while the young Latino and the angry black woman talk about the supervisor's attitude. We cut to waiting people and a woman changing a baby's diaper. In a confrontation with the angry black woman, the woman supervisor implies that the client and her mother are legal residents of North Carolina but are seeking welfare in New York. The Latino walks up to listen. The woman supervisor asks her superior and a guard to help her control the two clients. "They will be interviewed as soon as they lower their voices." The superior says he'll talk with the black woman himself, then turns to the Latino. The Latino complains, "Since October I been going back and forth. What should I do?" The woman supervisor snaps, "Get a job." The Latino says. "All I want is help to get on my feet, I wish I *had* a job then I wouldn't be here." The superior promises the Latino that his fiancee will get welfare and the Latino leaves after being promised an appointment for himself. We see a waiting room, a custodian. (14:00)

Part 11: Hirsch

In part 11, a prophet-like character (as in *Titicut Follies*) named Hirsch confronts the head supervisor (parts 3, 5, and 8) asking for assistance. He tells of stealing chocolate bars and canned goods. "I don't believe it's right; it's necessary." He claims someone stole his "billion dollars of original research on psychic phenomenon." The supervisor says, "There's nothing we can do for you." Hirsch says his situation is like "waiting for Godot," and he leaves to sit outside the supervisor's office while a custodian cleans nearby. Hirsch talks to himself, then looks upward and prays, "For seven years and seven months I've tried. How can you help anybody on 11 cents? You don't want me to eat or sleep, OK. And if You want me to keep wandering until You decide where I belong, I will." A woman seated next to him glances at him apprehensively. We return to hallways, faces, and the unmarried couple, still waiting. (7:30)

CREDITS AND NOTES

Producer:	Frederick Wiseman
Director:	Frederick Wiseman
Photography:	William Brayne
Editor:	Frederick Wiseman
Camera Assistant:	Oliver Kool
Synchronization:	Ken Sommer
Mix:	Richard Vorisek

Copyright 1975, Welfare Films Inc.

Distribution:	Zipporah Films
Running Time:	167 minutes
Released:	September, 1975.

10   MEAT (1975)

Meat was filmed at the Monfort Packing Company in Greeley, Colorado. Like *Primate*, the majority of the images are accompanied by wordless noise. This time we see a step-by-step account of the slaughtering and butchering of beef and sheep. Wiseman's depiction of the men and machinery involved produces haunting pictures of refrigerated carcasses, bloodied workers, and vise-like pincers that cut through bone. As in the other films, Wiseman shows the daily activities of the institution's employees — from slaughtering and butchering to the sales office, the workers' cafeteria, and a labor-management negotiation session. An interview with a company executive by a man we assume to be a journalist raises questions of the moral responsibility of the United States to reduce grain consumption, and the prospect of grain-oil wars. Unlike *Primate*, *Meat* stirred little controversy. (120 minutes)

SYNOPSIS

Part 1: Introduction

The film begins peacefully and quietly with shots of grazing cattle, cowboys on horseback, mountains in the distance, and cowboys herding several cattle along a road. In a corral, cowboys prod cattle into a semitrailer truck. In long shot we see dozens of cattle in huge corrals, a freight train passes in the background. Over images of cattle faces, we hear the voice of an auctioneer, then cut to a rhythmic sequence of shots, paced to the time of the cattle auctioneer's chant, of the faces and subtle bidding gestures of buyers. The auctioneer's chant fades out over shots of cattle running out of a pen, herded by a man and woman on horseback. In extreme long shot a cattle truck passes a large factory-like building. Cattle move about in huge outdoor corrals, herded by men on horseback.

A bulldozer scoops feed into a dump truck. The truck fills feed bins and dumps feed onto a conveyor belt. A computer reads out the ingredients of the feed, a voice says "OK," and the truck pulls away. We see a video image of a second truck arriving at the conveyor belt, as a woman reads the computer printout and says "OK," into a microphone. Trucks drive past the same factory-like building and a chartered bus arrives. Japanese "tourists" step off the bus carrying cameras, taking pictures, posing in front of cattle. The female tour guide tells them that the plant's capacity is 128,000 animals, and explains that the cattle arrive as yearlings and leave weighing 1,000 to 1,200 pounds. She poses for a snapshot with a "tourist." We return to cowboys and cattle in a fenced field. Men drive a truck along a feeding trough and watch the cattle eat. (16:00)

Part 2: Round-Up

Part 2 begins film day one. In quiet morning shots, with sun on the horizon, a cowboy grooms and saddles his horse, then rides across a hill in silhouette. Silhouetted cattle run past, herded by cowboys who whistle and call. The cattle enter pens and move between a line of fences. A truck pulls up and men prod the cattle up a ramp and into the truck. The cowboy rides off frame and the truck doors close. The truck drives up to a scale, then pulls away, passing in front of the large factory-like building. (6:00)

Part 3: Sales

In a modern office filled with desks and salesmen on telephones, we hear conversations of price lists, shipping dates, orders. In frenzied, aggressive, and sometimes violent tones, the salesmen wheel and deal. "This is the first complaint we've had of no taste in the hamburger, maybe you've got a cold." "I'm sold out of tri-tips but I could get you a few." "Sollie, that's it booby." "I know you're expanding, but banks loan money and we sell meat." (6:30)

Part 4: Slaughter

A truck arrives at a stall and cattle crowd out of the truck into a narrow pen. We see close-ups of their faces. Before the large factory-like building, men prod the cattle through a small dark door. From high angle we see a worker electrocute a bull by touching its head with a rod, and the bull drops. In a second room we watch from low angle as a stiff bull rolls through a swinging door and drops to the floor, eyes and mouth open. A worker twists a heavy chair around the bull's leg and the chain raises the animal toward the ceiling where it hangs with dozens more. Some of the carcasses jerk and wiggle. A worker enters and slits one bull's throat, blood rushes out onto the man and the floor. In a high angle shot, workers slit the throats of suspended cattle. One worker cuts the head off a bull. Standing ankle deep in blood and water, workers rinse the heads with hoses, detach the heads and hang them on hooks, while facial muscles twitch and tongues hang loose. Dozens of heads move slowly past, suspended from the ceiling on hooks. A row of workers cut out the tongues, sharpening their knives after each cut. The room is filled with the noise of rushing water. A worker washes a tongue with a hose, cuts the tongue out, throws it on a pile of other tongues. (9:00)

Part 5: Skinning

Back at the beheaded carcasses, workers cut away part of the skin and snap off the feet with huge pincers. One of the workers wears earphones. Above him, another worker on a high platform butchers the upper portion of the animal while the earphoned worker butchers the lower portion. Workers sharpen knives, a machine grips the skin of the animal and tears it completely off. One worker splits the belly of the animal and a machine pulls the rest of the skin away. A worker with a large saw cuts into the rib cage of a carcass. Again, a machine tears the skin away from the carcass and sends it down a conveyor belt. The room is filled with noises of machines. (4:45)

Part 6: Gutting

Back at the beheaded carcass, a worker slits the belly open, guts drop onto the floor and the worker kicks them aside with his boot. Another worker cuts the guts into parts, extracting the liver. He also wears earphones, apparently listening to the football game televised on a screen behind him. He glances up at the screen and throws a pile of guts into a receptacle. The room is filled with machine noise. (2:30)

Part 7: Quartering

Back at the skinned, gutted, beheaded carcasses, a worker stands on a platform and holds a huge electric saw. As he begins to split the carcass in two along the backbone, the whole platform descends, pulling the saw down through the backbone. Another worker sweeps waste from the floor into a drain. Another inspects the quartered carcass, feeling it as it moves by, suspended from the ceiling. The suspended carcass disappears through tall narrow doors. A worker wraps cloth around the quarters and pins it to the meat. The quarters move through another door and into a quiet room. Silently, the cloth-draped quarters move slowly into line with others. A worker wearing an overcoat and hat moves among the suspended quarters, through bright glaring white mist. (4:00)

Part 8: Shut Down

Workers punch timecards, rinse their aprons with water from hoses, and throw their boots into a pile. The machines and noise stop, hooks hang empty, custodians clean the floors with brooms and hoses. The scene becomes progressively quieter. Men hose the floor and stand in bright glaring mist. The room looks empty, mist rises, men hose the room in the background. Water pours into a floor drain. In a silent series of extreme close-ups we see abstract shots of tools, machines, instruments, all hanging silently and motionless. In an exterior shot of the factory-like building, a truck couples with a trailer. (2:30)

Part 9: Sales

Back in the sales office, we rejoin salesmen that we recognize from part 3. "Sollie, listen, I went to the Baby Huey . . . we're in trouble, that's all I can tell you."

A man walks into a meeting room filled with other men, some wearing cowboy hats. They talk about sales numbers and the price of corn, and discuss special promotion attempts. "Bad automobile years were good beef years, if people make no big purchases they have enough money for beef." We cut to people working at computer terminals, typing fingers, computer rooms, and computer printouts and buttons. (6:00)

Part 10: Lunch

Executives eat a lunch of processed food served and described by a representative of a food processing company. He displays processed eggs whose whites have been separated from the yolks, hard boiled, then rejoined in the shape of a sausage — whites on the outside, yolks inside. This saves wasted ends of individual eggs and makes it easier and faster to garnish salads, etc. "We see your company as a potential one for marketing these items."

We cut to workers eating lunch in the cafeteria, wearing hard hats and hair-nets. A man introduced as "Governor" walks in and shakes hands with the workers at their tables. One worker naps in the sunlight outside of the building. (4:35)

Part 11: Butchering

A conveyor belt drops skin into a truck, the truck pulls away and we see the exterior of the factory-like building. Back in the refrigerator, draped suspended quarters continue to move slowly through the room. A man strips off a cloth and the quarter leaves the refrigerator. A worker stamps the quarter in several places. In the background a radio plays, "What kind of man is this, an empty shell, a lonely cell in which an empty heart must dwell. What kind of lips are these, that lie with every kiss?" Rhythmically, the worker slaps plastic labels on the quarters and watches them go by. In a larger room, workers cut the quarters nearly in half and use pincers to make the final cut. Butchers cut the sections into ribs and trim off fat. They work fast and surely, using forks and claws as the meat moves along conveyor belts. At the next station workers sort and wrap the cuts and place them in plastic bags. They weigh them and put them in cardboard boxes. Outside, a large truck pulls away from the factory-like building while the sun rests low on the horizon, ending film day one. (9:00)

Part 12: Sheep Round Up

A worker sheers sheep and piles the wool on the floor. A machine stuffs the wool into huge bags and a truck takes the bags away. The only sound is of the sheering clippers. At crowded sheep pens, workers sort sheep into several pens, then load them into a truck. One sheep jumps the fence and runs off. A goat stands alone in the sheep yard, a man walks by and guides the goat off frame. We cut to the goat slowly leading unsheered sheep out of one pen into a larger pen, walking directly toward the camera. As men shake bells at the sheep, they pass through a doorway. The goat steps aside and allows them to enter the door. From high angle a worker electrocutes the sheep with a rod. The sheep drop, and a worker hangs them on hooks by one leg. The hook rises to the ceiling and the legs of the sheep kick. (9:30)

Part 13: Sheep Slaughter

In a reprise of the earlier beef slaughter scenes, workers slit sheep throats, skin the sheep by hand, pull skin off skulls with cleavers, and spray the carcass with jets of water. Like the bulls, the sheep move past workers, suspended from the ceiling. Workers gut the sheep and throw guts on conveyor belts. An inspector checks the carcasses by feeling them and looking at their backsides in a mirror. A worker sharpens his knife, cuts a sheep's head off, rinses the head, cuts out the tongue, and splits the skull. Another worker rests on the rungs of a ladder, a fan spins in the background, and we hear rushing water and machines. A worker weighs a carcass, stamps it, and swings it along the ceiling where it bumps into other carcasses. Another worker pushes a group of swinging carcasses toward the camera. In the refrigerator, a worker disappears through the mist and glare, where we see hundreds of carcasses hanging. The only sound is a quiet hum. (7:30)

Part 14: Union vs. Management

In a small office, union and management representatives meet to discuss a union grievance. The union insists that two men are needed to do a particular job, while the company believes only one man is needed. After much discussion the union agrees to try the company's arrangement for awhile. The company representative says he doesn't want workers to have too much free time on the line.

We cut to a union meeting in a large room, some men wear hard hats. They discuss where their union money is being invested and their control of investment decisions. An older worker says that by the time the younger workers are his age, they'll be very interested in where the money went. (14:00)

Part 15: Interview

In a comfortable office, a company representative talks with an interviewer who holds a pad and pencil. The executive explains that each animal eats 17 pounds of grain per day. If 25 days can be taken off of the maturing process, 3.6 million bushels of grain can be saved per year. The interviewer asks if it is the moral responsibility of the American consumer to reduce consumption of grain. The executive replies that the issue is whether we can produce enough grain to export in return for money to buy oil. He predicts that future wars won't be fought over ideology, but over the shortage of essentials. He predicts stable beef prices for three years, then the price could rise "50 to 75" . . . maybe 200 percent." Beef will become more and more of a luxury item. (5:00)

Part 16: To the Supermarket

Men and women workers package and wrap small cuts of meat in supermarket-like wrappings, pack them in boxes, and throw the boxes onto a conveyor belt. A hamburger-making machine with huge blades chops meat. In extreme close-up, chopped meat emerges from the machine and is squeezed into a large, narrow plastic bag. A worker shovels hamburger into a vibrating pattymaker. In closeup, the machine rhythmically presses out dozens of hamburger patties, and workers put them into boxes. Tenderizing needles pierce large cuts of meat. Women place labels on packages. Boxes are closed and labeled. A truck backs up to a loading dock and a conveyor sends boxes toward the truck. They're marked "Monfort Packaging Co., Greeley Colorado." This is the first time we learn the name of the company. The truck pulls away and from outdoors we watch it pull onto the highway. The sun is low on the horizon and we end film day two. Sound of the truck motor overlaps to the film credits. (5:20)

CREDITS AND NOTES

Producer:	Frederick Wiseman
Director:	Frederick Wiseman
Photography:	William Brayne
Editor:	Frederick Wiseman
Assistant Editor:	Oliver Kool
Camera Assistant:	Oliver Kool
Synchronization:	Ken Sommer

Copyright Zipporah Films, 1976, Kine Films, Inc.
Filmed on location in Greeley, Colorado.

Distribution:	Zipporah Films
Running Time:	120 minutes
Released:	November, 1976.

11   CANAL ZONE (1977)

Wiseman's contribution to the bicentennial observance is not a departure from his examination of American institutions, as the title might suggest. Rather, this time the institution is America itself, as observed in the Panama Canal Zone. David Eames writes that Wiseman became interested in doing a film of the zone after hearing a description of how Americans lived there. "They have bent every effort to create a life that resembles as much as possible life back home. They cling to their values and rituals, however out of step with time and place, with the tenacity of those British colonists a century ago who insisted on dressing for dinner in the jungles of India." (See 218). For nearly three hours, Wiseman profiles the activities of exaggereated Americans as they model exaggerated American fashions, customs, partriotism, and citizenship. *Canal Zone* is consistent with the style and structures of the previous films. (174 minutes)

SYNOPSIS

Part 1: Introduction

Like the ships that pass through the canal, the shots of part 1 are slow moving and quiet. We hear gulls call over the title and shots of ships moving through the canal. An American officer boards a Japanese cargo ship (*Toyota*) and asks about the cargo. He pilots the ship through the canal. Winches pull ships along the canal. Tourists on a tour boat snap pictures of ships and pose along decks. An officer practices putting golf balls on a ship's deck. Gates of a lock slowly open and a ship enters. The tour guide speaks into a microphone and explains the toll system. A huge, crane-like shovel dredges the canal bottom.

Part 2: Streets

As a transition from the canal to a Panama street scene, we cut to an extreme long shot of a ship in the canal seen from atop a cliff. In the foreground a Panamanian stoops to pick up objects from the slope. Cut to a long shot of a small boat where Panamanian men unload bananas by hand onto a pier. A group of men try to unload a live steer and chase it through the street yelling "Toro." They break the steer's tail in several places, and the animal stumbles off a pier into the water. It swims to the pier and climbs to the street. The men load it onto a truck and begin to drag a pig to the truck, kicking it and pulling its ears.

Part 3: Offices

In a busy urban street, cars pass, a Winnebago camper passes before a large white building. Inside an office, engineers work at drawing boards. American and Panamanian women operate computers and type. We hear the voice of the governor of the Canal Zone and president of the Panama Canal Company before we cut to his plush office, decorated with comfortable chairs. He explains the financial problems and obligations of the zone to a group of formally dressed American visitors. Vietnam was good for canal traffic and encouraged growth. But now inflation and negotiations to turn the canal over to the Panamanians is hurting business. By law the canal must break even. He suggests that the canal cut costs, raise tolls, and be subsidized by the American government. He refers to the canal as "the plant." "We need money to make it a place we're proud of."

Part 4: Law and Order

In a park, junior high school age Americans practice drill team formations while a Panamanian gardner picks up litter nearby. In the background, a fire truck leaves the station. In a courtroom, a judge makes a speech in observance of Law Day, after a chaplain offers a prayer, asking for guidance for judges and lawyers. The judge speaks of America's success in facing adversity in the tropics and Alaska. He praises the zone's "splendid law enforcement system" that enables people to walk the streets safely. Cut to police cars in streets, then to the cafeteria of a prison. All of the faces are Panamanian. Religious murals decorate the walls of the cafeteria. One is of the Last Supper, in the foreground inmates eat their meals. Cut to the street, where a native woman waits for a bus on the street corner. An American boy enters the frame riding a minibike. Cut to guns hanging in a rack. Americans shoot skeet alongside the canal. A Panamanian man stands silently and presses a button when Americans command "Pull!"

Part 5: Entertainment

In a studio, we watch a uniformed disc jockey air an Armed Forces Radio show. He plays Jimmy Buffett's "Havana Dreaming," and a crime prevention audio tape for "women listeners." He announces the movies that will be playing at bases in the zone: *Walking Tall Part 2, The Happy Hooker, Lenny, Mahogony.* Music from the show overlaps to a horse show. Americans sit in bleachers and on lawn chairs eating hot dogs and watching young people compete on horseback. Cut to a fashion show at an American women's club. One woman plays the organ, another describes the clothes made and modeled by the club members. One outfit is a suit with a bush jacket fastened by 1976 metal buttons. On the street, we see a theater marquee advertising *One Flew Over the Cuckoo's Nest.* Cut to a bingo game in a large hall. We see faces of the players and the caller. One woman plays with four cards. Cut to a television studio: on the monitor is a 30-second Spanish lesson that teaches viewers six words of Spanish by rote. After a short street scene, cut to "Ed," a ham radio operator, who is talking with someone in the "good country" (United States). Ed has been in the zone for 13 years and will retire from the navy in one year. The zone was the only place he could get a job with his training and have his family with him. Cut to a suburban street scene, a mosquito fogger drives down the street, a Panamanian man tends a flower garden. At a checkpoint, a woman sentry salutes as cars go by. Apparently they are entering a beach area. Cut to Americans lying on a beach, a man jogs past, children play in the surf, boys fish off a bridge. Cut to tennis courts and men playing doubles. We hear taps in the distance, the men stop in midgame, turn to the right and salute. A gun fires several shots. Cut to a street scene, a magazine stand.

Part 6: Stress Zone

An American female "youth officer" talks to a large audience in a hall about the problem of child abuse in the zone. The zone's reported child abuse cases number three times above the "national average." This is easily explained when you realize the "high stress" nature of living in the zone: fear of revolution and job insecurity. Cut to a street scene, palm trees and a large building in the background. Cut to extreme close up of a young American woman smoking a cigarette, talking to a man whom we assume is a psychiatrist. He shows her sketches of men and women in various communication situations and asks the woman to construct what is going on in the pictures. She speculates that the characters are unfaithful, lonely, and that the man is away from home for long periods of time. Cut to outdoor shot of a large building and the sign "Mental Health Center." A gardener works in the foreground. Inside the building, Panamanians sit in a crowded waiting room. They watch an Abbott and Costello movie on television (dubbed in Spanish) with commercials (in Spanish) for Kentucky Fried Chicken. The Abbott and Costello segment speaks of victims and a gun is fired. Faces of waiting patients are intercut with television images. Cut to a street scene, children ride skateboards past, a policeman walks by. A Panamanian artist paints pictures of a canal bridge. Panamanians and Americans stroll past craft displays. A young American boy wears six-guns and holster.

Part 7: Flag Ceremony

Cut to a long shot of a flagpole and a group of Americans at a VFW ceremony to retire a flag. The speakers talk of patriotism and praise the small group of "dedicated Americans" who have come for the ceremony. They pledge allegiance to the flag and leave for refreshments inside a building. A Panamanian caretaker walks past the empty chairs of the silent ceremony area.

Part 8: Privilege

At a union meeting of civilian workers, an American woman reads a letter protesting the fact that military Americans have more consumer and recreation privileges than do civilian workers. She asks, "Are we second class citizens?" Cut to a street scene, then to a modern, affluent supermarket where Americans shop and Panamanian workers stock and price items. Cut to a street scene, a policeman stands on a corner, cars pass by a theater marquee.

Part 9: Marriage

In a large room with tables arranged in a circle, an American husband and wife marriage counseling team leads a discussion with about a dozen American couples. The camera moves from faces to faces, following the conversation in close-up. The counselors ask participants to take turns telling the group what they "like" about their spouses. One husband says he likes his wife because she takes such good care of the kids. A wife says she likes her husband because he encourages her to be herself.

Part 10: Boy Scout Ceremony

Young American boys in 1776 costumes march into a large room playing "Yankee Doodle Dandy" on instruments, while adults stand, hands over hearts, as a flag is placed in front of the room. They pledge allegiance. Uniformed scout masters announce the presentation of the Silver Beaver Award to the adults who have contributed most to the troop during the year. He explains that even though they have recognized women's contributions in the past by giving them Silver Beavers, "women's lib" has caught up with them and the scouts now offer a Silver Fawn Award for women who have contributed much to the troop. But, he says, when given a chance to trade her Silver Beaver for a Silver Fawn, last year's female award winner declined. They conclude the meeting with a prayer.

Part 11: Boxing

Two Panamanian men fight in a boxing match. We see faces of Panamanian and American fans watching the fight. The camera rhythmically returns to the time-keeper, who rings the bell and stares at the stopwatch. A vender sells food. The match ends and the winner prances in the ring.

Part 12: Law and Order

In a television studio, we watch the taping of an Armed Services television show. Two men in uniform discuss the training and use of guard dogs in the zone. The zone has 12 guard dogs and two dogs that detect drugs. The dogs patrol the American living areas at night. Cut to street scene. A motorcycle parks along the curb.

Part 13: Sunday

In an extremely sexist sermon, we hear a preacher in a church service outline God's plan for relationships between men and women. The camera watches in extreme close-up. Women's lib "vexes" him, it is out of the "pit of hell." God gave Adam the choice of all of the animals as companions, but none satisfied him. So God made Eve, and the preacher pantomimes Adam's leers when he first sees Eve. A woman's proper place is subjugated to the authority of the husband. Cut to faces of the congregation, the choir sings, and the congregation files out of the church. The organ music overlaps to a soccer game in a park. We see a vollyball game, Americans swimming, women sunning themselves, and Americans racing motorcycles. The canal and ships are often in the background of the shots. At a zoo, Panamanians watch the animals and eat at a concession stand where dogs are fed scraps. Panamanians play baseball, a young couple and baby have a picnic, American boys ride the walkway on skateboards.

Part 14: High School Ceremony

We hear a band playing while we watch a Panamanian sweep a walkway in a park. We see the band and conductor in the park rehearsing in front of empty folding chairs. We see the faces of the high school band members. Cut to a night scene, graduating students seated before the same stage. A male student addresses the parents and graduates, speaking in cliches about friendship and responsibility.

Part 15: Military Games

In extreme long shot, hundreds of parachutes drop out of airplanes. In long shot we see one soldier land, men run past carrying guns. They wear camouflage and run through brush. They are American soldiers. We hear explosions. Soldiers throw grenades. They attack a small building and enter it. There is an explosion, men drop to the ground. They fly a flag from a tower. One soldier talks into a field radio. Men drop to the ground at the sound of explosions.

Part 16: Memorial Day

Long shot of a small boat passing a cargo ship in the canal. Well-dressed Americans sit in deck chairs on the small boat. Aboard, a chaplain reads a prayer for Memorial Day. The student speaker from part 14 reads the Gettysburg Address. The canal and mountains are in the background. A woman picks up a wreath, walks to the edge of the boat, and drops it into the canal. Other women throw flowers in the boat's wake. Cut to a graveyard. Brownies in uniform walk to graves and plant flags at the stones. Uniformed men plant flags at gravestones, stand at attention, and walk off. A group of Americans sit on a reviewing stand in the cemetery. A speaker eulogizes dead soldiers. VFW members carry wreaths to a monument. The same woman who threw a wreath from the small boat watches the ceremony. In long shot we see and hear a band play the National Anthem. Cuts to faces of Americans watching. A chaplain prays from the reviewing stand. People stand at attention for taps. One woman dabs her eyes. People carrying flags walk out of the cemetery as the band plays "Stars and Stripes Forever." In silence, Panamanians stand alongside the cemetery road, watching. Cut to long shots of graves. Panamanians bring flowers to graves. One woman washes a gravestone. Long shot of Panamanians grooming gravesites. Extreme long shot high angle of the cemetery. The credits roll over the quiet cemetery sounds.

CREDITS AND NOTES

Producer:	Frederick Wiseman
Director:	Frederick Wiseman
Photography:	William Brayne
Editor:	Frederick Wiseman
Camera Assistant:	James Hallowell
Assistant Editor:	Oliver Kool
Synchronization:	Stephanie Tepper

Copyright, Basic Training Co., Inc., 1977.
Filmed on location in the Panama Canal Zone.

Distribution:	Zipporah Films
Running Time:	174 minutes
Released:	October, 1977

IV   Writings About Frederick Wiseman

1963

12 Anon. "The Talk of the Town: New Producer." *The New Yorker*, 39 (14 September), 33-35.
In an interview, Wiseman describes his rush to edit *The Cool World* in time for presentation at the Venice Film Festival. He describes "documentary" techniques used in casting, choosing sets, and improvising dialogue.

13 Polt, Harriet R. *"The Cool World." Film Quarterly*, 17, No. 2 (Winter), 33-35.
Polt describes the documentary-like techniques director Shirley Clarke used in scripting, casting, and shooting the film.

1964

14 Anon. "The Sad Boppers." *Newsweek*, 63, No. 16 (20 April), 114.
Description and favorable review of *The Cool World*. The fiction structure is of minor importance – the film captures the reality of Harlem like the best of documentaries.

15 Hitchens, Gordon. *"The Cool World." Film Comment*, 2, No. 2, 52-53.
The author argues that director Shirley Clarke doesn't make us care about the characters, thus failing exactly where she wants to succeed.

16 Polt, Harriet. "Shirley Clarke at Venice: An Interview With Harriet Polt." *Film Comment*, 2 No. 2, 31-32.
Translation of an interview originally printed in *Film a Doba* (Prague). Clarke describes the making of *The Cool World* and its use of improvisation and non-professional actors.

17 Walker, Jess. *"The Cool World." Film Comment*, 2, No. 2, 51-52.
Favorable review describing the film's documentary-like style.

1967

18 Anon. "Bay State in Move to Bar Prison Film." *The New York Times* (27 September), p. 42.
The state of Massachusetts attempts to ban the screening of *Titicut Follies* because the film invades the inmates' right to privacy.

19 Anon. "Cinema: Festival Action, Side Show Action, *Titicut Follies.*" *Time*, 90, No. 13 (29 September), 101.

The film is a "raw, poorly edited report" that offers no comment and no solution to the subject and problem it reports. But as an exposé it deserves to stand with Sinclair's *The Jungle* as an accusation and plea for reform.

20 Anon. "Controversial Film to Have Six Day Run at Cinema Rendezvous." *The New York Times* (30 September), p. 27.

Announces screen of *Titicut Follies* in New York.

21 Anon. "Court Here Refuses to Bar Film at New York Film Festival." *The New York Times* (29 September), p. 55.

Titicut Follies will be shown at the festival.

*22 Anon. Review of *Titicut Follies. Films in Review,* 18, No. 9 (November), 580.

Cited in *Index to Critical Film Reviews.*

*23 Anon. Review of *Titicut Follies. Filmfacts,* 60, 314.

Cited in *Index to Critical Film Reviews.*

24 Anon. "Tempest in a Snakepit." *Newsweek*, 70 (4 December), 109.

Describes the legal battle over the right to show *Titicut Follies* in Massachusetts: does the inmates' right to privacy supersede the public's right to know what goes on in a public institution? Wiseman says he made the film so that his law students could "understand the kind of terrible things that came up in their law cases."

25 Anon. *"Titicut Follies." America,* 117 (11 November), 539.

The controversy around the film is not based on inmates' rights of privacy, but whether the film is an "objective documentary" or a "propaganda stunt." Wiseman should reedit *Titicut Follies* to give it needed balance.

26 Anon. "US Court Refuses to Ban *Titicut Follies* to Public." *The New York Times* (1 December), p. 56.

Federal judge refuses to ban public showings of the film.

27 Canby, Vincent. "The Screen: *Titicut Follies* Observes Life in a Modern Bedlam." *The New York Times* (4 October), p. 38.

This "extraordinarily candid picture" is honest, and observes life at Bridgewater "without comment."

28 Fenton, John H. "Film Stirs Furor in Mass., Legislators See *Follies* Made at Memorial Hospital." *The New York Times* (18 October), p. 40.

Gives background to the film's political fallout and the legal controversy that focuses on the inmates' right to privacy. Wiseman denies filming with hidden cameras.

29 Gill, Brendan. "The Current Cinema." *The New Yorker,* 43 (28 October), 166–67.

Gill calls *Titicut Follies* a "sickening picture from start to finish." It has no justification for existing except to have legislative and other "nonaesthetic consequences." The film should not be given an ordinary commercial run anywhere. It is not art.

30 Hatch, Robert. *"Films." Nation,* 205 (30 October), 446.
     Negative review of *Titicut Follies* that criticizes Wiseman for showing events out of context.

31 Knight, Arthur. "Cinema Verite and Film Truth." *Saturday Review,* 50 (9 September), 44.
     In an article primarily about Shirley Clarke, Knight suggests that *Titicut Follies* violates the rights of inmates and goes beyond decency by photographing their nudity.

32 Morgenstern, Joseph. "Movies: Bedlam Today." *Newsweek,* 70 (23 October), 100-101.
     A review of *Titicut Follies* that assesses the conditions of the hospital more than it assesses the film.

*33 Reilly, John L. Review of *Titicut Follies. Film Society Review*(October), 17-19.
     Cited in *Index to Critical Film Reviews.*

*34 Sarris, Andrew. Review of *Titicut Follies. Village Voice,* 13, No. 4 (9 November), 33.
     Cited in *Retrospective Index to Film Periodicals, 1930-1971.*

35 Schickel, Richard. "Sorriest Spectacle: *The Titicut Follies." Life*, 63 (1 December), 12.
     The film's adequate structure and sequences of inmates who somehow transcend their madness elevates the work from exposé to art, result in a shock of partial recognition and a sudden realization that insanity is a matter of degree. Unlike Weiss's *Marat/Sade,* which carefully reminded us of its artificiality, *Titicut Follies* doesn't let us forget that these inmates are there to stay. This gives the film a power more forceful than any artifice. "Therefore it must be regarded as art." *See also* 39, 105, 124, 215.

36 Yglesias, Jose. "Whose Truth?" *Nation*, 205, (23 October), 410-12.
     In this article assesssing the documentary films shown at Lincoln Center's New York Film Festival, Yglesias mentions that hundreds of people were turned away from the screening of *Titicut Follies.* He describes a panel discussion among cinema verite filmmakers Pennebaker, David Maysles, Al Wasserman, and Harold Mayer.

1968

37 Coles, Robert. "Stripped Bare at the *Follies." The New Republic.* 158 (20 January), 18, 28-30.
     Lists charges brought against the conditions at Bridgewater State Hospital before Wiseman filmed *Titicut Follies.* Gives background to Wiseman's reasons for producing *The Cool World* and directing *Titicut Follies.* Coles calls *Titicut*

Follies a "brilliant work of art" in which we "see ouselves in the professionals who hold the fort in the Bridgewaters of this|nation."

38 Kessler, Ronald. "Correspondence." *The New Republic,* 158 (10 February), 35.

Kessler deplores *Titicut Follies'* clear invasion of inmates' rights of privacy.

39 Schickel. "Sorriest Spectacle: *The Titicut Follies,"* in *Film 67/68, An Anthology by the National Society of Film Critics.* Edited by Richard Schickel and John Simon. New York: Simon & Schuster, pp. 246-48.

Reprint of Schickel's 1967 article. *See* 34, 214, 123, 104.

40 Sheed, Wilfred. "Films." *Esquire,* 69, No. 3 (March), 52, 55.

Review of *Titicut Follies* that focuses on the rights of privacy issue. "In a few scenes, the inmates come on as fun-house specimens; proving nothing but their own craziness and this, however you slice it is exploitation."

1969

41 Anon. "Cross Cuts at NY Fest." *Variety* (8 October), p. 26.

Wiseman attends the New York Film Festivan and presents *High School.*

42 Anon. "The High School: How Much Change — And How Fast?" *School Management,* 13, No. 12 (December), 56-62.

Description of *High School* and synopsis of Wiseman's remarks at a symposium of school administrators. The audience criticized his motives and techniques, especially the uncomplimentary close-ups of unattractive teachers. Wiseman answers that they have fallen for the Hollywood myth that everyone is physically attractive. He saw no creative classes when filming *High School.*

43 Anon. "High School, Telling It Like It Is (Sometimes)." *American Teacher,* 54, No. 3 (November), 10-11.

The writer visited Northeast High School to see if conditions "were really as Wiseman shows," and describes the school's positive and innovative programs that are "hardly recognizable in Wiseman's films." Quotes teacher criticisms about Wiseman's almost exclusive use of close-ups that emphasized physical defects of teachers and affected viewer response. "One criticizes films by looking at the film, and schools by looking at the school, not an artist's representation of it."

44 Anon. "Movies." *Playboy,* 16, No. 8 (August), 32.

Description of *High School.*

45 Anon. "*Titicut Follies* is Barred to Bay State Public." *The New York Times* (25 June), p. 41.

Massachusetts state supreme court bars the public screening of *Titicut Follies* because of "massive unrestrained invasion of the intimate lives of patients." Only special, professional audiences will be allowed to see the film.

46 Bradlow, Paul. "Two . . . But Not of a Kind. A Comparison of Two Controversial Documentaries about Mental Illness, *Warrendale* and *Titicut Follies."*

Film Comment, 5, No. 3, 60-61.

Favorable review of *Titicut Follies.* The film implies an "enormous hostility toward organized religion." *Warrendale* is for those "who wish to learn," *Titicut Follies* is for those "who wish to know."

47 Cass, James. "Education in America: Don't You Talk, Just Listen!" *Saturday Review,* 52 (19 April), 57.

High School documents visually the criticism that many educators have been directing toward the country's high schools. The film's most frightening aspect is "how many of the nation's teachers and administrators could view the film and see nothing wrong."

*48 Craddock, John. "*High School* Unless . . ." *Film Society Review,* 5, No. 1 (September), 30-38.

Cited in *Index to Critical Film Reviews.*

49 Dowd, Nancy Ellen. "Popular Conventions." *Film Quarterly,* 22, No. 3 (Spring), 28-31.

Dowd inappropriately compares the structure of *Titicut Follies* to that of Pontecorvo's *Battle of Algiers.* She describes Wiseman's technique of overlapping time, the absence of conventional characters, and how his editing reflects the disorientation and timelessness of the insane. "To its credit, (*Titicut Follies*) defies interpretation."

50 Fager, Charles E. "Movie: Sweet Revenge." *Christian Century,* 86, No. 36 (3 September), 1141-42.

Favorable review of *High School* that focuses on the image of the school as stifling, authoritarian, ridiculous.

51 Faucher, Charles A. "The Kids of *High School.*" *Media and Methods,* 6, No. 1 (September), 54-55.

There is not sufficient balance in the film to raise it above caricature. Wiseman's camera is cursory and drops a subject before the forces at work are played out. He suspects that Wiseman approached the film with preconceptions and although the film pretends to document, it is "in fact a very personal rhetoric." The film is a phenomenology of trivia that leaves answers on the cutting room floor.

52 Featherstone, Joseph. "Documentary: *High School.*" *The New Republic,* 160 (21 June), 28-30.

Discusses issues of sociology and class relations raised by the film. Wiseman confines himself to what the school elicits from the students, to the exclusion of interviews with students and teachers.

53 Ferretti, Fred. "NET Will Show *Hospital.*" *The New York Times* (31 December), p. 49.

National Educational Television will air *Hospital* late in the evening because of "extreme realism and strong but common language."

54 Gent, George. "Movie on Police Censored by NET, *Law and Order* Program Cut to Remove Obscenities." *The New York Times* (27 February), p. 83.

National Educational Television deletes audio segments of *Law and Order* that include obscenities against police. Wiseman protests the deletions.

55 Hechinger, F. M. "A Look at Irrelevent Values." *The New York Times* (23 March), Sec. IV, p. 5.
    Review of *High School*, criticizing the school's irrelevancy.

56 Janssen, Peter A. *"High School." Newsweek*, 73 (19 May), 102.
    As education editor of *Newsweek,* Janssen reviews the state of Northeast High School more than he does the film. The school takes "warm, breathing teenages and turns them into 40 year old mental eunuchs."

57 Kael, Pauline. "The Current Cinema." *The New Yorker,* 45 (18 October), 199-204.
    A disjointed discussion of *Law and Order*, focusing on the role of obscenities spoken by young people in the film, that leads into a longer discussion of *High School*: the social and class issues it raises, themes of power and authority, differences between Northeast High School and the high school she attended. "Wiseman sends us out wanting to know more, . . . and knowing there's more to know." See also 82, 141, 202, 209.

58 Morgenstern, Joseph. "Movies: The Last Bell." *Newsweek*, 73 (19 May), 102.
    In a review of *High School*, Morgenstern reviews Northeast High School more than he does the film.

59 Robinson, Donald. "A Slanted, Cruelly Middle Class Debunking Film." *Phi Delta Kappan,* 51, No. 1 (September), 47.
    Reviews the school more than the film, *High School*. While we do see some "good" teachers, the school is "woefully out of touch with its students" and fails at human communication.

60 Schickel, Richard. "A Verite View of High School." *Life,* 6/, No. 11 (12 September), regional.
    Favorable review of *High School*. Wiseman is the most distinguished practitioner of cinema verite. *See 61, 123.*

61 Schickel, Richard. "A Verite View of High School," in *Film 69/70, An Anthology by the National Society of Film Critics.* Edited by Joseph Morgenstern and Stefan Kanfer. New York: Simon & Schuster, pp. 209-211.
    Reprint of the 1969 *Life* review. *See 60, 123.*

62 Skolnick, Malcolm. "Is it Filmed Like it Is? A Commentary on the Film *High School." Audiovisual Instruction,* 14, No. 7 (September), 90-91.
    Favorable review. The film gives us a new "social base for the definition of insensitivity" and comments not only on education, but on environmental situations.

63 Wakefield, Dan. "Movies: American Close-up." *Atlantic Monthly,* 223, No. 5 (May), 107-108.
    Describes scenes from *High School* and the thematic significance of the letter read by the principal. Wiseman's style is that of "moving montage."

64 Wiseman, Frederick. "Reminiscences of a Filmmaker: Frederick Wiseman on *Law and Order*." *Police Chief,* 36, No. 9 (September), 32-35.
Wiseman describes his working relationship with the police while shooting the film, and several of his experiences while filming. Several of his stereotypes of police were changed during the process of making the film. "I think my film in tone and substance accurately portrays the realities of policing. If so, and if the police find it useful in transmitting these realitites to new recruits and the public, it may help to puncture some of those stereotypes about police which arise from false, misleading, or simply no information. I hope so. That is why I made the film."

65 Zimmerman, Paul D. "Movies: Shooting it Like it Is." *Newsweek,* 78 (17 March), 134-35.
Accurately outlines the working techniques, subjects, and styles of Maysles brothers, Wiseman, Pennebaker, and Barron. Their techniques are similar, but each filmmaker's "world" is distinctive and personal. Quotes the filmmakers on their techniques and problems of distribution. The growing impulse of artists to participate in what they're creating is shared by these filmmakers, making their work similar to poetry and literature.

1970

66 Anon. Review of *Hospital. Booklist,* 67, No. 3 (1 October), 131.
Slight favorable review.

67 Anon. Review of *Law and Order. Booklist,* 67, No. 2 (15 September), 87.
Slight review recommending the film for high school and college students.

68 Anon. "Wiseman's Controversial Film — II: How Do Teachers React to *High School*?" *American Teacher,* 54, No. 6 (February), 13.
Reports the results of a questionnaire given to Toledo teachers after they saw the film. Many teachers noted the authoritarianism of teachers and administrators and lack of communication between teachers and students.

69 Arnold, Gary. "*Law and Order*." *The Washington Post* (7 March), Section C, p. 6.
Favorable review of *Law and Order* with short Wiseman interview. Wiseman says the filming experience changed his preconceptions about police. Wiseman looks at the victims without shame and without sentimentality. Although scenes seem randomly arranged, they're ordered carefully for contrast and cumulative emotional impact.

70 Bennis, Warren G. "Letter to Editor." *Society for the Psychological Study of Social Issues, Newsletter, No. 126 (November).*
Bennis urges SPSSI members to see Wiseman's films. "Nothing I know of in literature . . . provides the microscopic and authentic detail of life better or more economically than Wiseman."

71 Berg, Beatrice. "I Was Fed Up With Hollywood Fantasies." *The New York Times* (1 February), Sec. II, p. 25.
Review of *Hospital* with a Wiseman interview. Gives background to earlier

films. Wiseman explains the thematic relationship between the "factory-like" first shots of *High School* and the letter read in the film's last shots ("I'm only a body doing a job"). He discusses the difficulty of conveying ideas on film, without narration, and his refusal to offer solutions to problems revealed in the films.

72 Berliner, Don. "TV Mailbag." *The New York Times* (1 March), Sec. II, pp. 21–22.
    In a letter to the editor, Berliner asks about camera awareness and how it affects the "reality" of Wiseman's films. Wiseman replies in print that the camera doesn't change behavior appreciably. "People don't have a repertory of alternative gestures and actions to act for the camera, and when they're nervous they fall back on familiar behavior." *See also 93.*

73 Byron, Christopher. "Metropolitan Follies." *New York*, 3, No. 4 (26 January), 60–61.
    Description of *Hospital* with a brief history of the earlier films.

74 Dancyger, Ken. *"Hospital." Take One*, 2, No. 6 (July/August), 21–22.
    Favorable review and description of scenes from the film.

75 Denby, David. "Documenting America." *Atlantic Monthly*, 225 (March), 139–42.
    Discusses *Titicut Follies, High School,* and *Hospital.* The films are political in the largest sense, they deal with power relations in our society and the way we're affected by the institutions we pass through. He accurately describes Wiseman's working methods and touches on the structures of the films. Wiseman arranges sequences subtly for contrast, balance, and thematic complexity. In a harsh way, the films are funny. Wiseman's bias seems to be not so much partisan as radically humanist and libertarian. *See also 105, 115, 203.*

76 Gould, Jack. "Apropos *Hospital*." *The New York Times* (4 February), p. 87.
    WNET New York postpones its telecast of *Hospital* until late evening because the word "shit" appears several times in the sound track.

77 Gould, Jack. "Real-Life Pathos." *The New York Times* (2 February), p. 67.
    Gould criticizes *Hospital* for not addressing the larger issue of "adequate medical care generally," but praises its "stark realism" that sets Wiseman's study apart from the "average namby pamby documentary."

78 Grahm, John. "There Are No Simple Solutions." *Contempora* 1, No. 4 (October/November), 10.
    Brief interview with Wiseman, touching on his purpose in filmmaking, editing, and selection processes, and his aversion to "propaganda" films. Wiseman wants to produce a film that presents a series of experiences and allows each individual to have a multiple response to the material. He wants people to realize the complexity of the problems shown. Narrators immediately separate the audience from the experience and force an attitude on the audience. *See 103, 202, 207.*

79 Handelman, Janet. "An Interview with Frederick Wiseman." *Film Library Quarterly,* 3, No. 3 (Summer), 5–9.
    A superficial interview touching on Wiseman's philosophy of filmmaking, his working techniques, the objectivity/subjectivity debate, and the ambiguities of

High School. Wiseman says *Titicut Follies* is often funny "and the inmates at least have some vitality which the *High School* students lack."

80 Hyman, Ronald. "Bringing the News: Three Apostles and Twelve Epistles." *Media and Methods*, 6, No. 9 (May), 43-44.
      Favorable review of *High School* as part of a review of 11 books and one film that have "influenced the new breed of teachers." The books include *Growing Up Absurd, How Children Fail,* and *Summerhill.*

81 Kael, Pauline. "The Current Cinema." *The New Yorker,* 45 (31 January), 74-76.
      Describes scenes from *Hospital* with little analysis of the film's structure or style. Wiseman is selective about what he shows, but not for the purpose of problem solving. The audience's response is not limited to an imposed point of view.

82 Kael, Pauline. "*High School*: A Movie Review." *This Magazine Is About Schools,* 4, No. 1 (Winter), 23-29.
      Essentially a reprint of the 1969 review. *See 57, 141, 202, 209.*

83 Katz, John S. "Film Review: *High School.*" *Interchange,* 1, No. 2, 105-07.
      Describes the film and reviews the atmosphere of repression in Northeast High School.

84 McWilliams, Donald E. "Frederick Wiseman." *Film Quarterly*, 24, No. 1 (Fall), 17-26.
      Interview with Wiseman after a brief introduction to cinema verite. Wiseman discusses the role of film in social change and concludes that "when you get into these things, you realize how infinitely complicated they are, and how they are tied into so many other aspects of the society." Reality is ambiguous and a filmmaker becomes suspect if he doesn't find that ambiguity. Wiseman explains how the structures of *Law and Order, Hospital,* and *High School* reflect these films' themes, and discusses cinema verite's ability to capture real people.

85 Mamber, Stephen. "The New Documentaries of Frederick Wiseman." *Cinema,* 6, No. 1 (Summer), 33-39.
      Analysis essentially repeated in Mamber's 1974 volume, of *Titicut Follies* (1967) through *Hospital* (1970). *See 170.* In an interview that follows the analysis, Wiseman discusses his purposes in filmmaking, his working techniques, the film's ambiguities and humor, and the problems of camera awareness.

86 Mamber, Stephen. "Reviews: *High School.*" *Film Quarterly*, 23, No. 3 (Spring), 49-51.
      High School demonstrates that cinema verite need not be a performer's medium. Mamber discusses the problem of camera awareness and touches on the film's "black comedy" heightened by Wiseman's playful tendency toward delaying establishing shots, giving bits and pieces of a slightly preposterous scene before letting us realize what's going on.

87 Morgenstern, Joseph. "Movies: 'It Don't Make Sense.' " *Newsweek,* 75 (9 February), 85-86.
      Hospital is a "horrifically beautiful study of life in a metropolitan center of

succor and mercy." He touches on the "woefully funny" aspects of the film and on the problem of camera awareness.

88 Rice, Susan. "The Movies: *Hospital." Media and Methods,* 6, No. 7 (March), 14.
Questions whether the film adds to experience or is simply voyeurism. Wiseman presents a positive and therefore dangerous portrait of the hospital because the film works neither as an instrument of criticism nor of reform.

89 Schickel, Richard. "TV Review: Where Misery Must Be Confronted." *Life,* 68 (6 February), 9.
Schickel favorably reviews *Hospital,* praising Wiseman's tact that never suggests the voyeur, no matter how intimate the scene. Wiseman's humanism is ironic, illuminating the gap between intensions and the job at hand. "The hospital staff is overmatched. The whole force of the film derives from this terrible, beautifully understated fact."

90 Schuth, Wayne H. "Review: *High School." Audiovisual Communication Review,* 18, No. 2 (Summer), 212-213.
Criticizes Wiseman's manipulation of the audience through the juxtaposition of one teacher's voice over the image of another teacher, using music for editorial comment, and showing fragments of events out of context. Wiseman approaches the film as prosecuter.

91 Sidel, Victor W., M.D. *"Hospital* on View." *New England Journal of Medicine,* 282, No. 5 (January), 279-80.
Favorable review of *Hospital.* Sidel criticizes the film for not showing anyone "blowing their cool," the doctors look like saints. Its main question is "Why do we allow these conditions to persist?"

*92 William, Paul. Review of *High School. Village Voice,* 15, No. 41 (8 October), 54, 64-65.
Cited in *Retrospective Index to Film Periodicals, 1930-1971.*

93 Wiseman, Frederick. "TV Mailbag." *The New York Times* (1 March), Sec. II. pp. 21-22.
Wiseman answers a letter to the editor. *See 72.*

1971

94 Anon. *"High School." Booklist,* 67, No. 18 (15 May), 784.
Slight review of *High School.* The film is "disturbing and thought provoking," the overwhelming tone is dullness and boredom with the futility of individuality.

95 Atkins, Thomas R. "Frederick Wiseman Documents the Dilemmas of Our Institutions." *Film News,* 28, No. 5 (October), 14-17, 37.
Focusing more on the institutions than on the films, Atkins reviews *Basic Training, High School, Law and Order,* and *Hospital,* and their thematic interconnections. *See also 52.*

96 Bill. "*Basic Training.*" *Variety* (6 October), p. 40.

Basic Training is a dodge of the *real* war story: the secret war in Cambodia and Laos. Its "tempo editing" and "shadowy photography" give it a phony look. Since this film lacks the shock value of the previous films, it lapses into cliches and is an example of "verite overkill."

97 Bromwich, David. "Movies: Documentary Now." *Dissent* (October), pp. 507-512.

Description and favorable review of *Titicut Follies, High School,* and *Law and Order* in a larger work that assesses representatives of current documentary, including *Gimme Shelter* (Maysles), *Ice* (Kramer), and Third World films like *Fidel* (Landau), *Ramparts of Clay* (Bertucelli), and *One Day in the Life of Ivan Denisovich* (Wrede). Documentarists must (as Wiseman does) avoid Eisenstein's artifice and concentrate instead on "everyday bread and butter."

98 Cyclops. "Snapshots of the Old Army Game." *Life*, 71, No. 14 (1 October), 10.

Basic Training is a "clutch of snapshots." The presence of the "smug" camera compromises the very truth it seeks to record. The film lacks the distance and sympathetic intelligence needed to transcend voyeurism.

99 Denby, David. "Television: Taps." *New York*, 4, No. 40 (4 October), 69.

Basic Training leaves us with an impression of "disintegrating morale and vacuous duties carried out in a void." At the center of each Wiseman film is the man who embodies the institution, "standing face to face with some poor bastard who has screwed up while passing through; he's always calm and reasonable, he makes troublemakers feel foolish, irrational, even insane."

100 Desilets, Michael. "Frederick Wiseman: *Titicut* Revisited." *Film Library Quarterly*, 4, No. 2 (Spring), 29-33.

Disilets toured Bridgewater State Hospital for himself and compares *Titicut Follies* with his own experience at the institution.

101 Friedenberg, Edgar Z. "Ship of Fools: The Films of Frederick Wiseman." *New York Review of Books*, 17, No. 6 (21 October), 19-22.

Critiques the institutions that Wiseman films, rather than the films themselves. Friedenberg assigns motives to the behavior of the characters in *Hospital* and *Law and Order* that can't be supported by evidence from the films. He touches on the interlocking nature of the institutions which sustain one another through a system of cross-referrals which serve to validate their existence.

102 Fuller, Richard. "Wiseman's *Basic Training.*" *Media and Methods*, 8, No. 3 (November), 40-41, 54-55.

Describes *Titicut Follies, High School, Hospital, Law and Order,* and Wiseman's use of editing and camerawork. Detailed description of *Basic Training* concludes by suggesting thematic interconnections between it and the earlier films. Reprinted in Atkins' volume. *See 202, 205.*

103 Grahm, John. "There Are No Simple Solutions." *The Film Journal*, 1, No. 1 (Spring), 33-47.

Reprint of his 1970 interview. *See 78, 202, 207.*

104 Issari, M. Ali. *Cinema Verite.* Ann Arbor: Michigan State University Press, 1971, pp. 125–129.

Wiseman can be situated in the American cinema verite because of his method: he uses no actors, script, direction, or preconceived story line. This work attempts to define cinema verite, trace its roots, and distinguish between the "French" and "Anglo Saxon" schools of cinema verite. Issari provides a cursory biography of Wiseman and brief descriptions of *Titicut Follies, High School, Law and Order,* and *Hospital.* He incorrectly dates *Law and Order* as 1968 instead of 1969. Wiseman's only "fault" is his blatant intercutting of scenes in the early films to manipulate opinion.

105 Jacobs, Lewis, ed. *The Documentary Tradition, Nanook to Woodstock.* New York: Hopkinson and Blake, pp. 459–61, 477–82.

Includes reviews of *Titicut Follies* by Schickel (see 35) and of *Titicut Follies, High School,* and *Hospital* by Denby (see 75).

1971

106 Levin, G. Roy. "Frederick Wiseman," in *Documentary Explorations.* Edited by G. Roy Levin. New York: Doubleday & Co., Inc., pp. 313–328.

Wiseman discusses *Titicut Follies* (1967) through *Basic Training* (1971), describing how he arrives at the themes and viewpoints that surface in the films, the problem of camera awareness, his procedure for getting verbal consent from people in the films, the objective/subjective debate, the ambiguity of camera angles and close-ups, and how he finances the films. His purpose in filmmaking: "The premise is the simple one that the more information you have, the more informed decision you can make." He would like to make a fiction film with the documentary technique.

107 Mamis, Robert. "The Media: Public Documents." *Newsweek,* 78 (4 October), 99.

Wiseman discusses *Basic Training*: the film breaks down the cliche that there's something "peculiar about men who choose to be soldiers. It turns out, there's nothing that puts professional soldiers at a distance from the rest of us." The film reverses the notion that in teaching how to kill, the army is forcing alien values on the recruits. He intends the films to share what he learns with other people.

108 Maynard, Richard A. *The Celluloid Curriculum: How to Use Movies in the Classroom.* New York: Haydan Book Co., Inc., Passim.

Maynard suggests how films can be used in the classroom for the "ideas" they communicate, not for technical cinematic study. *Titicut Follies, High School, Law and Order,* and *Hospital* can be used as primary classroom sources for historical and social content.

109 O'Connor, John H. "The Film is About Killing." *The New York Times* (3 October), p. 17.

Announces WNET New York's weeklong retrospective of Wiseman documenatries, plus the premier of *Basic Training. Law and Order* and *Hospital* signaled a change in Wiseman's style: they are less didactic than *Titicut Follies* and *High School.* Wiseman no longer intercuts scenes for immediate comment on the action and *Hospital* is actually sympathetic to the institution. Wiseman has discovered a symbiotic relationship between controller and controlled: each side is trapped by the other.

110 Rosenthal, Alan. "*High School*, Frederick Wiseman," in his *New Documentary in Action: A Casebook in Filmmaking.* Berkeley: University of California Press, pp. 67-75.

Wiseman interview recounts the making of *Titicut Follies*, its financing, preparation, purpose, and the lawsuits that followed. Detailed description of his working techniques while making *High School*, how he decides on a film's structure and how the school's superintendent reacted to the film. Wiseman avoids filmed interviews because they are "pompus bullshit." He makes films to satisfy his own internal standards, he doesn't have an audience in mind. His series on institutions is a search for larger societal issues, for "cultural spoors."

1972

111 Anon. Review of *Basic Training. Booklist*, 68, No. 17 (1 May), 757.
Brief, favorable review.

112 Anon. "The Wiseman Documentaries." *PTA Magazine*, 66, No. 10 (June), 34-35.
Description of *Titicut Follies* (1967) through *Basic Training* (1971) with a recommendation that they be used at PTA meetings.

113 Anon. "Wiseman Signs for WNET Shows." *The New York Times* (5 May), p. 82.
Wiseman agrees to do a documentary a year for five years.

114 Boyd, Malcolm. "To Worship and Glorify God." *The New York Times* (12 November), p. 17.
Review of *Essene*, "one of the best religious films ever made." Wiseman presents a point of view but does not provide an answer to the film's question: "Are these monks wise men or idiots, socially useful or detrimental, irrelevant dropouts from the mainstream of contemporary life or perhaps modern saints?"

115 Denby, David. "Documenting America," in *The Documentary Tradition, Nanook to Woodstock.* Edited by Lewis Jacobs. New York: Hopkinson & Blake, pp. 447-482.
Reprint of Denby's 1970 article. *See 75, 203.*

116 Fuller, Richard. "Frederick Wiseman's New Documentary, *Basic Training*." *The Film Journal*, 1, No. 3-4 (Fall-Winter), 74-79.
Fuller gives a detailed description of the film, drawing parallels to *High School*, but providing little analysis.

*117 Gay, K. "Documenatry." *Films and Filming*, 18, No. 10 (July), 78.
Report from a screening of Wiseman's films at the National Film Theatre, London. Cited in *International Index to Film Periodicals.*

118 Hecht, Chandra. "Total Institutions on Celluloid." *Society*, 9 (April), 44-48.
     A helpful analysis of *Basic Training*'s themes that employs the film's struc-
ture of subplots and minibiographies. *Basic Training* is a trip into the "aesthetics
of socialization," complete with status degradation ceremonies, etiquette and a
new reality in an institution that defines itself as good. The editing builds a sense
of the madness of institutional life by placing bits of misunderstanding on top of
confused ideology on top of complex activities.

119 Maynard, Richard. "Classroom Cinema: The Movies of '71 in Review."
     Scholastic Teacher (March), pp. 22-23.
     Favorable review of *Basic Training*, recommending it for classroom use.

120 Meehan, Thomas. "The Documentary Maker." *Saturday Review*, 55 (2
     December), 12-14, 18.
     Favorable review of *Essene*, with Wiseman interview on camera awareness,
working techniques, and choice of subjects.

121 O'Connor, John J. "TV: Strong Wiseman Documentary on Monastery." *The
     New York Times* (14 November), p. 94.
     Essene is one more step toward purification of Wiseman's form away from
editorializing and easy illustration and toward objective and sensitive recreation.
The film is a "superb human comedy."

122 Racine, Robert W. "16 mm Documentary: *Essene*." *Mass Media Bi-Weekly
     Newsletter*, 9, No. 7 (7 August), 7-8.
     Favorable review that focuses on the monastery's environment and activities
more than on the film.

123 Schickel, Richard. "A Verite View of High School," in *Second Sight, Notes
     on Some Movies 1965-1970*. New York, Simon & Schuster, pp. 256-258.
     Reprint of 1969 *Life* review. *See 60, 61*.

124 Schickel, Richard. "Sorriest Spectacle: The *Titicut Follies*," in *Second Sight,
     Notes on Some Movies 1965-1980*. New York, Simon & Schuster, pp. 155-59.
     Reprint of 1972 article with additional note about Schickel's testimoney at
the *Titicut Follies* censorship trial as expert witness asserting the artistic and
journalistic merits of the film. *See 35, 39, 215*.

125 Slavitt, David R. "*Basic Training*." *Contempora*, 2, No. 1 (September/Febru-
     ary), 10-11.
     An unfocused discussion of *Basic Training* that reviews the army more than
the film.

126 Sullivan, Patrick J. "What's All the Cryin' About? The Films of Frederick
     Wiseman." *Massachusetts Review*, 13, No. 3 (Summer), 452-69.
     Reviews *Titicut Follies* (1967) through *Hospital* (1970). Wiseman's vision in
High School is more caustic, exclusive, and anxious than it is in *Titicut Follies*.
Unlike *High School*, his point of view in *Law and Order* is dynamic and changing
and most faithful to the facts.

127 Swartz, Susan. "The Real Northeast." *Film Library Quarterly,* 6, No. 1 (Winter), 12–15.
Swartz, a graduate of Northeast High School and a filmmaker, criticizes Wiseman's biased portrait of Northeast. Wiseman placed too much emphasis on the teachers. It is presumptuous of him to spend less than a month at the institution and do no research on the subject. His involvement in recording sound during filming doesn't make him free to observe the institution. *High School* failed to reveal the "real mess" in the school: "the track system that fostered a class system."

1973

128 Anon. *"Essene." Landers Film Reviews,* 17, No. 8 (April), 210.
A cursory review of *Essene.*

129 Anon. *"Basic Training." Landers Film Reviews,* 17, No. 7 (March), 180.
Review of the film that is largely description of its content.

130 Anon. "Documentary to Change the Second Time Around." *The New York Times* (15 December), p. 63.
PBS will not air *Juvenile Court* in Memphis, hometown of some of the young people in the film, because of the "personal scandals revealed in the film."

131 Anon. "Filmlist: *Hospital." Sightlines,* 6, No. 4 (March/April), 21.
Cursory description of *Hospital.*

132 Anon. *"High School." Landers Film Reviews,* 17, No. 9 (May), 246.
Brief review that attributes attitudes and motives to students and teachers that cannot be supported with evidence from the film.

133 Anon. *"Law and Order." Landers Film Reviews,* 17, No. 7 (March), 188.
Attributes behavior to the police officers that cannot be supported with evidence from the film.

134 Anon. "Mixed Bag: *Essene." Sightlines,* 6, No. 5 (May/June), 18.
Short note describing *Essene.*

135 Anon. Review of *Juvenile Court. Booklist,* 70, No. 5 (1 November), 278.
Cursory review.

*136 Anon. "Wiseman on *Juvenile Court." University Film Association Journal,* 25, No. 3, 48–49+.
Cited in *Film Literature Index.*

137 Barsam, Richard Meran. "The New Nonfiction Films: 1960–1970: Frederick Wiseman," in *Nonfiction Film: A Critical History.* New York: E. P. Dutton & Co., Inc., pp. 271–80.
Barsam describes the ambiguity of Wiseman's style and the content and themes of *Titicut Follies, High School, Hospital, Law and Order,* and *Basic Training.* Wiseman yields films of "unquestionable value and merit in helping us to understand American society." His viewpoint is implicit in his choice of

subject, shooting of sequences, and editing. He understands injustice with the same intuitiveness that Leacock and Pennebaker understand creativity.

138 Coleman, John. "Walking Wounded." *New Statesman*, 86, No. 2229 (7 December), 878.

Note on *Juvenile Court* in a longer piece describing films of the 17th London Film Festival.

139 Crain, Jane Larkin. "TV Verite." *Commentary*, 56, No. 6 (December), 70-75.

This unclear and imprecise review discusses the themes and issues raised by *Essene, High School, Basic Training, Hospital,* and *Juvenile Court.*

140 Ferrer III, Jose M. "Don't Cry Yet." *Time*, 102, No. 15 (8 October), 94-95.

Slight review of *Juvenile Court.* Ferrer describes the controversy it provoked at the conference of juvenile court judges, the issues of privacy it raises, and Wiseman's technique and style.

141 Kale, Pauline. "*High School* and Other Forms of Madness," in her *Deeper into Movies.* Boston: Little Brown & Co., pp. 19-24.

Reprint of Kael's 1969 review. *See 57, 82, 202, 209.*

142 Kernan, Michael. "Revealing an Institution's heart." *The Washington Post* (1 October), Section B, p. 1.

Review of *Juvenile Court* that is mostly description of the film.

143 Lott, Nina Barbara. "*The Documentary Film: A Study of Communication.*" PhD dissertation, United States International University, pp. 152-223.

This dissertation contributes little to the understanding of Wiseman's films. Lott draws similarities and differences between Wiseman, Robert Flaherty, and Pare Lorentz through a content analysis of autobiographical and biographical works to answer the question: What is the intent of the filmmaker? The dissertation attempts to provide scholars with a systematic, objective, and organized method for the content analysis of subjective messages.

144 Mamber, Stephen. "Cinema Verite and Social Concerns." *Film Comment, 9,* No. 6 (November/December), 8-15.

Mamber analyzes *Basic Training, Gimme Shelter* (David and Albert Maysles and Charlotte Zwerin), and *Factory* (Arthur Barron) to answer the question: Is cinema verite a useful approach to investigating American society? Wiseman is the first filmmaker to attempt a systematic approach to applying cinema verite to social concerns. Because Wiseman's interests and concepts are not as narrow as other cinema verite filmmakers, his films manipulate the material to a much lesser degree. Cinema verite works best when the filmmaker has a precise sense of the special audience or when he is making an intracultural ethnographic film.

145 O'Connor, John J. "TV: Fred Wiseman's *Juvenile Court,* A Portrait." *The New York Times* (1 October), p. 71.

Wiseman continues his efforts to produce a pure product, to remove himself completely from the content, to avoid editorialization. This documentary does not advocate, it presents a portrait.

146 Rice, Eugene. "*Essene*: A Documentary Film on Benedictine Community Life." *American Benedictine Review*, 24, No. 3 (September), 381–83.
   A favorable review of the film and of the monastery describing Wiseman's technique.

147 Ross, Victoria. "Screenings: *Essene*." *Previews*, 2, No. 1 (September), 31.
   Cursory review and description of *Essene*.

148 Stelle, Robert. "Reviews and Previews: Religion and Interfaith, *Essene*." *Film News*, 30, No. 4 (September), 24.
   An inaccurate, unfocused review.

149 Sullivan, Patrick J. "*Essene*." *Film Quarterly*, 27, No. 1 (Fall), 55–57.
   Sullivan presents a plausible theory of how the themes of *Essene* relate to larger contemporary social questions. The antisocial Brother Wilfred symbolizes resistance to tides of change that diminishes the monastery's sense of collective authority. The "wild intensity and desperate theatricality" of the young monk asserts anarchic reform. "Any group which has accepted the necessity reconstitution in today's culture is battling with basic problems of social philosphy and practice" raised by *Essene*. *See 202, 216.*

1974

150 Anon. "Wiseman to Make 'Yes Yes, No No' First Fiction Film." *The New York Times* (6 December), p. 78.
   Wiseman has been developing a script for a fiction film that will have a documentary texture. Wiseman says that one of the major reasons a documentary works is that "the viewer believes the reality he sees."

151 Arlin, Michael J. "The Air." *New Yorker*, 50 (25 November), 149–155.
   Primate is fascinating and in some ways frightening, but humorous. Wiseman's special style is cool and clean, yet animated with passion and "a large vision of life."

152 Atkins, Thomas R. "American Institutions: The Films of Frederick Wiseman." *Sight and Sound*, 43, No. 4 (Autumn), 232–35.
   Essentially the same review as appeared in 1971 *Film News* with an added description of *Juvenile Court*. *See 94.*

153 Barnouw, Erik. "Observer," in *Documentary: A History of the Nonfiction Film*. New York: Oxford University Press, pp. 244–46.
   Brief description of the films from *Titicut Follies* (1967) through *Juvenile Court* (1973), and cursory outline of Wiseman's style and working techniques. The films are above all "destroyers of stereotypes."

*154 Bassan, R. "*Hospital*." *Telecine*, No. 191/192 (September/October), p. 37.
   Cited in *Film Literature Index*.

155 Bill. "PTV Goes Bananas Over *Primate*." *Variety* (18 December), p 48.
   An account of public television network's reaction to the *Primate* contro-

versy, including delayed broadcasts and panel discussions following the film. Outlines issues and reactions of scientists on panels.

156 Bourne, Geoffrey H. "Yerkes Director Calls Foul." *The New York Times* (15 December), p. 33.
    In a letter to the *Times*, Bourne, director of the Yerkes Primate Research Center, defends his "noble institution" and charges that Wiseman's technique actually "inverts the truth through lack of explanation."

157 Brown, Les. "Scientist Angrily Cancels TV Discussion of *Primate*." *The New York Times* (7 December), p. 59.
    Geoffrey Bourne, director of Yerkes Primate Research Center, claims that the film "bears no relationsip to reality." He refuses to appear on WNET discussion program with Wiseman after he sees the film a second time. WNET received 149 phoned complaints during their airing of *Primate*.

*158 Chevallier, J. Review of *Hospital*. *Revue du Cinema*. 187 (September), p. 125.
    Cited in *Film Literature Index*.

159 Combs, Richard. "Films." *The Listener,* 91, No. 2355 (May), 646.
    Slight review of *Juvenile Court*. Wiseman's approach seems "more strongly analytical than loosely cinema verite."

*160 Combs, Richard. Review of *Law and Order. Monthly Film Bulletin,* 41, No. 487 (August), p. 180.
    Cited in *Index to Film Periodicals*.

161 Etzioni, Amitai, "*Primate* is Unnecessarily Cruel to Scientists." *The New York Times* (15 December), p. 33.
    In *Primate*, Wiseman unveils the truth in a "truncated, and tortured way," leaving out the purpose of the research it shows. "Without some interpretation, virtually any area of human activity can be made to look grotesque." The film belongs on an editorial page.

*162 Glaessner, V. Review of *Hospital. Monthly Film Bulletin,* 41 (October), 224.
    Cited in *Film Literature Index*.

163 Halberstadt, Ira. "An Interview with Frederick Wiseman." *Filmmaker's Newsletter,* 7, No. 4 (February), 19-25.
    To date, the most detailed and comprehensive explanation by Wiseman of his shooting, editing, and distribution techniques. He discusses equipment, decisions made during shooting and editing, and the importance of structuring scenes to present a "theory" that guides the viewer's experience. "The abstractions you are dealing with are the abstractions that are related to the structure of the film and that emerge from the structure of the film." He discusses how he arrives at themes and points of view, and how and why he distributes his own films. *See 208.*

164 Kraemer, Chuck. "Frederick Wiseman's *Primate* Makes Monkeys of Scientists." *The New York Times* (1 December), Sec. II, p. 1.

The film is profound in the questions it raises about science, compassion, and the eternal tensions between the rational and spiritual. Kraemer visits and describes Wiseman's studio in Boston and quotes Wiseman on the film's humor: "The film is actually a rather bizarre comedy — I think it's a riot — but strangely, these guys don't see the humor in what's going on."

*165 LaJeunesse, J. Review of *Hospital. Revue du Cinema.* 288/289 (October), p. 163-64.
Cited in *Film Literature Index.*

166 Lefevre, R. *"Hospital." Cinema 74,* 190-191 (September/October), pp. 302-303.
Slight, favorable review of *Hospital* that touches on the theme it raises.

*167 Lewis, C. *"Essene." Monthly Film Bulletin,* 41 (September), 198.
Cited in *Film Literature Index.*

*168 Lewis, C. *"High School." Monthly Film Bulletin,* 41 (August), 177.
Cited in *Film Literature Index.*

*169 Lewis, C. *"Juvenile Court." Monthly Film Bulletin,* 41 (June), 129.
Cited in *International Index to Film Periodicals.*

170 Mamber, Stephen. "Frederick Wiseman," in *Cinema Verite in America: Studies in Uncontrolled Documentary."* Cambridge: The MIT Press, pp. 216-49.
In one of the most complete analyses of Wiseman to date, Mamber discusses *Titicut Follies* (1967) through *Essene* (1972) and places them within the tradition of American cinema verite. Wiseman's films are not chronological or presented from an intellectual distance, and this places them closer to propaganda documentary than to cinema verite. Still, they are not far from the mainstream of cinema verite, which Mamber defines by an examination of the work of Drew Associates, the Maysles brothers, Pennebaker, and Leacock. In *Titicut Follies.* Wiseman intercuts scenes that force us to consider each in terms of the other. This runs counter to the cinema verite notion of preserving the complexity of filmed events. He drops this technique in later films, making them more informational than didactic. Mamber mentions Wiseman's structural use of shots of hallways, waiting rooms, and the neutral connotations of close-ups when they are used consistently. The volume includes a seven-page bibliography, suggested course schedule, and filmographies.

171 O'Connor, John J. "TV: *Primate,* a Study by Wiseman." *The New York Times* (5 December), p. 124.
Although O'Connor asserts that *Primate* is a product of intelligence and insight rare in television, he criticizes the film for its lack of narration. "The audience is likely to be puzzled not only about the nature of a particular experiment but also as to what's happening at the specific moment." This works against the film's complexity.

*172 Rayns, T. *"Basic Training." Monthly Film Bulletin,* 41 (November), 246-47.
Cited in *Film Literature Index.*

173 Richardson, Elliot. "Letters: Focusing again on *Titicut*." *Civil Liberties Review*, 1, No. 3 (Summer), 148-51.

Richardson denies that the litigation surrounding *Titicut Follies* was intended to cover up conditions at the hospital. He outlines grounds for claiming that the film invades the patients' rights of privacy and alleges that Wiseman failed to follow the procedure of obtaining signed releases from prisoners. Wiseman replies to Richardson's charges in a letter, arguing that the public's right to know what is happening in public institutions transcends the right of privacy. *See 177.*

174 Tarrett, Margaret. "Review: *Juvenile Court*." *Films and Filming*, (20 August), pp. 43-44.

Description of the film.

175 Westin, Alan. "You Start Off with a Bromide: Wiseman on Film and Civil Liberties." *Civil Liberties Review*, 1, No. 2 (Winter/Spring), 56-57.

In this interview, Wiseman gives the most detailed account of his own philosophy of the social purpose and effects of his films. He is pessimistic about the capacity of institutions to administer legally enforceable rights on a large scale and doubts that people can be motivated toward large-scale social change, therefore he intends that the films function more as information to be used in making more informed decisions. He has grown away from the "simple minded social work view of help and intervention." He provides a detailed account of the *Titicut Follies* right of privacy controversy and the court actions surrounding it.

176 Wilkman, Jon. "Scanning." *Crawdaddy* (January), pp. 18-19.

In a favorable review of *Juvenile Court*, Wilkman unhelpfully situates Wiseman in the documentary-cinema verite-broadcast journalism traditions, and touches on the subjectivity-objectivity, reality-creativity split.

177 Wiseman, Frederick. "Letters: Focusing again on *Titicut*." *Civil Liberties Review*, 1, No. 3 (Summer), 148-51.

See 173.

1975

178 Anon. "The Price of Knowledge." *The Hastings Center Report*, 5, No. 1 (February), 6-8.

Excerpts from a televised discussion between Wiseman and *"Nova"* staff, about the ethical implications of the experiments shown in *Primate. See 196.*

*179 Anon. Review of *Primate. Booklist*, 71, No. 13 (1 March), 678.

Slight review. Wiseman may be using *Primate* to ask researchers to "reconsider their ethics governing all basic scientific research."

180 Anon. Review of *Welfare. Booklist*, 72, No. 7 (1 December), 522.

Favorable review of *Welfare*. The film's greatness is that for every scene, Wiseman includes a contradictory one that challenges any certainties that the viewer entertains.

181 Arnold, Gary. "Wiseman's *Welfare*: Compelling Case Study." *The Washington Post* (24 September), Sec. C, p. 1.

The additional running time of this film (three hours) seems to enhance Wiseman's approach, which depends on the steady accumulation of impressions and details. The larger issues emerge by implication, not as a thesis stated outright. The overlapping, repetitive structure of the film gives a bizarre fugal effect.

182 Brieland, Donald. "Film Reviews: *Welfare.*" *Social Work*. 20, No. 6 (November), 498.

The film needs narration to explain that it was made during the chaotic transition in New York from public welfare to supplemental security income. Brieland suggests how the upheaval could have been avoided or remedied by changes in office procedure. The film's inclusion of philosophical discussions of rascism and religion add human interest but destroy unity. The review is followed by a letter to the editor that praises the film and deplores the conditions of the welfare system.

183 Bunce, Alan. "Something different! Bored by Routine Series? There's a Compelling New Documentary to See." *The Christian Science Monitor* (25 September), p. 23.

Favorable review of *Welfare* with Wiseman interview. Wiseman uses no narration, because "in a narrated film, all you have to do is say: 'Some people feel that . . . and on the other hand other people feel that . . .' and then you've covered the waterfront, which is essentially phoney." He insists that *Welfare* might not be balanced, but it is fair.

184 Coleman, John. "Films: Long Look." *The New Statesman*, 90, No. 2329 (7 November), 589.

Favorable review and brief description of *Welfare*. "The clients are, to put it mildly, bizarre, but then, so are the staff." The film presents a reciprocity of alarm, helplessness, rage, and decency.

185 Coleman, John. "Films: *Primate.*" *The New Statesman*, 89, No. 2286 (10 January), 51.

Slight, favorable review.

186 Divoky, Dian. "*Juvenile Court.*" *Sightlines*, 8, No. 3 (Spring), 16.

Slight, favorable review.

187 Gay, Ken. "Review: *Primate.*" *Films and Filming*, 21, No. 6 (March), 37.

Favorable review. The film's ambiguities suggest larger themes and meanings.

188 Kilday, Gregg. "The Woes of Welfare." *Los Angeles Times* (22 September), Sec. IV, p. 1.

Welfare forces the viewer to experience the bewilderment and frustration of its characters. Wiseman refuses to sentimentalize. Despite its documentary approach, it bursts with black humor and theatricality because so many of its subjects stand on the brink of hysteria. In the thirties, a sense of impending social revolution encouraged photographers to ennoble their subjects by emphasizing traces of dignity and strength, presenting hints of ultimate triumph. Wiseman doesn't offer the same assurances. His camera captures only despair. Implicitly, he questions our society's apparent willingness to isolate and maintain a whole subculture of destitutes.

189 Kraemer, Chuck. "The *Primate* Controversy: Less Fun than a Barrel of Monkeys." Boston *The Real Paper* (22 January), pp. 6-7, 15.

Outlines the controversy over *Primate*; reactions of viewers who called television stations, and of the center's director. The charges that the film shows cruelly sadistic behavior by scientists are unjustified. Wiseman says the question the film really raises is: "Are there any limitations to research?" He sees the real danger of these institutions in their bureaucratic natures, their impersonality, tedium, blandness. Quotes an article by the center's director which advocates a policy of seeking out a country's most intelligent children and reproducing their kind.

*190 Lewis, C. "*Primate.*" *Monthly Film Bulletin,* 42 (January), 14.
Cited in *Film Literature Index.*

*191 Lindeborg, L. "Frederick Wiseman." *Chaplain,* 6, No. 141, 311-12.
Wiseman interview. Cited in *Film Literature Index.*

192 Meyer, Karl E. "Television: Report from Purgatory." *Saturday Review,* 2 (20 September), 52.

Reviewing the country's welfare system more than the film *Welfare,* Meyer says that Wiseman tends to amass rather than distill his material. "*Welfare* could have had twice the impact if it were half as long." But Meyer excuses this offense, the film is "strong stuff unflinchingly presented" with a pace that has the deliberation of a "dance macabre."

193 Morgenstern, Joseph. "Probing the Kafkaesque World of *Welfare.*" *The New York Times* (21 September), Sect. II, p. 1.
Essentially a description of the film.

194 O'Connor, John. "Wiseman's *Welfare* is on Channel 13 Tonite." *The New York Times* (24 September), p. 91.

The film is a catalogue of "human and institutional insanities of a system that has come to represent a landmark in colossal waste." It is "brilliantly representative, darkly funny, and finally frustrating."

195 Perrier, Patricia. "Audiovisual Reviews: *Hospital.*" *American Anthropologist,* 77, No. 1 (March), 185-86.

Favorable review describing the film and its themes. Touches on the religious theme of the film which questions what technological medicine does to the strong historical connections between medicine and religion.

196 Powledge, Tabitha. "*Primate* — Sensationalism for Subtlety." *Hastings Center Report,* 5, No. 1 (February), 5-6.

Wiseman's abstraction of experiments from their contexts works when the institution is familiar to the audience, but in this film it is a serious mistake. He chose cheap shots. The film is a simple antivivisection statement. *See also 178.*

197 Scott, James F. "The Advent of Magnetic Sounds," in *Film: The Medium and the Maker.* New York: Holt, Rinehart and Winston, Inc., pp. 153-54.

Wiseman's use of sound in *High School* builds its theme through the use of voice tracts that are oral capsules, confusing, competitive, incomplete, but create a tight weave that indicates a collective personality.

198 Stein, Benjamin. "Closeup on *Welfare*." *The Wall Street Journal* (24 September), p. 24.

Favorable review and description of *Welfare*. The people in the film are not only different from the middle class in that they have less money, but they are also psychologically disabled to a chilling extent. They are a group apart, a subculture that is parasitic, alienated, and largely devoid of hope.

199 Sullivan, Patrick. "Patrick Sullivan on TV: Frederick Wiseman's *Primate*." *The New Republic*, 172, No. 4 (25 January), 30–32.

Sullivan touches on the relationship between the film's style and its meaning. *Primate*'s final shot makes a visual connection between the government, the military, the air force, and the Pentagon, underlining Wiseman's theme of the madness of a massively financed scientific method.

200 Waters, Harry F. "Television: Wiseman on Welfare." *Newsweek*, 86 (29 September), 62–63.

Outlines Wiseman's working technique and style, comparing Wiseman's structuring of the material to that of a novelist.

201 Wolcott, James. "*Welfare* Must be Seen." *Village Voice*, 20, No. 39 (29 September), 126.

Camera awareness strains the documentary method and verges on performance. Wiseman should break through the "artifical objectivity" of documentary and begin to use actors in a documentary situation or create fictional situations for nonactors.

1976

202 Atkins, Thomas R., ed. *Frederick Wiseman*. New York: Monarch Press, 134 pp.

Atkins reprints interviews and reviews in the only volume devoted entirely to Wiseman. The volume includes a cursory biography to 1973, a filmography through *Welfare* (1975), a list of retrospective screenings, and a two page bibliography. Atkin's interview with Wiseman about *Primate* appears for the first time in this work. Wiseman describes his editing and shooting methods and discusses the problem of camera awareness. *See 205, 207, 209, 216, 217*.

203 Denby, David. "Documenting America," in *Nonfiction Film Theory and Criticism*. Edited by Richard Meran Barsam. New York: E. P. Dutton & Co., Inc., pp. 310–314.

Reprint of the 1970 article. *See 75, 115*.

204 Feldman, Silvia. "The Wiseman Documentary." *Human Behavior* 5 (February), 64, 69.

Descriptions of *Welfare* that critiques the system more than the film, followed by one of the most complete biographical interviews with Wiseman to date. The biography lapses into psychoanalysis, attributing Wiseman's unwillingness to share his personal self to growing up in a family of successful, verbally adept adults which make it easier to express himself indirectly through films.

205 Fuller, Richard. "Frederick Wiseman's New Documentary, *Basic Training*," in *Frederick Wiseman*. Edited by Thomas Atkins. New York: Simon and Schuster, pp. 103–12.
   Reprint of 1971 article. *See 78, 102, 202.*

206 Giannetti, Louis D. "Television and Cinema Verite," in *Understanding Movies*. Englewood Cliffs: Prentice Hall, Inc., pp. 260–62.
   Cursory treatment of Wiseman, his technique and themes, in textbook on film technique and theory.

207 Grahm, John. "There are No Simple Solutions," in *Frederick Wiseman*. Edited by Thomas R. Atkins. New York: Simon and Schuster, pp. 33–45.
   Reprint of 1970 article. *See 78, 103, 202.*

208 Halberstadt, Ira. "An Interview with Frederick Wiseman," in *Nonfiction Film Theory and Criticism*. Edited by Richard Meran Barsam. New York: E. P. Dutton & Co., Inc., pp. 296–309.
   Reprint of 1974 article. *see 163.*

209 Kael, Pauline. "*High School*," in *Frederick Wiseman*. Edited by Thomas R. Atkins. New York: Simon and Schuster, pp. 95–101.
   Reprint of Kael's 1969 article. *See 57, 141, 202.*

*210 Lewis, C. "*Welfare*." *Monthly Film Bulletin*, 43 (March), 65.
   Cited in *Film Literature Index.*

211 Mamber, Stephen. "One Man's *Meat*: Frederick Wiseman's New Film." *The New Republic*, 175, No. 23 (4 December) 21–22.
   Mamber helpfully demonstrates how *Meat*'s structure and imagery supports the film's themes. "A nightmare vision, *Meat* is one of Wiseman's studies (like *High School* and *Basic Training*) of things going far too well . . . We feel ourselves grasping for trivial indications of humanity." There's nothing necessarily evil about what goes on in *Meat*, the evil lies in potential.

212 O'Connor, John. "Wiseman's Latest Film is Another 'Reality Fiction.' " *The New York Times* (7 November), p. 27.
   In *Meat*, Wiseman creates a ficticious structure with the illusion of truth. The film has difficulty maintaining a focus and in the end gives the impression of reaching less of a conclusion than an exhaustion. Wiseman has contracted with WNET to do five more films.

213 LR. "*Welfare*." *Film* 35 (March), p. 9.
   Brief description of the film.

214 Russell, Cristine. "Science on Film: The *Primate* Controversy." *BioScience*, 25, No. 3 (March), 151–54, 218.
   Describes the airing of the film, public and critical reactions, and the battle between director of the Primate Research Center, Geoffrey H. Bourne, and Wiseman. Quotes antivivisection letters sent to Bourne and antifilm letters sent to WNET and the FCC. Describes WGBH follow-up program featuring a discussion between Wiseman and a "*NOVA*" science editor, a Yerkes researcher, and a

Harvard philosopher. Russell criticizes the film for falling short of its goal and failing to formulate themes in anything but the most ambiguous fashion. Bourne explains several of the experiments shown in the film. Russell concludes: "Posing complicated questions for the general public about little understood institutions requires a much more sophisticated and subtle approach than cinema verite seems capable of providing."

215 Schickel, Richard. "Sorriest Spectacle: The *Titicut Follies*," in *Frederick Wiseman*. Edited by Thomas R. Atkins. New York: Simon and Schuster, pp. 91-93.
Reprint of the 1967 article. *See 35, 39, 105, 124.*

216 Sullivan, Patrick J. *"Essene,"* in *Frederick Wiseman*. Edited by Thomas R. Atkins. New York: Simon and Schuster, pp. 113-20.
Reprint of the 1973 article. *See 149, 202.*

217 Westin, Alan. "You Start Off With a Bromide," in *Frederick Wiseman*. Edited by Thomas R. Atkins. New York: Simon and Schuster, pp. 47-66.
Reprint of the 1974 interview. *See 175, 202.*

218 Wolcott, James. "Blood on the Racks: Wiseman's *Meat*." *Village Voice*, 21, No. 46 (15 November), 95.
Wolcott shows how Wiseman's style and treatment leads to the film's themes. The formal design and detached black and white cinematography allows one to face the killing head on. The movie takes on a horrible majesty.

1977

219 Eames, David. "Watching Wiseman Watch." *The New York Times Magazine* (2 October), pp. 96-102, 108.
Eames assisted Wiseman in the making of *Titicut Follies* and gives a helpful, detailed description of Wiseman's working methods and history of the making of *Titicut Follies*. He describes *Canal Zone* and presents plausible interpretations of its themes. He speculates on the effect of boredom and the unconventional film length of *Canal Zone* on the viewer.

220 Rich, Frank. "A Sunny, Nightmare Vision." *Time*, 110, No. 15 (10 October), 103.
Favorable review of *Canal Zone*. The film shows that when Americanism is isolated and left to feed on itself, it becomes a desperate form of mass escapism.

221 Sourian, Peter. Review of *Canal Zone. The Nation*, 225, No. 12 (15 October), 181-82.
Favorable review with brief description and discussion of the themes it raises of colonialism and America's "butcherish efficiency" that may well be a mad efficiency. Wiseman is a closet fictionalist and should attempt making a fiction film.

*222 Wolcott, James. "Wiseman's Panamania." *Village Voice*, 22 (10 October), 45.
Cited in *Access: The Supplementary Index to Periodical Literature.*

1978

223 Nichols, Bill. "Fred Wiseman's Documentaries: Theory and Structure." *Film Quarterly*, 31, No. 3 (Spring), 15–28.

In the only serious attempt to analyze Wiseman's films according to contemporary theory and critical concerns to date, Nichols addresses the form and structure of Wiseman's films in an attempt to "tease open" larger ideological implications of style embedded in the organizing principles of the parts, the whole, and the part/whole relationships of the films. Wiseman's mosaic structure of the whole, with narrative structure of the parts, assumes that social events are multiply caused and must be analyzed as a web of interconnecting influences and patterns. Nichols suggests how the spatiotemporal flow of scenes can be interpreted according to classifications in Christian Metz's grande syntagmatique and Vladimir Propp's "functions." Wiseman's mosaic structuring of the films and the supplementary nature of the facets frequently demand a retroactive relationship to the text, making the viewer participate in the film's process of becoming a text. Nichols closely analyzes a segment of *Hospital*, employing Noel Burch's categories of spatial and temporal articulation to determine how Wiseman constructs imaginary continuity in a situation where the filmmaker controls the "profilmic" event so weakly. He concludes that the impression of continuity depends on an active and retroactive reading of cues embedded in shots and their articulations.

V Award Summary
and Festival Screenings

224 TITCUT FOLLIES

Best Film, Mannheim International Filmweek, 1967.
Best Film Dealing with the Human Condition, Festival dei Popoli, 1967.
New York Film Festival, 1968 (noncompetitive).
Edinburgh Film Festival, 1968 (noncompetitive).

225 HIGH SCHOOL

Festival dei Popoli, 1969.
Spoleto Film Festival, 1969.
San Francisco International Film Festival, 1969.
New York Film Festival, 1969.
Festival du Cinema Americain-Deauville, 1975.

226 LAW AND ORDER

Emmy Award, Best News Documentary, 1969.
Spoleto Film Festival, 1969.
Venice Film Festival, 1969
Festival dei Popoli, 1970.
Edinburgh Film Festival, 1970.
Award for Exceptional Merit, Philadelphia International Festival, 1971.
Festival du Cinema Americain-Deauville, 1975.

227 HOSPITAL

Emmy Awards, Best News Documentary and Best Director, 1970.
Catholic Filmmakers Award, Mannheim, 1970.
Dupont Award for Excellence in Broadcast Journalism, 1970.
Red Ribbon, American Film Festival, 1972.
Edinburgh Film Festival, 1970.
Festival dei Popoli, 1970.
National Education Film Festival, 1969.

228 BASIC TRAINING

Edinburgh Film Festival, 1971.
London Film Festival, 1972.
Festival du Cinema Americain-Deauville, 1975.
Award for Exceptional Merit, Philadelphia International Festival, 1971.

229 ESSENE

Gabriel Award, Catholic Broadcasters' Association, 1972.
Edinburgh Film Festival, 1972.
Festival dei Popoli, 1972.
London Film Festival, 1972.

230 JUVENILE COURT

Silver Phoenix, Atlanta International Film Festival, 1974.
Cine Golden Eagle, 1974.
Dupont Award, Columbia School of Journalism, 1975.
Emmy nomination for Best News Documentary, 1974.
Festival dei Popoli, 1973.
London Film Festival, 1973.

231 PRIMATE

International Film Festival-Nyon, 1975.
London Film Festival, 1974.
Festival du Cinema Americain-Dauville, 1975.
Wellington Film Festival, New Zealand, 1975.

232 WELFARE

Best Documentary Award, Athens International Film Festival, 1976.
Gold Medal, Special Jury Award, Virgin Islands International Film
  Festival, 1975.
International Film Festival-Nyon, 1975.
American Film Festival, 1976.
London Film Festival, 1975.
Wellington Film Festival, New Zealand, 1976.
Festival dei Popoli, 1975.
Melbourne and Sydney Festivals, Australia, 1976.

233 MEAT

London Film Festival, 1976.
Festival dei Popoli, 1977.
Wellington (New Zealand) International Film Festival, 1977.
Melbourne and Sydney Festivals, Australia, 1977.

234 CANAL ZONE

London Film Festival, 1977.
Athens International Film Festival, Golden Athena Award for Best
  Feature, 1977.
Wellington and Auckland Festivals, New Zealand, 1977.
Mostra Internazionale del film D'Autore, Sanremo, 1978.

235 INDIVIDUAL AWARDS

Golden Hugo Award, Chicago International Film Festival, 1972, presented
  in conjunction with a retrospective screening.
Personal Achievement Gabriel Award, presented by the Catholic
  Broadcasters' Association, 1975.

236 RETROSPECTIVE SCREENINGS

Chicago International Film Festival, 1972.
London Film Festival, 1972.
Filmex, Los Angeles International Film Festival, 1976.
Spanish Film Cinematheque, Madrid and Barcelone, 1978.
Swedish Film Cinematheque, 1975.
Danish Film School, 1975.
Paris Film Cinematheque, 1975.
Norwegian Film Cinematheque, 1976.

237 TELEVISION BROADCASTS

Public Broadcasting System, national broadcasts of *Law and Order,
Hospital, Juvenile Court, Essene, Basic Training, Primate, Welfare, Meat,
Canal Zone, Sinai Field Mission.*
Additional broadcasts in Sweden, The Netherlands, Japan, Italy, Norway,
  and Denmark.

VI   Archival Sources
for Further Research

238   Boston, Massachusetts
Zipporah Films
  Zipporah makes transcripts and stills of the films it distributes available to researchers upon request.

239   Washington, D.C.
Library of Congress
Motion Picture, Broadcasting, and Recorded Sound Division
  Each of Wiseman's films is available for screening at the Library of Congress.

VII   Film Distributors

240   Grove Press, Inc.
53 East 11th St.
New York, New York 10003
   Titicut Follies (1967)
   (Distributed by Grove from 1967 until 31 December 1977.)

241   Zipporah Films
54 Lewis Wharf
Boston, Massachusetts 02110
   Basic Training (1971)
   Canal Zone (1977)
   Cool World, The (1964)
   Essene (1972)
   High School (1968)
   Hospital (1970)
   Juvenile Court (1973)
   Law and Order (1969)
   Meat (1975)
   Primate (1974)
   Sinai Field Mission (1978)
   Titicut Follies (1967)
   Welfare (1975)

Film Title Index

Note: numbers in indices refer to entry numbers rather than pages.

Author Index